Financial Regulation in the
Global Economy

Integrating National Economies: Promise and Pitfalls

Barry Bosworth (Brookings Institution) and Gur Ofer (Hebrew University)
Reforming Planned Economies in an Integrating World Economy

Ralph C. Bryant (Brookings Institution)
International Coordination of National Stabilization Policies

Susan M. Collins (Brookings Institution/Georgetown University)
Distributive Issues: A Constraint on Global Integration

Richard N. Cooper (Harvard University)
Environment and Resource Policies for the World Economy

Ronald G. Ehrenberg (Cornell University)
Labor Markets and Integrating National Economies

Barry Eichengreen (University of California, Berkeley)
International Monetary Arrangements for the 21st Century

Mitsuhiro Fukao (Bank of Japan)
Financial Integration, Corporate Governance, and the Performance of Multinational Companies

Stephan Haggard (University of California, San Diego)
Developing Nations and the Politics of Global Integration

Richard J. Herring (University of Pennsylvania) and Robert E. Litan (Department of Justice/Brookings Institution)
Financial Regulation in the Global Economy

Miles Kahler (University of California, San Diego)
International Institutions and the Political Economy of Integration

Anne O. Krueger (Stanford University)
Trade Policies and Developing Nations

Robert Z. Lawrence (Harvard University)
Regionalism, Multilateralism, and Deeper Integration

Sylvia Ostry (University of Toronto) and Richard R. Nelson (Columbia University)
Techno-Nationalism and Techno-Globalism: Conflict and Cooperation

Robert L. Paarlberg (Wellesley College/Harvard University)
Leadership Abroad Begins at Home: U.S. Foreign Economic Policy after the Cold War

Peter Rutland (Wesleyan University)
Russia, Eurasia, and the Global Economy

F. M. Scherer (Harvard University)
Competition Policies for an Integrated World Economy

Susan L. Shirk (University of California, San Diego)
How China Opened Its Door: The Political Success of the PRC's Foreign Trade and Investment Reforms

Alan O. Sykes (University of Chicago)
Product Standards for Internationally Integrated Goods Markets

Akihiko Tanaka (Institute of Oriental Culture, University of Tokyo)
The Politics of Deeper Integration: National Attitudes and Policies in Japan

Vito Tanzi (International Monetary Fund)
Taxation in an Integrating World

William Wallace (St. Antony's College, Oxford University)
Regional Integration: The West European Experience

Richard J. Herring and
Robert E. Litan

Financial Regulation
in the
Global Economy

THE BROOKINGS INSTITUTION
Washington, D.C.

Library of Congress Cataloging-in-Publication data:
Herring, Richard.
Financial regulation in the global economy / by Richard J. Herring
and Robert E. Litan.
p.   cm.—(Integrating national economies)
Includes bibliographical references and index.
ISBN 0-8157-5284-9 (alk. paper)—ISBN 0-8157-5283-0 (pbk.)
1. Financial services industry—State supervision.   2. Banks and
banking—State supervision.   3. International finance.   4. Financial
services industry—State supervision—International cooperation.
I. Litan, Robert E., 1950–   . II. Title. III. Series.
HG173.H47   1994
332.1—dc20   94-32769
                                                                    CIP

9 8 7 6 5 4 3 2 1

The paper used in this publication meets the minimum requirements of
American National Standard for Information Sciences—Permanence of Paper
for Printed Library Materials, ANSI Z39.48-1984

Typeset in Plantin

Composition by Princeton Editorial Associates
Princeton, New Jersey

Printed by R. R. Donnelley and Sons Co.
Harrisonburg, Virginia

Foreword

TECHNOLOGICAL advances have reduced the costs of cross-border transactions in all sectors of the economy. Spectacular reductions in the costs of transportation, telecommunications, and computation have greatly increased the ease with which firms can bridge the natural barriers of time and space that separate national markets, especially in financial services.

Restrictions against cross-border financial transactions are almost always unwise, both for the countries that impose them and for the world as a whole. At root, financial instruments—whether bank deposits, loans, stocks, bonds, or complicated derivative contracts— are ultimately claims on real resources, goods, or services. Efforts to restrict flows of financial instruments therefore hinder exchanges of goods and services, thus impeding the transfer of resources to their best uses. The result is reduced economic efficiency and growth. More and more countries around the world have recognized the harm from such restrictions by dropping controls on movement of capital.

The principal concerns of financial regulators and policymakers thus should be the ability of the financial institutions—banks, insurers, mutual funds, securities firms—to do business in different countries and the rules and conditions under which they are allowed to operate there. Among the central issues the authors explore in this book are: What should be the rights of access to markets in different countries? Whose rules should apply? And which national or regulatory bodies should enforce these rules?

In the most ambitious international effort to date, the European Union has tried to address all three questions—rights of access, rules, and supervisors. The members of GATT wrestled with right of access in the Uruguay Round negotiations, although provisions relating to the financial services sector ultimately were dropped from the agreement. And Canada, Mexico, and the United States have negotiated right-of-access rules for financial institutions in North America as part of the North American Free Trade Area.

In 1988 the Basel Accord set common capital standards for the major banks doing business across national borders. Initially signed by twelve countries—including the United States, Japan, and most member states of the European Union—these standards have subsequently been adopted by many other countries, including all the world's major banking centers. Financial regulators have continued to refine the standards to take account of additional risks. Many countries have also been negotiating to establish a similar regulatory framework for securities firms.

In short, regulators have put considerable effort into coordinating and harmonizing the rules governing the financial marketplace around the world. But markets are dynamic, presenting a moving target.

Richard Herring and Robert Litan try to provide a framework for understanding the measures to regulate international financial institutions that countries have agreed on so far. They project potential changes in the international marketplace and the implications of those changes for regulatory policy. They discuss how policymakers should respond and, given the relevant political constraints, how they are likely to respond. The book concludes with proposals designed to emphasize discipline of financial institutions by the market rather than by regulators.

Richard J. Herring is professor of finance at the Wharton School at the University of Pennsylvania and director of the Wharton Financial Institutions Center. He is grateful to his colleagues Jamshed Ghandi, Jack Guttentag, Richard Marston, and Anthony Santomero for numerous discussions on many of the topics addressed in this book. In addition he would like to acknowledge help from several past and present members of the Basel Committee on Banking and Supervision and to experts at the Bank for International Settlements, the Bank of England, and the Federal Reserve who shared their insights in interviews conducted in the preparation of this book. He is also grateful to members of the Biennial Multinational Banking Seminar and the Shadow Financial Regulatory Committee who have contributed to his understanding of financial regulation. Keith Norieke provided research assistance at several stages in the project along with Jallal Akhavein and Tom Grevens. Theresa DiNardo guided the successive drafts of the manuscript through word processing. Herring's work on the book was funded by the Alfred P. Sloan Foundation.

Robert E. Litan, formerly a Senior Fellow in the Economic Studies Program at the Brookings Institution, is a Deputy Assistant Attorney General in the Antitrust Division of the United States Department of Justice. He is grateful to Kacy Collons and Kirsten Wallenstein for research assistance.

The authors would like to thank Ralph Bryant, Stephan Haggard, Myron Kwast, Robert Lawrence, Larry Promisel, and the participants in a Brookings review conference held on October 15, 1993, and their discussants, Yasuhiro Maehara and Richard Webb, for their constructive criticisms and suggestions. Robert Litan completed the draft of this book, which was reviewed at the conference, while he was at Brookings and before he joined the Department of Justice.

Deborah Styles edited the manuscript, David Bearce and Zhiqin Zhou verified its factual content, and Carlotta Ribar proofread it. Princeton Editorial Associates prepared the index.

Funding for this project came from the Center for Global Partnership of the Japan Foundation, the Curry Foundation, the Ford Foundation, the Korea Foundation, the Alfred P. Sloan Foundation, the Tokyo Club Foundation for Global Studies, the United States-Japan Foundation, and the Alex C. Walker Educational and Charitable Foundation. The authors and Brookings are grateful for their support.

The views expressed in this book are those of the authors and should not be ascribed to any of the persons or organizations mentioned or acknowledged above, or to the trustees, officers, or staff members of the Brookings Institution.

BRUCE K. MAC LAURY
President

December 1994
Washington, D.C.

To Chris, Laura, and Michael
and
Avivah, Ari, and Alisa

Contents

Preface   xvii

1. **Introduction and Overview**   1

   The Internationalization of Finance: Implications
   for Regulation 4
   Harmonization of Financial Rules: Opportunities
   and Limits 7
   Recommendations 9

2. **International Financial Integration:
   The Continuing Process**   13

   Effect on Users of Financial Services 14
   Effect on Financial Service Institutions 18
   Effect on Regulators 19
   Expanding International Flows of Capital 23
   Increasing International Asset Price Integration 29
   Covered Interest Rate Parity in the Eurocurrency Market 29
   Conclusion: The Extent of International
   Financial Integration 44

3. **Financial Regulation in Domestic and
   International Environments**   49

   Rationales for Financial Regulation in a Domestic Setting 49
   Financial Regulation in an International Environment 64
   The Appropriate Size of the Supervisory and
   Regulatory Domain 79

4. International Efforts in Financial Regulation
   to Date   86

Rights of Access   88
Systemic Risk and Solvency   95
Common Bank Capital Standards: The Basel Accord   107
Consumer Protection   113
Other Objectives   115

5. Prospects for International Cooperation in the
   Regulation and Supervision of Financial Services   120

The Willingness to Cooperate   121
Emergency Liquidity Assistance for Internationally
   Active Banks   126
Refinements and Extensions of the Basel Concordat
   and Accord   132
Rules for Securities Firms   137
Dealing with Financial Conglomerates   142
Market Alternatives to Regulatory Harmonization   147
Competitive Equity   151

Comments   153

Yasuhiro Maehara   153
Richard Webb   163

Appendix: Permissible Activities for Banking
Organizations in Various Financial Centers   167

References   171

Index   179

Tables

2-1. Costs of Air Transportation and Telephone Calls,
     Selected Years, 1930–90   14
2-2. Five Levels of International Financial Integration   30
3-1. Objectives and Tools of Financial Regulation   50
3-2. Illustrative List of Bank Deposit Insurance Schemes   54
3-3. Permissible Activities for Banking Organizations in
     Various Financial Centers   58
4-1. International Financial Regulatory Initiatives   87

Figures

2-1. Direct Issues of Securities in International Flows of Credit,
1981–92   15

2-2. Life Insurance, Pension, and Mutual Fund Assets as a
Percentage of Household Assets, Selected Countries,
1980, 1985, 1990   17

2-3. Indexed Value of World Exports and World GDP, 1963–90   23

2-4. Indexed Value of World Exports and CHIPS Payments,
1970–92   24

2-5. Daily Turnover in Foreign Exchange, Selected Countries,
1986, 1989, 1992   25

2-6. International Bank Lending, 1973–92   26

2-7. International Issues of Bonds, 1981–92   27

2-8. Gross Cross-Border Equity Flows, 1979–90   27

2-9. Swap Market Growth, 1987–92: Outstanding Notional
Principal of Interest Rate and Currency Swaps   28

2-10. External and Internal Money Markets in the
Deutsche Mark, January 1973–August 1974   33

2-11. External and Internal Money Markets in the French Franc,
1982–91   35

2-12. Uncovered Interest Differentials, Four Countries,
1973–92   38

2-13. Real Interest Rate Differentials, United States and
Four Other Countries, 1977–92   41

4-1. The Corporate Structure of Banco Ambrosiano   102

Preface to the Studies on Integrating National Economies

E CONOMIC interdependence among nations has increased sharply in the past half century. For example, while the value of total production of industrial countries increased at a rate of about 9 percent a year on average between 1964 and 1992, the value of the exports of those nations grew at an average rate of 12 percent, and lending and borrowing across national borders through banks surged upward even more rapidly at 23 percent a year. This international economic interdependence has contributed to significantly improved standards of living for most countries. Continuing international economic integration holds out the promise of further benefits. Yet the increasing sensitivity of national economies to events and policies originating abroad creates dilemmas and pitfalls if national policies and international cooperation are poorly managed.

The Brookings Project on Integrating National Economies, of which this study is a component, focuses on the interplay between two fundamental facts about the world at the end of the twentieth century. First, the world will continue for the foreseeable future to be organized politically into nation-states with sovereign governments. Second, increasing economic integration among nations will continue to erode differences among national economies and undermine the autonomy of national governments. The project explores the opportunities and tensions arising from these two facts.

Scholars from a variety of disciplines have produced twenty-one studies for the first phase of the project. Each study examines the heightened competition between national political sovereignty and increased cross-border economic integration. This preface identifies background themes and issues common to all the studies and provides a brief overview of the project as a whole.[1]

Increasing World Economic Integration

Two underlying sets of causes have led nations to become more closely intertwined. First, technological, social, and cultural changes have sharply reduced the effective economic distances among nations. Second, many of the government policies that traditionally inhibited cross-border transactions have been relaxed or even dismantled.

The same improvements in transportation and communications technology that make it much easier and cheaper for companies in New York to ship goods to California, for residents of Strasbourg to visit relatives in Marseilles, and for investors in Hokkaido to buy and sell shares on the Tokyo Stock Exchange facilitate trade, migration, and capital movements spanning nations and continents. The sharply reduced costs of moving goods, money, people, and information underlie the profound economic truth that technology has made the world markedly smaller.

New communications technology has been especially significant for financial activity. Computers, switching devices, and telecommunications satellites have slashed the cost of transmitting information internationally, of confirming transactions, and of paying for transactions. In the 1950s, for example, foreign exchange could be bought and sold only during conventional business hours in the initiating party's time zone. Such transactions can now be carried out instantaneously twenty-four hours a day. Large banks pass the management of their worldwide foreign-exchange positions around the globe from one branch to another, staying continuously ahead of the setting sun.

Such technological innovations have increased the knowledge of potentially profitable international exchanges and of economic opportunities abroad. Those developments, in turn, have changed consumers' and producers' tastes. Foreign goods, foreign vacations, foreign financial investments—virtually anything from other nations—have lost some of their exotic character.

1. A complete list of authors and study titles is included at the beginning of this volume, facing the title page.

Although technological change permits increased contact among nations, it would not have produced such dramatic effects if it had been countermanded by government policies. Governments have traditionally taxed goods moving in international trade, directly restricted imports and subsidized exports, and tried to limit international capital movements. Those policies erected "separation fences" at the borders of nations. From the perspective of private sector agents, separation fences imposed extra costs on cross-border transactions. They reduced trade and, in some cases, eliminated it. During the 1930s governments used such policies with particular zeal, a practice now believed to have deepened and lengthened the Great Depression.

After World War II, most national governments began—sometimes unilaterally, more often collaboratively—to lower their separation fences, to make them more permeable, or sometimes even to tear down parts of them. The multilateral negotiations under the auspices of the General Agreement on Trade and Tariffs (GATT)—for example, the Kennedy Round in the 1960s, the Tokyo Round in the 1970s, and most recently the protracted negotiations of the Uruguay Round, formally signed only in April 1994—stand out as the most prominent examples of fence lowering for trade in goods. Though contentious and marked by many compromises, the GATT negotiations are responsible for sharp reductions in at-the-border restrictions on trade in goods and services. After the mid-1980s a large number of developing countries moved unilaterally to reduce border barriers and to pursue outwardly oriented policies.

The lowering of fences for financial transactions began later and was less dramatic. Nonetheless, by the 1990s government restrictions on capital flows, especially among the industrial countries, were much less important and widespread than at the end of World War II and in the 1950s.

By shrinking the economic distances among nations, changes in technology would have progressively integrated the world economy even in the absence of reductions in governments' separation fences. Reductions in separation fences would have enhanced interdependence even without the technological innovations. Together, these two sets of evolutionary changes have reinforced each other and strikingly transformed the world economy.

Changes in the Government of Nations

Simultaneously with the transformation of the global economy, major changes have occurred in the world's political structure. First, the number of governmental decisionmaking units in the world has expanded markedly, and political power has been diffused more broadly among them. Rising nationalism and, in some areas, heightened ethnic tensions have accompanied that increasing political pluralism.

The history of membership in international organizations documents the sharp growth in the number of independent states. For example, only 44 nations participated in the Bretton Woods conference of July 1944, which gave birth to the International Monetary Fund. But by the end of 1970, the IMF had 118 member nations. The number of members grew to 150 by the mid-1980s and to 178 by December 1993. Much of this growth reflects the collapse of colonial empires. Although many nations today are small and carry little individual weight in the global economy, their combined influence is considerable, and their interests cannot be ignored as easily as they were in the past.

A second political trend, less visible but equally important, has been the gradual loss of the political and economic hegemony of the United States. Immediately after World War II, the United States by itself accounted for more than one-third of world production. By the early 1990s the U.S. share had fallen to about one-fifth. Concurrently, the political and economic influence of the European colonial powers continued to wane, and the economic significance of nations outside Europe and North America, such as Japan, Korea, Indonesia, China, Brazil, and Mexico, increased. A world in which economic power and influence are widely diffused has displaced a world in which one or a few nations effectively dominated international decisionmaking.

Turmoil and the prospect of fundamental change in the formerly centrally planned economies compose a third factor causing radical changes in world politics. During the era of central planning, governments in those nations tried to limit external influences on their economies. Now leaders in the formerly planned economies are trying to adopt reforms modeled on Western capitalist principles. To the extent that these efforts succeed, those nations will increase their economic involvement with the rest of the world. Political and economic alignments among the Western industrialized nations will be forced to adapt.

Governments and scholars have begun to assess these three trends, but their far-reaching ramifications will not be clear for decades.

Dilemmas for National Policies

Cross-border economic integration and national political sovereignty have increasingly come into conflict, leading to a growing mismatch between the economic and political structures of the world. The effective domains of economic markets have come to coincide less and less with national governmental jurisdictions.

When the separation fences at nations' borders were high, governments and citizens could sharply distinguish "international" from "domestic" policies. International policies dealt with at-the-border barriers, such as tariffs and quotas, or responded to events occurring abroad. In contrast, domestic policies were concerned with everything behind the nation's borders, such as competition and antitrust rules, corporate governance, product standards, worker safety, regulation and supervision of financial institutions, environmental protection, tax codes, and the government's budget. Domestic policies were regarded as matters about which nations were sovereign, to be determined by the preferences of the nation's citizens and its political institutions, without regard for effects on other nations.

As separation fences have been lowered and technological innovations have shrunk economic distances, a multitude of formerly neglected differences among nations' domestic policies have become exposed to international scrutiny. National governments and international negotiations must thus increasingly deal with "deeper"—behind-the-border—integration. For example, if country A permits companies to emit air and water pollutants whereas country B does not, companies that use pollution-generating methods of production will find it cheaper to produce in country A. Companies in country B that compete internationally with companies in country A are likely to complain that foreign competitors enjoy unfair advantages and to press for international pollution standards.

Deeper integration requires analysis of the economic and the political aspects of virtually all nonborder policies and practices. Such issues have already figured prominently in negotiations over the evolution of the European Community, over the Uruguay Round of GATT negotiations, over the North American Free Trade Agreement (NAFTA), and over the bilateral economic relationships between Japan and the United States. Future debates about behind-the-border policies will occur with increasing frequency and prove at least as complex and contentious as the past negotiations regarding at-the-border restrictions.

Tensions about deeper integration arise from three broad sources: cross-border spillovers, diminished national autonomy, and challenges to political sovereignty.

Cross-Border Spillovers

Some activities in one nation produce consequences that spill across borders and affect other nations. Illustrations of these spillovers abound. Given the impact of modern technology of banking and securities markets in creating interconnected networks, lax rules in one nation erode the ability of all other nations to enforce banking and securities rules and to deal with fraudulent transactions. Given the rapid diffusion of knowledge, science and technology policies in one nation generate knowledge that other nations can use without full payment. Labor market policies become matters of concern to other nations because workers migrate in search of work; policies in one nation can trigger migration that floods or starves labor markets elsewhere. When one nation dumps pollutants into the air or water that other nations breathe or drink, the matter goes beyond the unitary concern of the polluting nation and becomes a matter for international negotiation. Indeed, the hydrocarbons that are emitted into the atmosphere when individual nations burn coal for generating electricity contribute to global warming and are thereby a matter of concern for the entire world.

The tensions associated with cross-border spillovers can be especially vexing when national policies generate outcomes alleged to be competitively inequitable, as in the example in which country A permits companies to emit pollutants and country B does not. Or consider a situation in which country C requires commodities, whether produced at home or abroad, to meet certain design standards, justified for safety reasons. Foreign competitors may find it too expensive to meet these standards. In that event, the standards in C act very much like tariffs or quotas, effectively narrowing or even eliminating foreign competition for domestic producers. Citing examples of this sort, producers or governments in individual nations often complain that business is not conducted on a "level playing field." Typically, the complaining nation proposes that *other* nations adjust their policies to moderate or remove the competitive inequities.

Arguments for creating a level playing field are troublesome at best. International trade occurs precisely because of differences among nations—in resource endowments, labor skills, and consumer tastes. Nations specialize in producing goods and services in which they are relatively most efficient. In a fundamental sense, cross-border trade is valuable because the playing field is *not* level.

When David Ricardo first developed the theory of comparative advantage, he focused on differences among nations owing to climate or technology. But Ricardo could as easily have ascribed the productive differences to differing "social climates" as to physical or technological climates. Taking all "climatic" differences as given, the theory of comparative advantage argues that free trade among nations will maximize global welfare.

Taken to its logical extreme, the notion of leveling the playing field implies that nations should become homogeneous in all major respects. But that recommendation is unrealistic and even pernicious. Suppose country A decides that it is too poor to afford the costs of a clean environment, and will thus permit the production of goods that pollute local air and water supplies. Or suppose it concludes that it cannot afford stringent protections for worker safety. Country A will then argue that it is inappropriate for other nations to impute to country A the value they themselves place on a clean environment and safety standards (just as it would be inappropriate to impute the A valuations to the environment of other nations). The core of the idea of political sovereignty is to permit national residents to order their lives and property in accord with their own preferences.

Which perspective about differences among nations in behind-the-border policies is more compelling? Is country A merely exercising its national preferences and appropriately exploiting its comparative advantage in goods that are dirty or dangerous to produce? Or does a legitimate international problem exist that justifies pressure from other nations urging country A to accept changes in its policies (thus curbing its national sovereignty)? When national governments negotiate resolutions to such questions—trying to agree whether individual nations are legitimately exercising sovereign choices or, alternatively, engaging in behavior that is unfair or damaging to other nations—the dialogue is invariably contentious because the resolutions depend on the typically complex circumstances of the international spillovers and on the relative weights accorded to the interests of particular individuals and particular nations.

Diminished National Autonomy

As cross-border economic integration increases, governments experience greater difficulties in trying to control events within their borders. Those difficulties, summarized by the term *diminished autonomy*, are the second set of reasons why tensions arise from the competition between political sovereignty and economic integration.

For example, nations adjust monetary and fiscal policies to influence domestic inflation and employment. In setting these policies, smaller countries have always been somewhat constrained by foreign economic events and policies. Today, however, all nations are constrained, often severely. More than in the past, therefore, nations may be better able to achieve their economic goals if they work together collaboratively in adjusting their macroeconomic policies.

Diminished autonomy and cross-border spillovers can sometimes be allowed to persist without explicit international cooperation to deal with them. States in the United States adopt their own tax systems and set policies for assistance to poor single people without any formal cooperation or limitation. Market pressures operate to force a degree of de facto cooperation. If one state taxes corporations too heavily, it knows business will move elsewhere. (Those familiar with older debates about "fiscal federalism" within the United States and other nations will recognize the similarity between those issues and the emerging international debates about deeper integration of national economies.) Analogously, differences among nations in regulations, standards, policies, institutions, and even social and cultural preferences create economic incentives for a kind of arbitrage that erodes or eliminates the differences. Such pressures involve not only the conventional arbitrage that exploits price differentials (buying at one point in geographic space or time and selling at another) but also shifts in the location of production facilities and in the residence of factors of production.

In many other cases, however, cross-border spillovers, arbitrage pressures, and diminished effectiveness of national policies can produce unwanted consequences. In cases involving what economists call externalities (external economies and diseconomies), national governments may need to cooperate to promote mutual interests. For example, population growth, continued urbanization, and the more intensive exploitation of natural resources generate external diseconomies not only within but across national boundaries. External economies generated when benefits spill across national jurisdictions probably also increase in importance (for instance, the gains from basic research and from control of communicable diseases).

None of these situations is new, but technological change and the reduction of tariffs and quotas heighten their importance. When one nation produces goods (such as scientific research) or "bads" (such as pollution) that significantly affect other nations, individual governments acting sequentially and noncooperatively cannot deal effectively with the resulting issues. In the absence of explicit cooperation and political leadership, too few collective goods and too many collective bads will be supplied.

Challenges to Political Sovereignty

The pressures from cross-border economic integration sometimes even lead individuals or governments to challenge the core assumptions of national political sovereignty. Such challenges are a third source of tensions about deeper integration.

The existing world system of nation-states assumes that a nation's residents are free to follow their own values and to select their own political arrangements without interference from others. Similarly, property rights are allocated by nation. (The so-called global commons, such as outer space and the deep seabed, are the sole exceptions.) A nation is assumed to have the sovereign right to exploit its property in accordance with its own preferences and policies. Political sovereignty is thus analogous to the concept of consumer sovereignty (the presumption that the individual consumer best knows his or her own interests and should exercise them freely).

In times of war, some nations have had sovereignty wrested from them by force. In earlier eras, a handful of individuals or groups have questioned the premises of political sovereignty. With the profound increases in economic integration in recent decades, however, a larger number of individuals and groups—and occasionally even their national governments—have identified circumstances in which, it is claimed, some universal or international set of values should take precedence over the preferences or policies of particular nations.

Some groups seize on human-rights issues, for example, or what they deem to be egregiously inappropriate political arrangements in other nations. An especially prominent case occurred when citizens in many nations labeled the former apartheid policies of South Africa an affront to universal values and emphasized that the South African government was not legitimately representing the interests of a majority of South Africa's residents. Such views caused many national governments to apply economic sanctions against South Africa. Examples of value conflicts are not restricted to human rights, however. Groups focusing on environmental issues characterize tropical rain forests as the lungs of the world and the genetic repository for numerous species of plants and animals that are the heritage of all mankind. Such views lead Europeans, North Americans, or Japanese to challenge the timber-cutting policies of Brazilians and Indonesians. A recent controversy over tuna fishing with long drift nets that kill porpoises is yet another example. Environmentalists in the United States whose sensibilities were offended by the drowning of porpoises required U.S. boats at some additional expense to amend their fishing practices. The U.S. fishermen, complaining about imported tuna caught with less regard for porpoises, persuaded the U.S. government to ban such tuna imports (both direct imports from the countries in which the tuna is caught and indirect imports shipped via third countries). Mexico and Venezuela were the main countries affected by this ban; a GATT dispute panel sided with Mexico against the United States in the controversy, which further upset the U.S. environmental community.

A common feature of all such examples is the existence, real or alleged, of "psychological externalities" or "political failures." Those holding such views reject untrammeled political sovereignty for nation-states in deference to universal or non-national values. They wish to constrain the exercise of individual nations' sovereignties through international negotiations or, if necessary, by even stronger intervention.

The Management of International Convergence

In areas in which arbitrage pressures and cross-border spillovers are weak and psychological or political externalities are largely absent, national governments may encounter few problems with deeper integration. Diversity across nations may persist quite easily. But at the other extreme, arbitrage and spillovers in some areas may be so strong that they threaten to erode national diversity completely. Or psychological and political sensitivities may be asserted too powerfully to be ignored. Governments will then be confronted with serious tensions, and national policies and behaviors may eventually converge to common, worldwide patterns (for example, subject to internationally agreed norms or minimum standards). Eventual convergence across nations, if it occurs, could happen in a harmful way (national policies and practices being driven to a least common denominator with externalities ignored, in effect a "race to the bottom") or it could occur with mutually beneficial results ("survival of the fittest and the best").

Each study in this series addresses basic questions about the management of international convergence: if, when, and how national governments should intervene to try to influence the consequences of arbitrage pressures, cross-border spillovers, diminished autonomy, and the assertion of psychological or political externalities. A wide variety of responses is conceivable. We identify six, which should be regarded not as distinct categories but as ranges along a continuum.

National autonomy defines a situation at one end of the continuum in which national governments make decentralized decisions with little or no consultation and no explicit cooperation. This response represents political sovereignty at its strongest, undiluted by any international management of convergence.

Mutual recognition, like national autonomy, presumes decentralized decisions by national governments and relies on market competition to guide the process of international convergence. Mutual recognition, however, entails exchanges of information and consultations among governments to constrain the formation of national regulations and policies. As understood in discussions of economic integration within the European Community, moreover, mutual recognition entails an explicit acceptance by each member nation of the regulations, standards, and certification procedures of other members. For example, mutual recognition allows wine or liquor produced in any European Union country to be sold in all twelve member countries even if production standards in member countries differ. Doctors licensed in France are permitted to practice in Germany, and vice versa, even if licensing procedures in the two countries differ.

Governments may agree on rules that restrict their freedom to set policy or that promote gradual convergence in the structure of policy. As international consultations and monitoring of compliance with such rules become more important, this situation can be described as *monitored decentralization*. The Group of Seven finance ministers meetings, supplemented by the IMF's surveillance over exchange rate and macroeconomic policies, illustrate this approach to management.

Coordination goes further than mutual recognition and monitored decentralization in acknowledging convergence pressures. It is also more ambitious in promoting intergovernmental cooperation to deal with them. Coordination involves jointly designed mutual adjustments of national policies. In clear-cut cases of coordination, bargaining occurs and governments agree to behave differently from the ways they would have behaved without the agreement. Examples include the World Health Organization's procedures for controlling communicable diseases and the 1987 Montreal Protocol (to a 1985 framework convention) for the protection of stratospheric ozone by reducing emissions of chlorofluorocarbons.

Explicit harmonization, which requires still higher levels of intergovernmental cooperation, may require agreement on regional standards or world standards. Explicit harmonization typically entails still greater departures from decentralization in decisionmaking and still further strengthening of international institutions. The 1988 agreement among major central banks to set minimum standards for the required capital positions of commercial banks (reached through the Committee on Banking Regulations and Supervisory Practices at the Bank for International Settlements) is an example of partially harmonized regulations.

At the opposite end of the spectrum from national autonomy lies *federalist mutual governance*, which implies continuous bargaining and joint, centralized decisionmaking. To make federalist mutual governance work would require greatly strengthened supranational institutions. This end of the management spectrum, now relevant only as an analytical benchmark, is a possible outcome that can be imagined for the middle or late decades of the twenty-first century, possibly even sooner for regional groupings like the European Union.

Overview of the Brookings Project

Despite their growing importance, the issues of deeper economic integration and its competition with national political sovereignty were largely neglected in the 1980s. In 1992 the Brookings Institution initiated its project on Integrating National Economies to direct attention to these important questions.

In studying this topic, Brookings sought and received the co-operation of some of the world's leading economists, political scientists, foreign-policy specialists, and government officials, representing all regions of the world. Although some functional areas require a special focus on European, Japanese, and North American perspectives, at all junctures the goal was to include, in addition, the perspectives of developing nations and the formerly centrally planned economies.

The first phase of the project commissioned the twenty-one scholarly studies listed at the beginning of the book. One or two lead discussants, typically residents of parts of the world other than the area where the author resides, were asked to comment on each study.

Authors enjoyed substantial freedom to design their individual studies, taking due account of the overall themes and goals of the project. The guidelines for the studies requested that at least some of the analysis be carried out with a non-normative perspective. In effect, authors were asked to develop a "baseline" of what might happen in the absence of changed policies or further international cooperation. For their normative analyses, authors were asked to start with an agnostic posture that did not prejudge the net benefits or costs resulting from integration. The project organizers themselves had no presumption about whether national diversity is better or worse than international convergence or about what the individual studies should conclude regarding the desirability of increased integration. On the contrary, each author was asked to address the trade-offs in his or her issue area between diversity and convergence and to locate the area, currently and prospectively, on

the spectrum of international management possibilities running between national autonomy through mutual recognition to coordination and explicit harmonization.

HENRY J. AARON   SUSAN M. COLLINS
RALPH C. BRYANT   ROBERT Z. LAWRENCE

Financial Regulation in the
Global Economy

Chapter 1

Introduction and Overview

*I*F THERE IS any arena of economic activity that has become global in recent decades, it is finance. Modern means of communication—telephones and computers—help transfer vast sums of money across national boundaries every day. Money moves faster and in response to smaller price differentials than do goods or people.

Nevertheless, regulation of financial activities and the institutions that conduct them continues to be carried out mostly by national, and in some countries subnational, governments. By the same token, the problems countries have experienced in financial institutions have so far been confined largely to national borders. The now infamous savings and loan debacle in the United States had essentially no international ramifications. The same is generally true for this country's rash of bank failures since the early 1980s and for the troubles of banks in Japan and the Scandinavian countries in the early 1990s.

There have been important exceptions to this pattern, however, and the prospect that more of them might occur has aroused concern among financial regulators and policymakers in many countries. The potential spillovers from bank failures in one country to others were first highlighted in 1974 when the closure of a relatively small German bank, Herstatt, that was active in foreign exchange markets caused substantial disruptions in international interbank markets. Ten years later, U.S. bank regulators were forced to take over the Continental Illinois Bank, then the ninth largest in this country, in large part because of a run on the bank that began with foreign depositors. Most recently, the scandal surrounding the

1

failure of the Bank of Commerce and Credit International (BCCI) demonstrated how unscrupulous bankers can exploit gaps in domestic and international banking regulations to cause losses to depositors around the world. Although BCCI's failure did not at any time pose a significant threat to the orderly operation of global financial markets, it served as yet another warning to policymakers to pay attention to the growing interdependence of the international financial system.

Even when financial institutions do not fail, their increasing presence in many countries has aroused other concerns. Domestically owned institutions complain when they perceive that foreign institutions are given special tax or regulatory advantages by their home governments. For example, through much of the 1980s some large U.S. banks argued that they were losing market share to Japanese banks because U.S. regulators imposed more restrictive capital standards than their counterparts in Japan. Such arguments about unfairness have grown increasingly common in many areas of international trade and investment, but they have become especially intense in the financial arena.

In this book we attempt to address how in the years and decades ahead countries should best take account of the increasingly international character and interdependence of financial activities and markets. Given the relevant policy objectives, we attempt to identify those financial regulatory policies that are most likely to advance the economic interests of individual nations and of the world economy (recognizing that what may be good for one or more countries may not be in the interest of the expanding global economy). Of course, what may be desirable may not be politically possible. For this reason, we also speculate on what outcomes are most likely, given our view of the prevailing political realities.

We proceed on the premise that restrictions against cross-border financial transactions are almost always unwise, both for the countries that maintain them and for the world as a whole. At bottom, financial instruments—whether currencies, loans, stocks, bonds, or complicated derivative contracts (instruments whose value is "derived" from other instruments)—are nothing more than claims on real resources, goods, or assets. When nations restrict the flows of financial instruments, therefore, they are ultimately restricting exchange in goods and assets, impeding the transfer of resources to their best uses. The result is reduced economic efficiency and growth.[1] Increasingly, countries around the world have recognized this by dropping controls on movements of capital.

The principal challenges for financial regulators and policymakers thus pertain less to measures required to facilitate the transfer of resources from one country to another than to restrictions on the ability of the financial *institutions* that arrange and carry out these transfers—banks, insurers, mutual funds, securities firms—to do business in different countries and to the rules and conditions under which they are allowed to operate once there. More specifically, the central issues we explore in this book are: What should be the *rights of access* for firms in the financial services industry to markets in different countries? Whose *rules* should apply to the institutions that do business there? And which nations or regulatory bodies should *enforce* those rules? Each country must answer these questions for its domestically chartered institutions that do business within that nation's borders. In an increasingly integrated world, how will countries answer these questions for financial institutions that cross national borders?

We are not the first to take up these subjects, of course, nor will we be the last. In the mid-1980s, when financial markets were not as integrated internationally as they are now, Ralph Bryant published a pioneering study of these issues. Richard Cooper has addressed similar and even broader questions in his years of writing about economic interdependence. More recently, both Richard O'Brien and Benn Steil have tackled the regulatory issues raised by the increasingly international nature of financial activities.[2]

Governments, too, have devoted increasing attention to this subject, in the seven years since the publication of Bryant's book. In the most ambitious effort to date, the European Union has attempted to address all three issues—rights of access, which rules, and which supervisors—in various directives issued in connection with its single market initiative. The members of the General Agreement on Tariffs and Trade (GATT) have wrestled with rights of access in the Uruguay Round negotiations, although provisions relating to the financial ser-

1. For evidence, see Alesina, Grilli, and Milesi-Ferrett (1993).
2. Bryant (1987). Cooper has had a long history of writing in this area. For a sampling of some of his important contributions, see Cooper (1986). O'Brien (1992); and Steil (1992).

vices sector ultimately were dropped from the agreement. And Canada, Mexico, and the United States have negotiated right-of-access rules for financial institutions in North America as part of the North American Free Trade Area (NAFTA).

Attention also has been given by regulators from major industrialized countries both inside and outside the European Union (EU) to the potentially more difficult matters of rules and enforcement. In 1988 twelve countries—including the United States, Japan, and most member-states of the EU—agreed to the Basel Accord, which set common capital standards for "international banks," or the major banks doing business across national borders. Since then these standards have been adopted by a large number of other countries, including all the world's major banking centers. Financial regulators have continued to attempt to refine the standards to take account of additional risks. Many countries have also been negotiating for several years to establish a similar regulatory framework for securities firms.

In short, much effort already has gone into coordinating and harmonizing the rules governing the financial marketplace around the world. Indeed, it is our impression that nations have made more progress in addressing the questions of access, rules, and enforcement in the financial arena than in any other sphere of cross-border activity. But markets are dynamic and present a moving target for policymakers. In this book we try to provide a framework for understanding what measures countries have agreed on so far to regulate financial institutions active in international finance and to project how the international marketplace may change and what implications those changes may hold for regulatory policy. Then we discuss how policymakers should respond and, given the relevant political constraints, how they are likely to respond.

The Internationalization of Finance: Implications for Regulation

Notwithstanding the clear trend toward globalized finance, integration across national boundaries is still uneven, as we demonstrate in chapter 2. Roughly speaking, large companies seeking wholesale financial services can readily cross borders to get them, and, by the same token, so can firms that provide these services. For example,

American firms that want to borrow can do so in any major currency and from virtually any institution or market. The removal of capital controls and major advances in communications and transportation make this possible. As a result, nations that attempt to regulate providers of financial services to the wholesale market must confront regulatory arbitrage as a fact of life. If regulation is excessively restrictive, providers and users will simply go to less restrictive, cheaper jurisdictions.

There are limits, however, to which nations can and will engage in a competition in laxity. Users of financial services will not choose to deal with institutions or markets in countries with excessively lax regulation, imperfect legal systems, or inadequate communications and transportation facilities. There is a reason, in other words, why all banks, insurers, and securities houses have not moved to the Cayman Islands but choose to remain in the United States, Europe, or Japan, where they may complain about excessive regulation or taxation but nevertheless continue to conduct business. Accordingly, even in markets where financial integration seems more or less complete, individual nations may still have the ability to maintain different, and perhaps more restrictive, regulatory regimes—provided that any such additional regulatory protections are valued by investors and users of the financial services offered in those countries.

The same is true in retail financial markets, where financial integration is far less complete. Individuals and small firms still customarily patronize financial service providers located in their countries. They want to see and to interact with local personnel. And communications and transportation costs are not so low that customers can inexpensively obtain equivalent services from providers abroad.

Why then do countries regulate and supervise their financial institutions and markets?[3] We attempt to answer this question in chapter 3, first solely in a domestic context. We suggest that the principal

3. Quinn has provided a useful distinction between regulation and supervision: "Regulation . . . is about rules and about the precise formulation and policing of those rules. . . . Supervision is different, both in content and in style: the laws set the framework within which authorized companies may operate, rather than prescribing in detail how the relevant goods and services should be provided. Within that context, the companies providing those goods and services are, broadly speaking, left to make their own business decisions. . . . The role of the banking supervisor is to seek to enforce prudent conduct by banks, not customer satisfaction. . . . The supervisor's task is not to look after the interest of shareholders or of borrowers." Quinn (1993).

reason is that failures of individual financial institutions may pose systemic risks to the broader financial system and from there to the real economy. Of course, central banks and the presence of government insurance for bank (and perhaps other financial) liabilities can virtually eliminate systemic risk, but at the price of creating a moral hazard for private participants to take risks at the expense of governments and the taxpayers who finance them. Properly designed regulation can and should be able to avoid this danger.

Other rationales for financial regulation also are commonly advanced, with different emphases in different countries. In the United States, where distrust of financial institutions has strong historical roots, various types of regulation have been justified as necessary to protect consumers from excessive prices and discrimination; to prevent an undue concentration of economic and even political power; and to encourage the allocation of credit to favored industries, activities, and regions. In Japan regulation of interest rates and commissions has been maintained with the ostensible purpose of protecting consumers and discouraging excessive competition. Governments of the EU countries also have long displayed interest in allocating credit to achieve certain social objectives. And less developed countries historically have tightly regulated their financial sector—often providing for government ownership of many key financial institutions—to achieve some or all of the purposes for which industrialized countries have maintained financial regulation.

In chapter 3 we explore how these rationales for financial regulation change, or should be modified, when financial activities and firms cross national borders. In brief, we conclude that just as countries are concerned about systemic risk within their borders, they have every reason to maintain that concern in a global market where financial difficulties experienced in one country can be transmitted to others. Another way in which countries may suffer from unwelcome financial spillovers is through money-laundering activities that facilitate criminal enterprise. Countries that permit such activities reduce the costs of criminal enterprise that can affect or be conducted within other countries. In short, so-called direct spillovers justify not only domestic regulation, but also, where they cross national borders, at least some degree of multinational coordination or harmonization.

More difficult are what we (and elsewhere in this series, Richard Cooper) call indirect spillovers, or the effects of regulatory regimes in one country on the abilities of firms domiciled in that country to compete against firms domiciled in other countries. The unlevel playing field created by different bank capital standards, for example, was a major impetus for the attempted harmonization of those rules in the Basel Accord. Yet, as we discuss in chapters 4 and 5, harmonizing simply for the sake of leveling the playing field can be dangerous if in the process nations lose sight of other important objectives. In the financial arena in particular, we are concerned that in their quest to harmonize capital standards and other regulations, regulators may compromise the central objective of strengthening the international financial system.

Harmonization of Financial Rules: Opportunities and Limits

Still, the international character of financial activity has produced some notable efforts by various countries at harmonizing their financial rules and enforcement efforts. When we speak of harmonization, however, we do not refer to a single concept, but rather to the continuum of efforts by which countries take account of the policies of other countries. How much account they take depends on how they choose to resolve an inevitable tension: between accommodating economic forces that drive money and institutions across national borders with increasing speed and preserving the autonomy of national governments, reflecting the preferences and objectives of local citizens.

Thus where countries can enforce local rules cost-effectively and without significant evasion, it is likely that countries will develop and enforce those rules autonomously, reflecting only the preferences of their citizens. However, the easier and more desirable it is for firms and individuals to engage in regulatory arbitrage—moving from jurisdictions with strict regulatory regimes to those with lax regulation—the greater will be the demand both within and across countries to coordinate or in some way harmonize their rules and enforcement with other nations. In the limit, of course, regulatory arbitrage can be stopped by common rules binding on many countries and enforced by multinational or international agencies, just as federal law and courts apply to interstate commerce within the United States.

So far, the harmonization efforts that have occurred in the financial sector have fallen well short of this extreme. The weakest form of harmonization is coordination of domestic enforcement efforts to catch violators of the domestic laws of individual countries. This has occurred among banking and securities regulators from predominantly industrialized countries.

The European Union has adopted a stronger form of harmonization for its financial activities: a policy of mutual recognition whereby member states within the union have agreed to allow firms from other states to operate under home country rules and supervision. Thus, for example, British banks can do business in Germany or France, exercising powers authorized under British law and supervised by British banking regulators. This state of affairs could not exist, however, unless member states had confidence in the appropriateness of each other's local rules and the effectiveness of their supervisors. One way to develop that confidence is for countries to agree on minimum standards. As a result, policies of mutual recognition also typically entail some agreement on minimum standards of conduct, which is the case in the EU.

The most ambitious efforts at financial harmonization so far have been the bank capital rules developed by the Basel Committee on Banking Supervision. The Basel standards are expressly common minimum standards, although they continue to be enforced by individual countries. Common rules, especially when enforced by a single body, obviously hold the greatest promise for preventing regulatory arbitrage. But the very process that produces common rules—potentially lengthy negotiations between representatives of different countries—also demonstrates their greatest disadvantage: their potential inflexibility and difficulty in being corrected. Simply put, international regulators can just as easily agree on the wrong standards as the right ones, especially in finance, where market developments move so rapidly.

The Basel Accord for banks is a good example. Although the Basel Committee made some progress in agreeing on minimum capital standards, those rules contain arbitrary elements, as we discuss in chapter 4, that do not necessarily advance overall economic welfare. The Committee has tried to correct some of the flaws in the original Accord by developing rules to handle interest rate and market risks (among others), but the complicated outcome that may finally be agreed on may not improve bank safety or may instead simply increase regulatory burdens. We believe the Basel Committee should return to its original role of serving as an information clearinghouse and forum in which regulators from different countries can exchange views about how to measure and control various sorts of risks.

The case for adopting Basel-like standards for the securities industry also has yet to be supported, even if obtaining agreement on such standards were possible (an outcome that has thus far proved elusive). Proponents of this course point to the dangers exhibited by the collapse of Drexel Burnham Lambert and how, but for active intervention by U.S. regulatory authorities in particular, the international payments system could have been jeopardized. We challenge this view in chapter 3, demonstrating that the dangers from Drexel's collapse were overstated and that, in any event, the regulatory system as it existed was fully capable of responding to the crisis.

More fundamentally, the case for harmonizing capital standards for securities firms across countries fails to recognize a fundamental fact: to the extent that failures of securities firms pose risks to the international financial system, they do so principally because of their linkages with banks. But many other types of firms also expose banks to risk; banks lend to nonsecurities firms also. We see no compelling case why *international* capital standards should be set for nonsecurities firms, and so we believe the same logic applies to securities firms.

Recommendations

What then is and should be the future of efforts by countries to harmonize their rules and enforcement activities in the financial arena? We believe that, despite the difficulties, countries will continue to have strong interest in coordinating their regulation and supervision of financial activities and institutions to minimize financial spillovers or their effects. In chapter 5, we outline a number of steps that nations might take to improve their efforts in this regard.

We take up first the role of central banks in dealing with actual or potential breakdowns of the international payment system or the systemic risk that all nations have an interest in preventing. Yet the current policy of calculated ambiguity practiced by most central banks—an uncertain commitment to provide emergency liquidity assistance to any particular depository institution to preserve market discipline—is deeply flawed and contributes to the problem it is meant to solve.

On the one hand, calculated ambiguity provides an unwarranted competitive advantage to large banks, whose deposit liabilities market participants expect to be fully guaranteed by the central bank in a crisis. This is not the case for smaller banks. On the other hand, ambiguity cannot halt runs once they occur. Indeed, uncertainty about a central bank's intentions to provide emergency assistance can accelerate runs.

For these reasons, we suggest in chapter 5 that central banks in at least the large industrial countries—the Basel Committee would be a good place to start—explicitly acknowledge all the specific banks for which they stand ready to provide emergency liquidity assistance. The commitment would not protect shareholders against loss or the creditors of a parent or affiliates of the bank, however. In addition, the central banks would announce publicly how responsibilities for dealing with liquidity problems of international banks will be apportioned. We believe such a precommitment policy would make clear which banks do not have access to emergency liquidity assistance, thus ensuring a meaningful role for market discipline for those banks. At the same time, the policy would help prevent runs at large banks.

To be sure, a precommitment policy may appear to give up on market discipline for the large banks that make the list. But this can and should be rectified by requiring these institutions to back their assets not just by shareholders' funds, but also by funds from subordinated or unsecured, and uninsured, creditors. Unlike depositors, who can run at any time, holders of subordinated debt cannot run until their instruments mature. For this reason, they are likely to exert significant, continuous market discipline.

There also may be a role for nations to move toward greater harmonization of their financial structures, although we recognize that our particular suggestion may be even more controversial than the one we have advanced with respect to lender of last resort.

Countries now differ significantly in the extent to which they permit their banks to affiliate with or be owned by nonbanks. At one extreme, the United States has attempted to wall off its banks from many types of nonbank activity, although these barriers have been falling slowly. At the other extreme, countries such as Germany endorse universal banking, in which banks may directly underwrite securities and may invest in equities of nonbank corporations. Recently several European banks have combined universal banking activities with insurance activities in a phenomenon known as *allfinanz* or *bancassurance.*

Given the strong political and cultural differences that have led to these differences in national financial structures, we do not believe harmonization of structures will occur any time soon. Nevertheless, in our concluding chapter, we suggest one way in which such structures could be harmonized that addresses the fundamental problem of systemic risk. Financial institutions could be required to collateralize transactions accounts with marketable securities or to separate such accounts completely from nonbank affiliates in a "narrow bank."

In any event, the central challenge for financial regulators in the future will be the same as it has been in the past: to minimize systemic risks without dampening useful innovation or encouraging counterproductive innovation. This is a difficult line to walk, especially in the financial arena, where innovation is a routine mode of competition.

Ultimately, the best way to walk that line may be to place greater emphasis on discipline by the market rather than by regulators, a judgment reinforced by the failures of U.S. regulation of banks and savings and loans during the 1980s. Improved market discipline requires more timely disclosure of meaningful financial information. Harmonization of financial reporting systems may help in this regard by making it easier for market participants to compare the performance of firms from different countries. But, if the Basel negotiations for minimum capital standards are any guide, reaching such agreement among regulators may be especially difficult. Progress is more likely to be made by market participants themselves—especially large institutions with the most substantial stake in the system and the greatest capacity for analysis—who press for better quality disclosure. Removing central bank guarantees for smaller institutions and instituting a stronger and more stable degree of market discipline for larger institutions through a subordinated debt requirement, for example, would encourage efforts in this direction.

Finally, given the nature of the risks involved, we concentrate primarily in this book on financial markets and institutions in the developed world. Our analysis and recommendations largely ignore the special problems that financial activities may pose in developing countries. A challenge for policymakers in the future will be to extend to other countries that succeed in joining this club the rules and frameworks for coordinating and harmonizing financial policies that are now in place among developed countries.

Chapter 2

International Financial Integration: The Continuing Process

*T*ECHNOLOGICAL advances have reduced the costs of cross-border transactions in all sectors of the economy. The dramatic reductions in transportation, telecommunications, and computation costs have greatly increased the ease with which firms can bridge the natural barriers of time and space that separate national markets (table 2-1). Nowhere has technology had a greater effect on cross-border activity than in financial services.

The fundamental function of financial service firms is to gather and process information. The sharp reductions in the costs of telecommunications and in the costs of compiling, storing, and analyzing information have broadened the geographic areas over which financial service institutions and their customers make decisions. Advances in computer hardware and software have dramatically reduced the costs of collecting and analyzing data, initiating and confirming transactions, clearing and settling payments, and monitoring financial flows through management information and accounting systems. Indeed, technological advances have made it possible for sophisticated firms to raise or invest funds, exchange currencies, or change the attributes of assets around the globe and around the clock.

In this chapter we sketch the effect of these technological advances on users of financial services, providers of financial services, and regulators of financial services in the industrialized countries that have been most affected by these advances. Next we document the increasing volume of international financial transactions. Finally, we evaluate the extent to which financial prices are integrated across

Table 2-1. *Costs of Air Transportation and Telephone Calls, Selected Years, 1930–90*

1990 dollars, unless otherwise indicated

Year	Average air transportation revenue per passenger mile	Cost of a three-minute call, New York to London	Department of Commerce computer price deflator (1990 = 1,000)
1930	0.68	244.65	n.a.
1940	0.46	188.51	n.a.
1950	0.30	53.20	n.a.
1960	0.24	45.86	125,000
1970	0.16	31.58	19,474
1980	0.10	4.80	3,620
1990	0.11	3.32	1,000

Source: Gary Hufbauer, "World Economic Integration: The Long View," *International Economic Insights*, vol. 11 (May-June 1991).

countries. In short we demonstrate how technology is creating an increasingly integrated financial market that ignores national boundaries.

Effect on Users of Financial Services

Although the same customer may be both a provider of funds and a user of funds, it is useful to distinguish the two roles when assessing the effects of technological advances on customer behavior. Users of funds have sought to broaden their funding base internationally as a means of increasing their liquidity and lowering their costs. Multinational corporations and governments have financial needs sufficiently large to justify substantial search costs to identify the cheapest source of funds. Some of these needs continue to be satisfied by traditional international bank loans, albeit often in the form of new kinds of loan contracts that include a variety of embedded options. But increasingly, large borrowers have found that they can place issues of securities in markets more cheaply than they can borrow from international banks. Figure 2-1 shows that since 1983 direct issues of securities have dominated international flows of credit intermediated through banks.

This trend has been facilitated in part by an improved flow of information. News services provide a continuous flow of information relevant to valuing securities. In addition, analytic software can transform raw financial data into a format useful for making decisions.

Figure 2-1. *Direct Issues of Securities in International Flows of Credit, 1981–92*[a]

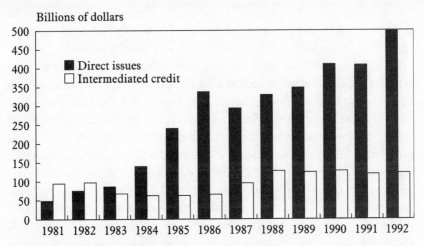

Source: *OECD Financial Market Trends* (February 1993), pp. 6, 117.

a. International intermediated credit includes Euroloans and foreign loans. International direct issues include issues of fixed, floating-rate bonds.

Security analysts and ratings agencies continually prod borrowers to improve their disclosure practices. Both have invested significant resources in analyzing a wider range of foreign borrowers to help potential investors make better decisions. Accountants and regulatory authorities in some countries have also required that more data be disclosed on a more timely basis. And borrowers who are eager to tap international sources of savings have voluntarily disclosed more data relevant to evaluating their creditworthiness.

These trends have generally favored investment banks and universal banks that have specialized in facilitating the access of borrowers to world financial markets. But commercial banks have also participated, sometimes with striking success. Because commercial banks in the United States and Japan have had broader securities powers outside their domestic markets, they have been particularly active in helping their clients gain access to foreign markets.[1] In addition some

1. This is one of many examples of the attempt of regulatory authorities to improve the international competitiveness of their regulatees. As Richard Dale notes, the Federal Reserve Board's "willingness to pare down the constraints imposed by Glass-Steagall reflects, among other considerations, the U.S. regulatory authorities' concern to maintain the international competitiveness of the U.S. banking system." Similarly, "Japanese financial institutions can

of the largest corporations have formed in-house banks to serve their international financial needs.

Financial institutions have introduced a variety of innovations to reduce transaction costs and to broaden the range of options available to borrowers in national and international financial markets. In general these innovations have permitted institutions to unbundle and repackage financial attributes so that both borrowers and lenders end up with the financial instruments they prefer and risks are redistributed to those investors who are most willing to bear them. For example, a firm that wants a ten-year, floating-rate, U.S. dollar-denominated loan may find that the cheapest alternative is to issue a ten-year, fixed-rate, Australian dollar-denominated bond combined with a currency swap from Australian dollars into U.S. dollars and an interest rate swap from fixed interest rates to floating interest rates. The information systems and analytic capacity to compare such borrowing alternatives are formidable; they require virtually instantaneous information about global developments that can be factored into investment, funding, and credit evaluation decisions. But sophisticated international borrowers have come to expect that they can select from an extremely broad menu that includes a multitude of indirect ways to achieve the desired result.

Large customers have also demanded a variety of noncredit services to facilitate international transactions. These include global management of cash flows through integrated computer networks; global custody, record-keeping, and trustee services for pension, savings, and other sorts of employee benefit plans worldwide; and fiduciary and agency services in connection with capital and debt financing for entities throughout the world.

Providers of funds have also become increasingly international in their outlook. In almost every major country, more and more funds are being managed by a smaller number of decisionmakers (see figure 2-2). Institutional investors—pension funds, insurance companies, and mutual funds—have come to dominate financial markets. This trend is particularly apparent in the United States. Forty years ago individuals held 90 percent of corporate equity. Even ten years ago they owned more than 65 percent. Today

combine banking and securities business in foreign financial centers [even though] they are denied this privilege in their home market." Dale (1992, pp. 70, 90).

Figure 2-2. *Life Insurance, Pension, and Mutual Fund Assets as a Percentage of Household Assets, Selected Countries, 1980, 1985, 1990*

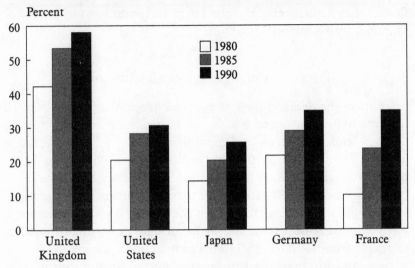

Source: Simon Brady, "Why Equities Will Dominate the 1990s," *Euromoney* (July 1993), p. 31.

institutional investors control more than half of the shares of American public corporations.[2]

Institutional investors often behave differently from individual investors. They are able to reduce their transactions costs per unit relative to individual investors by pooling transactions, negotiating commissions, and, on occasion, dealing directly with issuers of securities. They can follow market developments closely throughout the world, analyze investment prospects, and execute decisions promptly. Moreover, they are under intense pressure to earn competitive risk-adjusted returns. Just as ratings agencies have arisen to help investors analyze the issuers of securities, advisory services have developed to help savers evaluate the performance of institutional investors.

Increasingly, institutional investors are diversifying internationally as a means of boosting their returns and reducing the volatility of their portfolios.[3] Although prudential regulations have constrained the

2. New York Stock Exchange (1993, p. 1).

3. Morningstar Mutual Funds, an advisory service that compares the performance of hundreds of mutual funds, observed that even within the category "domestic fund," "only one domestic fund in four now fails to own a foreign stock." Indeed a number of equity funds, including the Fidelity Magellan Fund and the Vanguard/Windsor Fund,

amounts some can invest abroad, these restrictions are being relaxed. Regulators are becoming convinced that careful international diversification can actually enhance the safety and soundness of portfolios managed by institutional investors.

Effect on Financial Service Institutions

To meet the demand for international financial services, financial institutions have invested heavily in the technical infrastructure to compete effectively in international markets. They have also established offices in foreign financial centers. By 1986 foreign banks operated more than 600 offices in the United States, triple the number from the mid-1970s. And more than 400 foreign banks operated in London, a fourfold increase from the mid-1970s.[4] The number of foreign banking offices tripled in Japan and nearly quadrupled in Germany from 1970 to 1985.[5] This competition is largely focused on wholesale institutional markets because foreign financial institutions have usually found it difficult to acquire large, local retail bases.

Foreign banks have made deep inroads in several major markets. In the United States, by 1991 they had gained nearly a 45 percent share of the market for commercial loans.[6] These competitive inroads have undoubtedly been facilitated by technology. Fax machines, for example, have enabled Japanese banks to respond quickly to U.S. loan customers. The U.S. office of a Japanese bank can take a loan application during the U.S. business day, fax the information to Japan, where the loan application can be evaluated during the Japanese business day, and the decision can be faxed back to the United States to communicate to the loan applicant by the start of the next U.S. business day.

Just as direct investment in the manufacturing sector often embodies transfers of technology, foreign financial establishments often introduce financial innovations in local markets. European banks

---

two of the largest actively managed equity mutual funds, hold more than 10 percent of their equity in non-U.S. issues. Rekenthaler (1993).

4. J. P. Morgan & Co. Incorporated (1986).

5. Bank for International Settlements (1986, p. 151).

6. This estimate made by Robert N. McCauley and Rama Seth combines loans made from U.S. offices of foreign banks and loans extended from their offshore offices. See McCauley and Seth (1992, p. 52).

have improved the quality of foreign exchange services available to U.S. residents, and U.S. banks have introduced derivative instruments in several markets abroad.

Increased competition among financial services firms has led to increased international specialization of labor. Systems analysts and computer programmers in India are providing services for financial firms in many other parts of the world. Ireland, which has invested substantial resources in developing a computer-literate work force, has become an important exporter of back office services to several financial service firms in North America.

Effect on Regulators

Perhaps most important for the issues we address in this book, technological advances have diminished the ability of financial regulators in each country to maintain more burdensome regulations that increase the cost of financial services relative to that in other countries. This has occurred in two ways.

First, as noted, technological advances have facilitated the unbundling and repackaging of individual financial products. Consequently, regulations that prohibit one kind of activity can easily be circumvented by product redesign to produce a close substitute. These financial innovations may occur in the domestic market—the development of money market mutual funds, for example—and they may also involve international financial transactions such as Eurodollar deposits or offshore commercial paper facilities.

Second, technology has undermined the significance of geopolitical boundaries. Regulation that distorts prices creates profit opportunities for customers of financial institutions and for financial institutions themselves. They can often avoid onerous regulation by moving the locus of activity to a more congenial regulatory domain. In short, technology has allowed participants in the financial marketplace to engage in regulatory arbitrage.

Heightened global competition thus exposes differences in national regulatory structures to an exacting market test. Policies designed to raise revenue or to redistribute wealth from one sector of the economy to another or from one class of institutions to another have become increasingly untenable because users of financial services turn to foreign sources of supply whenever domestic financial products are not competitively priced.

In recent decades some tax and regulatory initiatives have been more effective in shifting the location of financial activity than in accomplishing their objectives. For example, when the United States attempted to impose an interest equalization tax to discourage foreign borrowing in dollar capital markets, it created an active market in dollar-denominated bonds—the Eurobond market—outside the United States. Similarly, during the 1960s and 1970s, each time market interest rates rose above deposit interest rate ceilings in the United States, an enormous volume of dollar deposits shifted from the United States to Eurodollar centers. When U.S. bank customers found they could not roll over their certificates of deposit in U.S. banks at the market rate of interest, many simply transferred their deposits to Eurobanks—often shell branches of their American banks but located beyond the reach of interest-rate ceiling regulations.

Examples of this phenomenon are apparent in other parts of the world as well. In the early 1980s Japanese investors faced high tax rates on interest income but no taxes on capital gains. This led to a strong demand for zero-coupon Eurobonds until the Japanese tax laws were reformed.[7] In 1988 several billion dollars of German investment funds flowed into the Luxembourg bond market following the announcement that a German 10 percent withholding tax would take effect in January 1989.[8] The establishment of organized markets for derivative instruments has been so inhibited in Germany by the interpretation of gambling laws that most futures trading in German government bonds has taken place in London. Similarly, the imposition of a transfer tax in the Swedish market caused market activity to relocate to London. The tax mainly succeeded in shifting market activity rather than in raising revenue for the government or dampening volatility in market prices.

Of course, regulatory authorities often try to anticipate or respond to regulatory arbitrage. International competition among national regulatory authorities is a long-standing tradition; it has become more intense as the costs of traversing time and space have fallen.[9] In some

7. IMF Staff Team, Exchange and Trade Relations and Research Departments (1990, p. 65).

8. For additional details, see Bank for International Settlements (1989, p. 71) and IMF Staff Team, Exchange and Trade Relations and Research Departments (1990, p. 64).

9. For example, in the Middle Ages, the king of France tried to attract commercial and financial business to Lyons by forbidding merchants to travel to the rival center, Geneva.

important financial centers, regulatory authorities have reacted to competitive pressures by relaxing regulations covering both financial markets and depository institutions. Indeed, some countries have taken active measures to attract a larger share of international business by improving the infrastructure to support financial services and by virtually eliminating regulatory burdens on international financial transactions.[10] In addition, Canada, France, New Zealand, and the United Kingdom have relaxed traditional restrictions on the permissible scope of operations of domestic depository institutions to permit them greater flexibility in responding to changing market conditions.[11]

The liberalization of domestic financial systems and the dismantling of capital controls has often been attributed to the rise of conservative ideology. Indeed, the trend is often associated with President Ronald Reagan of the United States and Prime Minister Margaret Thatcher of Great Britain. But in the United States the first important initiative to phase out interest rate ceilings, the Depository Institutions Deregulation and Monetary Control Act of 1980, was introduced by and enacted during the Carter administration. Similarly, the deregulation efforts of the Conservative government in Great Britain have been largely matched by the actions of the Socialist governments in other parts of Europe. In short, market developments are at least as important as ideology in motivating policymakers to change the financial regulatory landscape.

Regulatory competition has recently intensified because of the European Union's bold initiative to enhance the efficiency of financial regulation within the EU.[12] The Second Banking Directive, approved in December 1989 by the European Parliament, ensures that European institutions can choose to become universal banks. European banks will be permitted to accept deposits, make long-term loans, issue and underwrite corporate securities, and take equity positions. The EU's approach to harmonization of banking regulation among the member states, which combines the adoption of a single banking license with the principles of mutual recognition and home country control, will create a competitive dynamic that makes it likely that the European regulatory system will remain flexible and efficient.[13] These

10. Kane (1987).
11. Bröker (1989).
12. Herring (1993b).
13. Key (1989).

principles have been largely adopted in the directives covering investment services, life insurance, and nonlife insurance.[14]

European financial institutions will have the freedom to select from regulatory regimes in any of the current twelve member countries. This will cause each national regulatory authority to assess carefully the competitive impact of its regulatory structure. The approach deliberately encourages national regulatory authorities to compete, subject to basic safety and soundness constraints, in providing the most efficient regulatory system. As Sir Leon Brittan observed, "In one bound [the European] Community has moved from twelve fragmented and confusing structures of national [banking] regulation to a single market of a size and simplicity unmatched anywhere else in the world." He emphasized that the motive was not "merely to benefit banks" but "to increase the competitiveness of European industry by giving it access to the cheapest most efficient and most innovative financial products in the world."[15] The European Community has estimated that financial integration would yield gains equal to one-third to one-half of the total benefits of completing the European single-market initiative.[16]

Technological advance thus has had a powerful effect on international financial integration. It has broadened the financial horizons of users of financial services and enhanced the ability of financial institutions to provide international solutions to financial problems. Regulators have faced a stark choice. They can regulate domestic financial institutions heavily, but that is likely to drive business to less heavily regulated domestic firms or foreign institutions. Alternatively, regulators can liberalize domestic rules and relax international capital controls. Most countries have chosen the second course.

In the process, government policies have heightened international financial competition and deepened international financial integration. The hope is that better international integration of financial markets will facilitate the pricing and reallocation of a broader range of risks, thereby enhancing the international allocation of resources.

It is instructive, however, that efforts at financial policy integration have proceeded both unilaterally and multilaterally. Whether and to what extent future financial regulatory policies should be coordinated

14. "The EC Single Market in Financial Services" (1993).
15. Brittan (1990).
16. Catinant, Etonnai, and Italianer (1988, chap. 10).

Figure 2-3. *Indexed Value of World Exports and World GDP, 1963–90*

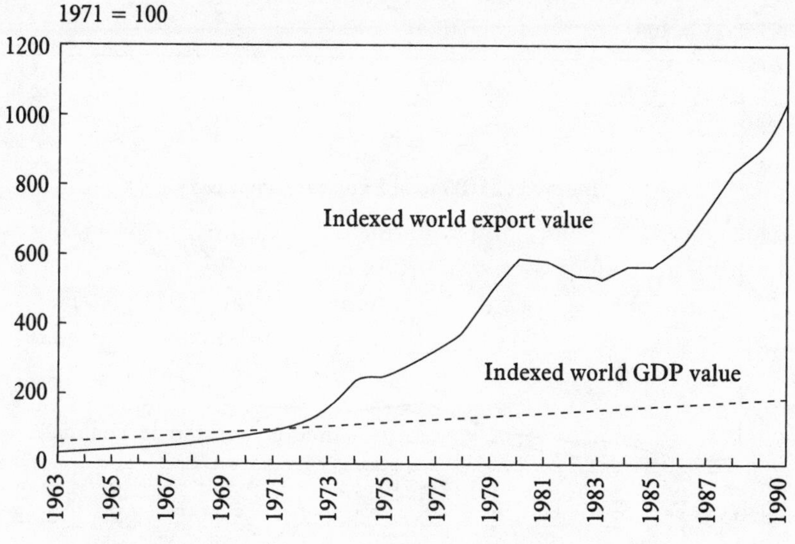

1971 = 100

Source: Author's calculations using data from IMF, *International Financial Statistics*, various issues.

across national boundaries is an issue we explore more fully in sub-sequent chapters.

Expanding International Flows of Capital

Can the trends toward increased financial integration be quantified? Unfortunately, no comprehensive measure of gross international financial flows exists, but there is little doubt that they have increased over the past two decades. International trade has continued to grow faster than GDP (see figure 2-3). (Even in the absence of the technical advances and liberalization of regulation, the volume of international transactions would have increased relative to GDP, if only to support the growth in world trade.) International financial transactions have grown much faster than world trade. One plausible though admittedly imperfect proxy for the volume of international financial transactions is the value of payments cleared through the Clearing House Interbank Payment System. CHIPS is the electronic payment system that transfers and settles international transactions based on U.S. dollars, the paramount currency vehicle for inter-

Figure 2-4. *Indexed Value of World Exports and CHIPS Payments, 1970–92*

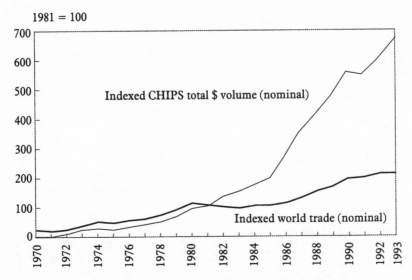

1981 = 100

Indexed CHIPS total $ volume (nominal)

Indexed world trade (nominal)

Sources: Author's calculations using unpublished CHIPS data from New York Clearing House Association; trade data from International Monetary Fund *International Financial Statistics,* various issues.

national finance and commerce.[17] CHIPS handles more than 90 percent of all dollar payments moving among countries, including foreign exchange transactions, Eurodollar transactions, Eurosecurities settlements, and international disbursements of dollar-denominated loans.[18] The dollar value of clearings through the system has grown much faster than the dollar value of world trade; by 1993, the average daily volume of transactions cleared through CHIPS was just over $1 trillion (figure 2-4).[19]

17. In the colorful prose of the CHIPS brochure, "the world is evolving into a single, seamless financial marketplace that functions around the clock. Decisions involving megasums are communicated electronically in nanoseconds. And, in the overwhelming majority of the transactions, the denominator is the U.S. dollar. . . . [CHIPS] is the central clearing system in the United States for international transactions." New York Clearing House Association (1986, p. 1).

18. This measure presents a useful indicator of trends, but it cannot be regarded as a precise measure of the volume of international financial transactions for several reasons. First, it includes trade as well as financial transactions. Second, domestic U.S. transactions account for a minor portion of the volume. Third, an estimated 10 percent of international dollar payments do not flow through CHIPS. Fourth, although the dollar is usually the currency against which any other currency is traded, this is not invariably the case. Finally, as other currencies become more important in international financial transactions, displacing to some extent the vehicle role of the dollar, the flow of transactions through CHIPS understates the volume of international transactions.

19. Unpublished data on CHIPS provided to the author from New York Clearing House.

Figure 2-5. *Daily Turnover in Foreign Exchange, Selected Countries, 1986, 1989, 1992*

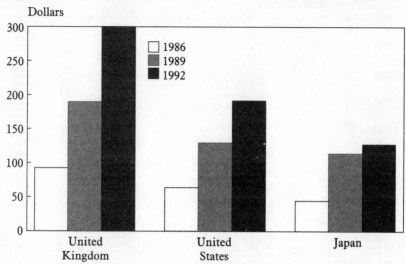

Source: *Bank of England Quarterly Bulletin,* September 1986 (pp. 531–82), November 1989 (pp. 531–35), November 1992 (pp. 408–15).

The increasing volume of international financial flows can be seen in the rising volume of foreign exchange trading in three major centers that conducted surveys of their foreign exchange markets during March 1986 and April 1989 and 1992 (figure 2-5). In each interval the increase has exceeded the increase in GDP and merchandise trade. Undoubtedly a substantial part of the increase in foreign exchange turnover has been generated by the greater cross-border capital flows stimulated by the relaxation of capital controls and continued deregulation of domestic financial markets. A central bank survey showed that the global turnover in the world's foreign exchange markets was $1 trillion on each business day in April 1992.[20] This average daily turnover during a very placid period in the foreign exchange markets was virtually identical to the total stock of official foreign exchange reserves for all countries reported at the end of April 1992.[21]

The stock of international bank lending as reported by the Bank for International Settlements also has grown steadily (figure 2-6).

20. Goldstein and others (1993, p. 24).

21. The stock of foreign exchange reserves for all countries was SDR 648,330 million or about $900 trillion. International Monetary Fund (1992, p. 24).

Figure 2-6. *International Bank Lending, 1973–92*

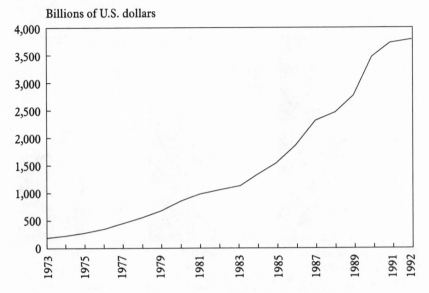

Billions of U.S. dollars

Source: Goldstein, Mathieson, and Lane (1991, p. 6); Bank for International Settlements, *Annual Reports*, various years.

Nonetheless, the rate of growth of international bank lending has been eclipsed in the past decade by the growth in international issues of securities and in derivative instruments.

The dramatic growth of international bond issues is depicted in figure 2-7. In fact, new issues of international bonds began to exceed the flow of bank loans in 1983 (figure 2-1). Since that time they have continued to dominate new bank lending. Over the decade several kinds of bonds were introduced that had equitylike characteristics. During periods when equity prices were expected to rise, issuers found that they could reduce interest costs dramatically by issuing convertible bonds or bonds with equity warrants attached. Japanese borrowers made especially aggressive use of these instruments in the later part of the decade. During 1989, equity-related issues accounted for more than 40 percent of all bonds issued on international markets.[22]

Cross-border flows of equities have become increasingly important over the last decade as well (see figure 2-8). Professional traders continually monitor prices for the same securities quoted on different markets to profit from discrepancies. In addition, investment manag-

22. Bank for International Settlements (1990, p. 41.)

Figure 2-7. *International Issues of Bonds, 1981–92*

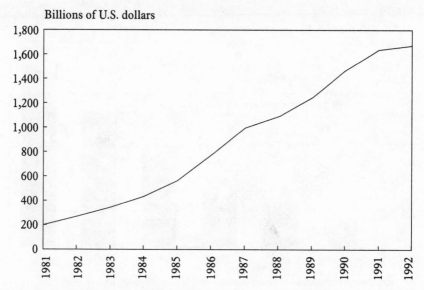

Billions of U.S. dollars

Source: Author's calculations using the sources given in figure 2-6. For 1981, the stocks were combined, subtracting the previous year flows from the previous year stocks.

Figure 2-8. *Gross Cross-Border Equity Flows, 1979–90*

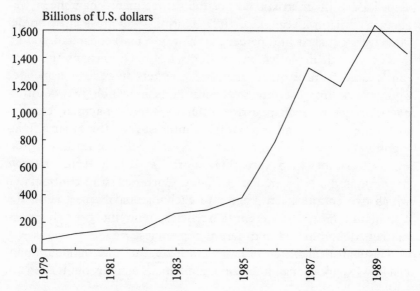

Billions of U.S. dollars

Source: Howell and Cozzini (1990, p. 21).

Figure 2-9. *Swap Market Growth, 1987–92: Outstanding Notional Principal of Interest Rate and Currency Swaps*

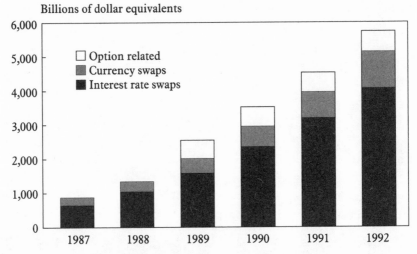

Source: Author's calculations using unpublished data from J. P. Morgan Guaranty Trust.

ers attempt to exploit what they perceive to be valuation discrepancies for comparable companies traded in different national markets. Gross cross-border equity flows—the sum of equity purchases and sales associated with international portfolio investment—have been well above $1 trillion a year since 1987. During 1989 gross cross-border flows were equal to 14.8 percent of the world market capitalization.[23]

The growth in derivative products has been perhaps the most remarkable feature of international markets in recent years (see figure 2-9). Interest rate swap contracts in which two counterparties agree to exchange two different interest payment streams over time—one usually pays a fixed interest rate, the other a floating interest rate—account for the largest volume of trading. Interest rate swaps help integrate short- and long-term markets denominated in a particular currency. Currency swap contracts, in which two counterparties agree to exchange payment streams denominated in two different currencies, help integrate financial markets denominated in different currencies.

This statistical sketch of large and increasing international financial flows suggests high international financial activity, but it does not

23. Howell and Cozzini (1990, p. 13).

clearly indicate how much financial integration has been achieved. Moreover, even if comprehensive and reliable statistics on gross international capital flows and derivative transactions were available, they could shed only limited light on the extent of international financial integration.

Increasing International Asset Price Integration

As markets become more highly integrated, asset prices often adjust in anticipation of capital flows that would otherwise occur. Indeed, it is possible to imagine a perfectly integrated international market in which capital never actually flows from one market to another. Instead, market participants adjust equilibrium prices instantaneously to new information because they know that they would experience losses if they were to conduct transactions at the preceding price. If prices do not diverge from equilibrium levels, no arbitrage flows will take place. Thus an additional way of evaluating the extent of international financial integration is to measure the extent of asset price integration.

Table 2-2 summarizes five different degrees of international financial integration as reflected by asset prices, starting from the most superficial level and extending to the deepest level. Each level will be considered in turn to measure how deeply international financial integration has progressed.

Covered Interest Rate Parity in the Eurocurrency Market

The first and most superficial level of international financial integration is integration of the offshore markets—covered interest rate parity among Eurocurrency deposits. This implies that, when deposits are adjusted for the cost of protecting against a change in the foreign exchange rate (the forward premium), investors receive precisely the same return regardless of the denomination of Eurocurrency they choose to hold. For example, if interest rate parity holds, investors will earn the same return whether they invest in a Eurodollar deposit or convert dollars into sterling, investing in a Eurosterling deposit of comparable maturity and simultaneously

Table 2-2. *Five Levels of International Financial Integration*[a]

Level	U.S. market ($)	Offshore market		Foreign market (*)	
1		$i_{E\$} = fp + i_{E\star}$			Covered interest rate parity among Eurocurrency rates
2	$i_\$ =$	$i_{E\$}$	$i_{E\star}$	$= i_\star$	Integration of offshore and onshore markets
3		$i_\$ = fp + i_\star$ $\rightarrow i_\$ - (fp + i_\star) = 0$			Covered interest rate parity among national rates[b]
4		$i_\$ = sp' + i_\star$ $\rightarrow i_\$ - (sp' + i_\star) = 0$			Uncovered interest rate parity among national rates[c]
5	$r_\$ = i_\$ - \%\Delta P'_\$$			$r_\star = i_\star - \%\Delta P'_\star$	Real interest rate parity among national rates[d]

$$r_\$ - r_\star = i_\$ - i_\star + \%\Delta P'_\star - \%\Delta P'_\$ = 0$$
$$\rightarrow r_\$ - r_\star = (fp - sp') + sp' - (\%\Delta P'_\$ - \%\Delta P'_\star) = 0$$

Source: Authors' summary of the literature.

a. Definitions of symbols.

$i_{E\$}$ = the Eurodollar rate on a Eurodollar deposit that matures in one year.

i_{E*} = a nondollar Eurocurrency rate on a nondollar-denominated Eurocurrency deposit that matures in one year.

fp = the forward premium stated as the difference between dollar price of a unit of foreign currency for delivery in one year less the dollar price of a unit of foreign currency for spot delivery scaled by the spot price of foreign currency.

$'$ indicates that a variable contains a nonobservable, expected component.

i_x = the national interest rate in country X on an instrument that is comparable in all other aspects to the Eurocurrency deposit denominated in the same currency.

sp' = the speculative premium stated as the expected dollar price of a unit of foreign currency in one year less the actual dollar price of a unit of foreign currency for spot delivery scaled by the spot price of foreign currency.

$\%\Delta P'_x$ = the anticipated annual percentage change in the price index of country X.

r_x = the real (inflation-adjusted) interest rate in country X for a one-year maturity. The real interest rate is conventionally expressed as $r_x = i_x - \%\Delta P'_x$ but this omits a term. For precision, the product of the real interest rate and the anticipated inflation rate should also be included.

b. The precise covered interest rate parity relationship includes an additional term, the product of the forward premium and the foreign interest rate, $fp \cdot i_*$, that is customarily omitted for simplicity. This omission becomes more important the higher the foreign interest rate and the larger the forward premium.

c. The precise uncovered interest rate parity relationship includes an additional term, the product of the speculative premium and the foreign interest rate, $sp' \cdot i_*$, that is customarily omitted. The omission becomes more important the higher the foreign interest rate and the larger the speculative premium.

d. The term $sp' - (\%\Delta P'_\$ - \%\Delta P'_*)$ can be interpreted as an approximation to the anticipated deviation from purchasing power parity or the anticipated real depreciation of the dollar. If the exchange rate is currently at purchasing power parity, the current price of a bundle of goods priced in dollars ($P_\$$) is equal to the current price of the same bundle priced in the foreign currency (P_*) translated into dollars at the spot dollar price of a unit of foreign currency (e): $P_\$ = P_0 \cdot e$. If the exchange rate is expected to remain at purchasing power parity, the expected exchange rate (e') will adjust by precisely enough to offset the anticipated difference in inflation between the dollar and the foreign currency: $P'_\$ \cdot (1 + \%\Delta P'_\$) = P_* \cdot (1 + \%\Delta P'_*) \cdot e'$. This implies that the anticipated change in the exchange rate (sp') must be precisely equal to: $sp' = \%\Delta P'_\$ - \%\Delta P'_* - sp' \cdot \%\Delta P'_*$. The last term in this expression is customarily omitted.

selling the sterling proceeds in the forward market for dollars (thus locking in a dollar-sterling exchange rate in advance).[24] Several studies have shown that forward exchange rates have remained at interest rate parity with respect to Eurocurrency interest rates since the mid-1960s.[25] The highly integrated Eurocurrency markets offered large, sophisticated international investors and borrowers an important alternative to national markets that were often highly regulated and insulated from other national markets and the international market by capital controls.

Interest rate parity holds in the Eurocurrency markets because Eurocurrency deposits are nearly ideal vehicles for interest arbitrage. Four features explain why arbitrage is so effective in integrating the Eurocurrency markets. First, arbitrage need not be inhibited by differences in credit risk. Eurocurrency deposits issued by a particular bank in different currency denominations have equal credit risk. Moreover, they are free of taxes and sinking fund or call provisions that complicate comparisons of returns among other assets. Second, Eurocurrency rates are market determined, so they fully reflect prevailing market conditions, unlike interest rates that are administered or subject to regulatory ceilings or floors. Third, the Eurocurrency markets are free from capital controls and other restrictions that have often inhibited arbitrage between national markets. Fourth, the Eurocurrency markets share a negligible and equal vulnerability to future capital controls. Even a country that is inclined to impose capital controls on transactions denominated in its own currency lacks incentive to regulate securities denominated in foreign currencies because Eurocurrency activities can readily shift to another center. Moreover, a country is especially unlikely to have a motive to discriminate among Eurocurrency deposits denominated in different foreign

24. In this example, as in all subsequent examples, routine transactions costs are neglected. It should be noted, however, that as competition increases, transactions costs tend to decline, thus enhancing incentives for arbitrage. For example, Goldstein, Mathieson and Lane present evidence that bid-ask spreads on some of the lesser traded Eurocurrency deposits have declined over the 1980s to a fifth of the level at the beginning of the decade, so that now bid-ask spreads are relatively uniform across all major Eurocurrency deposits. Goldstein, Mathieson, and Lane (1991, p. 7).

25. Aliber (1973) and Marston (1976). For a model that analyzes the simultaneous determination of forward exchange rates and Eurocurrency rates, see Herring and Marston (1977).

Figure 2-10. *External and Internal Money Markets in the Deutsche Mark, January 1973–August 1974*[a]

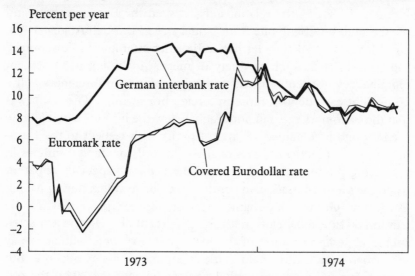

Percent per year

Sources: Author's calculations using various issues of *Money Manager* for Euromark rate, and Federal Reserve Board data for all other interest and exchange rates.

a. Euromark rate: Wednesday quotations on three-month deutsche mark deposits in London. German rate: rate of interest in the Frankfurt interbank loan market for three-month funds. Covered Eurodollar rate: Wednesday quotations on the bid rate on three-month, U.S. dollar-denominated time deposits in London minus the Wednesday deutsche mark premium quoted in Frankfurt.

currencies, so all Eurocurrencies share the same low risk of future controls.[26]

Integration of Offshore and Onshore Markets

Offshore markets have been integrated since the early days of the Eurocurrency market, but integration of offshore and onshore markets has been a more sporadic development. Capital controls and domestic bank regulations have often separated Eurocurrency markets from the corresponding national markets. Two historical examples suggest the importance of these restrictions.

26. In this regard, the U.S. sanctions against Iran and Libya were exceptions that prove the rule. In both instances the United States attempted to freeze the Eurodollar deposits held in offshore branches of U.S. banks. The Iranian freeze was ended before it could be tested in court, but the Libyan freeze was challenged in British courts in two cases against U.S. money center banks. In each case the British court required that the U.S. branch repay the Eurodollar deposit in full. Herring (1991).

The first example illustrates the importance of controls on capital inflows designed to keep a strong currency from becoming stronger. Figure 2-10 shows the relationship between the Euromark rate and the German interbank rate from January 1973 through August 1974. Until January 1974 the German authorities attempted to discourage capital inflows through a variety of means, including a 60 percent marginal reserve requirement on bank liabilities to foreigners and a 50 percent cash deposit ratio on foreign borrowing.[27] The result was that the Euromark rate fell noticeably below the internal German rate even though it remained at interest parity with respect to the Euro-dollar rate. The effectiveness of these controls on capital inflows in separating the internal and external market was especially apparent when the German mark came under speculative attack during March 1973. The German interbank rate rose above 8 percent while the Euromark rate fell below negative 2 percent. Foreigners expected such a large appreciation of the mark that they were willing to pay more than 2 percent to hold mark-denominated assets offshore. But when Germany removed capital controls in January 1974, the off-shore and onshore rates became virtually identical.

The second example illustrates the importance of controls on capital outflows intended to support a weak currency. Figure 2-11 shows the Eurofranc rate alongside the domestic French rate to illustrate the effect of controls on capital outflows on the differential between offshore and onshore rates. Capital controls were maintained in France for one and one-half decades longer than in Germany; indeed, they were tightened substantially early in the Mitterrand regime. Regulation of trade credits, however, was sufficiently loose so that the internal and external money markets moved together relatively tightly unless the franc was under speculative attack.[28] During speculative periods the controls were binding, and the speculative demand for franc-denominated loans caused the Eurofranc rate to rise far above the internal French rate. The speculative attack against the franc during March 1983 provides a good example. The differen-

27. If capital controls were merely taxes on cross-border flows it would be possible to identify a precise wedge between interest rates in the onshore and offshore markets. But in Germany, as in most other countries that have imposed capital controls, taxlike regulations were combined with quantitative limitations on some activities. Since it is also very difficult to know how capital controls function in practice, it is usually not possible to specify a precise, meaningful arbitrage band.

28. For further details, see Giavazzi and Giovannini (1989, chap. 7).

Figure 2-11. *External and Internal Money Markets in the French Franc,*
1982–91

Percent per year

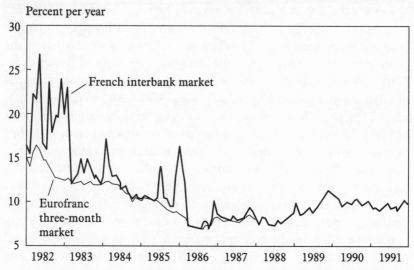

Sources: Author's calculations using on-line service (Reuters, Datastream) for data; Organization for Economic Cooperation and Development; and J. P. Morgan Guaranty Trust.

tial between the external and internal franc rate rose above 9 percent.[29] When France removed capital controls as a prelude to entering the European Community's single market in financial services, the offshore and onshore franc-denominated rates merged.

Covered Interest Parity among National Rates

By 1993 offshore money markets had been integrated with onshore money markets in most industrial countries. For large, sophisticated transactors, the Eurocurrency markets have merged with the corresponding domestic currency markets. Capital controls were relaxed during three different periods. In 1974, with the abandonment of fixed exchange rates, Canada, Germany, the Netherlands, Switzerland, and the United States shed their capital controls. In 1979 the United Kingdom abandoned its controls, and Japan began the process of dismantling its controls.[30] And during 1990 France and Italy

29. Marston shows that the interest differential responded significantly to the anticipated realignment of the exchange rate. Marston (1994, chap. 3).

30. Japanese capital controls were somewhat unusual because they applied to both inflows and outflows of capital.

abolished their capital controls as part of the step-by-step approach to economic and monetary union in the European Community.

Once offshore and onshore markets became integrated, covered interest rate parity among national rates was also achieved.[31] Since the Eurocurrency rates were at interest rate parity and were equal to the corresponding national rates, the national rates were at interest rate parity. More fundamentally, capital controls and domestic financial regulations no longer inhibited arbitrage flows between national markets. This third level of international financial integration permits virtually frictionless capital mobility: investors perceive national assets that are insured against possible changes in exchange rates as virtually perfect substitutes. This can happen only when all barriers between national markets except exchange rates have become negligible. These include transactions costs, perceptions of default risk, current capital controls, and the expectation of future capital controls. Jeffrey Frankel calls these factors the country premium.[32] Elimination of the country premium does not, however, ensure that uncovered funding costs—those in which no exchange rate protections have been purchased—will be the same in all countries.

Uncovered Interest Rate Parity

The next deeper level of international financial integration—uncovered interest rate parity—implies that the difference in nominal interest rates is equal to the anticipated change in exchange rates. If this condition holds, expected returns on investments in different currencies are identical when measured in the same currency. Uncovered interest rate parity is much more difficult to verify because it incorporates a variable that is not directly observable, the speculative premium or expected change in the exchange rate.

Most major countries have reached the third level of integration, in which covered interest rate parity holds. If uncovered interest

31. For recent evidence, see Frankel (1991); and Marston (1994, chap. 3). It is difficult to demonstrate covered interest parity for longer-term instruments because forward exchange markets become very thin as the maturity of the contract increases and disappear altogether for long-term maturities. Forward cover is available for long-term transactions, but it is an over-the-counter product for which data are not readily available. Swap contracts can be viewed as bundles of forward contracts, so the growth of interest rate and foreign exchange swap markets in longer maturities is expanding the opportunities for covered interest arbitrage.

32. Frankel (1992, p. 199).

rate parity also holds for these countries, the forward premium must equal the expected change in the exchange rate (or the speculative premium), $fp = sp'$. Although the forward premium can be computed from market rates, investors' expectations of the corresponding speculative premium cannot be observed. Consequently most tests of uncovered interest rate parity use the forward premium as a proxy for the speculative premium and are really joint tests of two hypotheses: first, uncovered interest parity and, second, the efficiency of the forward premium as a forecast of the exchange rate change. Tests almost always reject the joint hypothesis.[33] Most investigators infer that uncovered interest parity does not hold, but rejection of the joint test could also be attributable to the inefficiency of the forward premium as a predictor of exchange rate changes. Figure 2-12 shows uncovered interest rates under the naive assumption that actual exchange rates were expected by market participants.

In a recent study Marston reaffirms that forward premiums (or nominal interest differentials) are biased predictors of actual changes in exchange rates.[34] He then uses survey data on exchange rate expectations as a direct measure of the speculative premium that does not depend on the assumption that the forward premium is an efficient estimate of the speculative premium. This enables him to compute measures of the forecast error and the risk premium. His analysis of the two series leads him to conclude that both systematic forecast errors and time-varying exchange risk premiums cause deviations from uncovered interest rate parity and explain why the forward premium is not equal to the speculative premium. Uncertainty over changes in the nominal exchange rate thus prevents the major industrial countries from reaching the fourth level of integration.

Real Interest Rate Parity

The fifth and deepest level of integration assumes that uncovered interest parity holds and makes the additional assumption that the expected change in the exchange rate just offsets the anticipated

33. The uncovered interest rate parity relationship has been widely investigated in literally hundreds of published studies. For an excellent recent survey and extension, see Marston (1994, chap. 4).

34. Marston (1994, chap. 4).

Figure 2-12. *Uncovered Interest Differentials, Four Countries, 1973–92*

United Kingdom

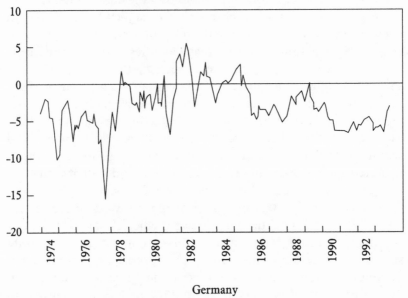

Germany

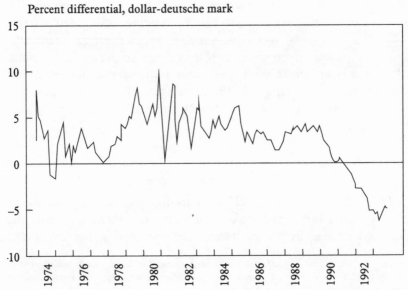

Sources: See figure 2-11.

Figure 2-12. *(continued)*

France

Percent differential, dollar-franc

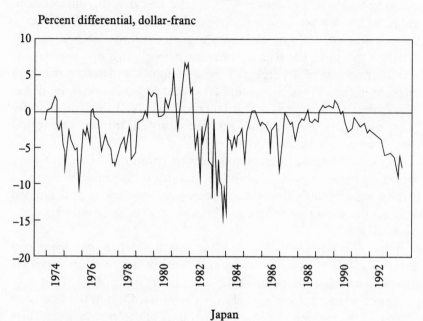

Japan

Percent differential, dollar-yen

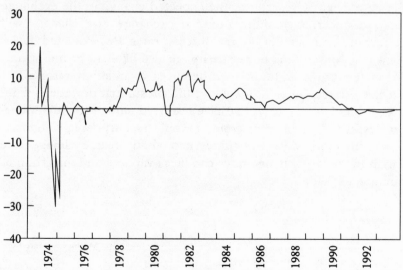

inflation differential in both countries, thus maintaining real exchange rates.[35] Real interest rate parity implies that capital flows equate real interest rates across countries and that the difference in nominal interest rates is precisely equal to the anticipated difference in inflation rates.[36] For example, a one-year U.S. interest rate of 5 percent would be at real interest rate parity with a one-year Japanese interest rate of 4 percent if the anticipated inflation rate was 3 percent in the United States and 2 percent in Japan and if the dollar was expected to depreciate by 1 percent relative to the yen. Under these circumstances the real (inflation-adjusted) interest rate would be 2 percent in both countries.

Figure 2-13 shows international comparisons of real interest rates based on the simplistic assumption that the actual inflation rate was the anticipated inflation rate. This ex-post measure of real interest spreads indicates that differences between real interest rates are large and variable.

It is difficult to quantify the reasons for departures from real interest rate parity because the relationship depends on variables that are not directly observable: the anticipated inflation rates in both countries and the speculative premium. Deviations from uncovered interest rate parity are clearly part of the explanation. Tests of uncovered interest rate parity imply that the forward premium is not an efficient forecaster of the expected change in the exchange rate, so uncertainty about nominal exchange rate changes will contribute to differences in real interest rates. But expected deviations from purchasing power parity are also likely to be important. Many factors in addition to differences in inflation rates affect exchange rates. Indeed, in view of the substantial deviations from purchasing power parity that have occurred among the major currencies in the past fifteen years, it would be surprising if international investors were not concerned about real exchange rate variability. Real exchange rates can be as variable and uncertain as nominal exchange rates.

35. A similar analytic framework can be found in Goldstein, Mathieson, and Lane (1991, pp. 1–45); and Frankel (1992).

36. For discussion of purchasing power parity as an ex-ante relationship see Roll (1979); and Adler and Lehmann (1973). For evidence on real interest rate differentials see Cumby and Obstfeld (1984); and Frankel and MacArthur (1988).

Figure 2-13. *Real Interest Rate Differentials, United States and Four Other Countries, 1977–92*

United States–United Kingdom

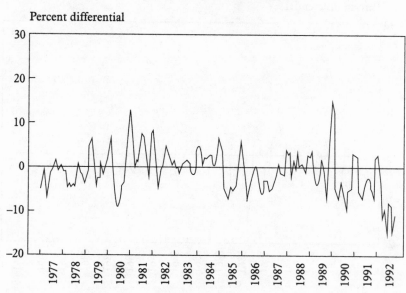

United States–Germany

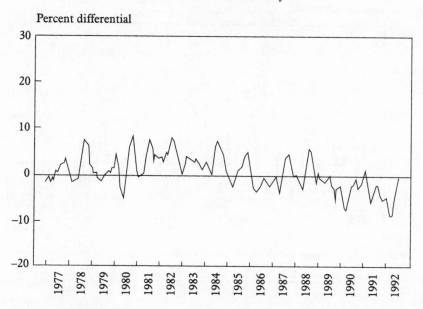

Sources: See figure 2-11.

Figure 2-13. *(continued)*

United States–France

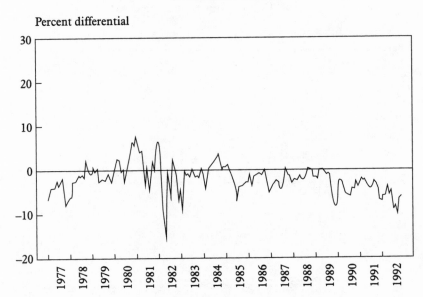

United States–Japan

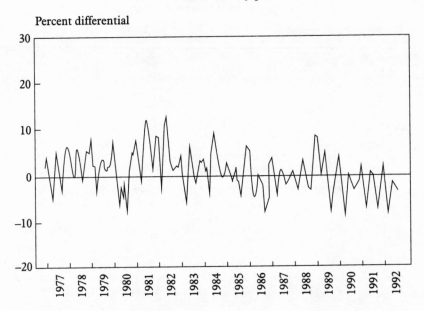

Summary and Implications

The implication of the failure of real interest parity is that the current level of international financial integration falls short of what would prevail in a truly integrated financial market. For example, the real interest rate in one region of the United States is likely to be virtually identical to the real interest rate in any other region of the United States even if the regions are three thousand miles apart. In contrast several obvious barriers to flows of financial capital exist between nations that are of little importance inside nations. The preceding analysis emphasizes the risk of nominal and real exchange rate changes, but other sources of friction may also be relevant.

Although country premiums have largely disappeared for high-quality, short-to-medium-term financial investments, they may still be an important inhibition to international substitutability between long-term bonds, equities, and real investments. Information and transactions costs are higher for assets that are not traded in broad, deep, liquid markets. Different countries have different legal systems that assign different rights to creditors in the event that a borrower defaults; indeed, rules for winding down a failed business may discriminate against foreign residents.[37] And differences in tax laws may discriminate against foreign residents.[38] Moreover, differences in language, business traditions, disclosure laws, taxes, political traditions, macroeconomic stability, and the risks of future interferences with international capital flows become more important in international comparisons of longer-term investments and equity than in comparisons of short-term, nominally risk-free assets that underlie the preceding attempt to quantify the level of financial integration.

Since international financial integration does not appear to have advanced to the fourth level, much less the fifth, it should not be surprising that the supply of national savings still seems to influence the quantity of national investment. In an integrated national financial market, interregional capital flows quickly bridge regional imbalances between savings and investment. International capital flows, in contrast, are inhibited by exchange rate variability and, probably, for some categories of transactions, by residual country premiums as

37. For a comparison of bankruptcy laws in the United Kingdom and the United States see Franks and Torous (1993, pp. 95–103).

38. Mitsuhiro Fukao discusses important international differences in bankruptcy procedures and tax laws. Fukao (1993).

well. In the international system, unlike a financial system in which real interest rate parity prevails, imbalances between national savings and investment may lead to changes in the national real interest rate. A shortfall in private savings or an increase in the government deficit may crowd out private investment.

Studies of national savings and investment are consistent with inferences about the level of international financial integration based on arbitrage relationships. The pathbreaking study by Martin Feldstein and Charles Horioka showed that national savings and investment rates tend to be highly correlated.[39] Their results have been replicated for a wide range of countries. A number of subsequent studies have suggested additional reasons why national savings and investment rates might be highly correlated even if real interest rate parity held.[40] National savings and investment tend to respond positively to the national income and to the growth in population or productivity. Government policy may accentuate the correlation if it attempts to limit current account surpluses by boosting national savings. And a large country that can influence real interest rates throughout the world will have positively correlated savings and investment even if real interest rate parity holds. These factors undoubtedly contribute to the observed positive correlation between national savings and investment. But until real interest rate parity is achieved, national investment will necessarily depend to some extent on the supply of national savings.

Conclusion: The Extent of International Financial Integration

Our analysis of the effect of technological advances in telecommunications and information technology has shown that the costs of surmounting natural impediments to international financial transactions have fallen sharply. Financial information flows almost instantaneously throughout the industrial world, twenty-four hours a day. This has had an important effect on the behavior of users of financial services, producers of financial services, and regulators of financial services.

39. Feldstein and Horioka (1980).
40. See Frankel (1992) for a detailed discussion and analysis of the literature.

Cross-border flows of financial transactions have grown more rapidly than income or international trade. These flows have undoubtedly tightened international linkages between national financial markets in leading industrial countries. The growth of cross-border flows has been supported by the international expansion of financial institutions headquartered in leading industrial countries. Although these foreign offices must comply with local regulations, they inevitably intensify competition and introduce new kinds of financial products and practices that often lead to changes in local regulations. The menus of financial choices in different national markets are consequently becoming more similar. This trend has been most pronounced with regard to large wholesale transactions. But the same forces of innovation and technological advance that are integrating offshore and onshore markets are also breaking down barriers within traditionally segmented national financial markets.

International comparisons of returns on assets indicate that international financial integration has advanced to the third level, in which short-to-medium-term fixed-income assets insured against foreign exchange risk are virtually perfect substitutes across the leading industrial countries. But uncertainty about movements in nominal and real exchange rates presents an obstacle to achieving the deeper level of financial integration that prevails within leading industrial countries. For longer-term, more heterogeneous financial instruments, residual country premiums may also interfere with international substitutability of otherwise comparable assets.

Large sophisticated institutions dealing in short-to-medium-term financial instruments enjoy a degree of international financial integration that is without precedent in the post–World War II era. This is in striking contrast to the tightly insulated, heavily controlled national markets that prevailed just after the war. Even before all leading industrial nations had achieved external convertibility, the development of the Eurocurrency markets gave the largest investors and borrowers access to an offshore market in which covered interest rate parity prevailed. But domestic financial regulations and capital controls continued to impede the integration of offshore and onshore markets.

Since the 1970s the major industrial countries have liberalized their domestic financial regulations and relaxed controls on international flows of capital. The correspondence of the two trends was not coincidental. Growing cross-border flows put pressure on restrictive domestic regulations, and the liberalization of domestic regulations further increased cross-border flows. These developments tended to be sporadic; but by 1990, covered interest differentials were negligible for all major industrial countries.

Are these changes irreversible? The answer is clearly no. Indeed, it is arguable that the world has not yet returned to the level of financial integration that prevailed in the late nineteenth century, when real interest rates differed little across major countries.[41] Moreover, the behavior of France in the 1980s indicates that decisions to liberalize can be reversed for at least short periods.

But even though a retreat from international financial integration is possible, the costs of withdrawing from an integrated world financial market are rising. Technological advances have limited the scope for autonomous regulatory action that raises the cost of financial services. The introduction of personal computers, modems, and international direct-dial telephone systems has sharply limited a government's options for insulating its financial sector from the integrated international financial system. Unless a government chooses to impose draconian controls on cross-border flows of information and people, sophisticated transactors can readily shift from costly domestic financial services to cheaper foreign substitutes. And controls of that stringency on movements of people and information would impose heavy costs, not just on the financial sector but on the whole economy. Governments may still choose to impose costly regulations, but these regulations may no longer accomplish the policy goals they are intended to achieve.

Will the world economy proceed to higher levels of integration, ultimately approaching real interest parity? The answer depends in part on the kind of exchange rate system that countries choose. The policy changes that have reduced country premiums and advanced the industrial nations to the third level of integration have required only autonomous policy decisions to liberalize domestic financial regulations and lower capital controls. To a considerable extent, tech-

41. Philip Turner concludes from his analysis of the gold standard era (1881–1913) that "nominal long-term interest rates in the major industrial centers (Belgium, France, Germany, the Netherlands, the United Kingdom and the United States) did not diverge from each other by more than one percentage point. Because prices in different countries also tended to move together, there was a marked tendency for real rates of return to be equalized internationally." Turner (1991, p. 17).

nological advances have driven this process by facilitating innovations that permit sophisticated transactors to evade costly regulations. Liberalization and deregulation have as often been an admission that traditional policies no longer work as an attempt to achieve welfare gains from a more competitive financial system. This process is likely to continue to integrate internal markets between maturities, between sectors, between institutions, and between instruments to facilitate international substitutability over a wider range of assets.

The main barrier to the next higher levels of integration, however, is exchange rate uncertainty. Reduction of exchange rate uncertainty requires a very high degree of international cooperation. It cannot be accomplished by the actions of a single country. Although groups of countries may choose to adopt a common currency—and in mid-1994 even the plans of the European Union in this regard seem highly uncertain—it is doubtful that all major countries would choose this option.

Even if international financial integration does not advance to the next higher levels, the current level of integration raises important challenges for policymakers. The extent of substitutability between domestic financial instruments and international alternatives is already great enough to constrain the discretion of national policymakers with respect to macroeconomic, regulatory, and prudential policies. Other monographs in this series consider the way in which international financial integration affects monetary policy, fiscal policy, exchange rate policy, and the regulation of multinational enterprises. This book focuses on the implications of international financial integration for prudential policies—measures designed to protect the safety and soundness of the financial system.

As we argue in chapters 3 and 4, international financial integration affects both policies devised to prevent threats to financial stability and prudential policies designed to limit the damage to the financial system and the real economy once a shock has occurred. Ex ante the authorities face increasing difficulties in monitoring the safety and soundness of financial institutions as they become more involved in international financial transactions. Information on foreign transactions is often more costly to obtain and interpret. Moreover, notwithstanding the substantial potential benefits of international diversification, financial institutions engaged in international transactions may face three kinds of risk that do not occur in purely domestic financial transactions. First is foreign exchange risk. Foreign exchange positions, like other speculative positions in assets with volatile prices, may jeopardize the solvency of an institution. Second is transfer risk, the possibility that residents of a particular foreign country will be unable to pay a promised amount because the central bank on which they depend for foreign exchange is unable or unwilling to permit local currency to be converted into the currency in which the contract is denominated. Third is international settlement risk, the possibility that the quid pro quo in a foreign exchange transaction that an institution paid out earlier in the Greenwich-mean-time day will not be received when the relevant market settles later in the Greenwich-mean-time day.[42]

After a shock to the solvency of an important financial institution has occurred, either because of the realization of a foreign risk or a traditional domestic risk, the authorities may experience greater difficult in organizing an effective response when markets are highly integrated internationally. An effective ex-post response may require cooperation among national authorities in several different countries to gather information and perhaps to perfect collateral and provide resources. Moreover, the increased capital mobility that has accompanied deeper international financial integration means that the authorities have a much shorter time to perceive and react to a shock. And the acceleration of financial innovation that has gone along with greater international financial integration has increased the complexity of interconnections among financial market participants. This would make it more difficult to implement an effective prudential policy if an important market participant were to fail. We will address these aspects of international financial integration in the chapters that follow.

42. This intraday risk is sometimes known as Herstatt risk (see chapter 3).

Chapter 3

Financial Regulation
in Domestic and
International Environments

W HY DO governments regulate financial institutions and markets?
It is a useful question to answer in order to assess the policy
implications of the forces driving financial interdependence and integration described in chapter 2. To provide that answer, we first
address in this chapter why governments might have an interest in
regulating financial activity even if it is solely domestic in nature—that
is, if all the parties are domestic nationals and the funds transferred
remain within the country. We then take up the question of how, if at
all, the rationales for regulation might change once financial activities
and the parties that engage in them cross national borders. Our
concluding section outlines alternatives for addressing these rationales in a multicountry context, thus providing the foundation for the
central issues we emphasize in subsequent chapters: in an increasingly
international environment, who should do the regulating and how?

Rationales for Financial Regulation in a Domestic Setting

Although we do not necessarily agree with all of them, three broad
reasons appear to have motivated countries to subject their financial
institutions and markets to regulation and supervision: preventing
disruptions in financial markets and troubles experienced by financial
institutions from posing wider systemic risks; protecting consumers
from excessive prices and opportunistic behavior by providers of
financial services and other participants in the financial marketplace
(thus helping to ensure the integrity and efficiency of the financial

Table 3-1. *Objectives and Tools of Financial Regulation*

Tools	Systemic risk	Consumer protection	Broader social objectives
Antitrust enforcement		✓	
Asset restrictions	✓		✓
Capital standards	✓	✓	
Conflict rules (including restrictions on insider transactions)		✓	
Disclosure standards and requirements	✓	✓	
Entry restrictions:			
Geographic			✓
Product line	✓		✓
Interest rate ceilings			✓
Investment requirements			✓
Reporting requirements (antisecrecy)			✓

markets); and achieving various social objectives, such as allocating credit to specific sectors of the economy, preventing undue concentration of political power, and inhibiting illicit activity. Table 3-1 shows the various regulatory instruments that have been used to reach these objectives. Countries have placed different degrees of emphasis on these objectives at different times and have used different regulatory tools to achieve them.

Systemic Risk

Historically, perhaps the overriding reason for regulating financial institutions and markets has been the desire to avoid systemic risk—the possibility of a contagious spread of losses across financial institutions that threatens to harm the real economy (the production of goods and services).[1] Michael Hewitt, an official with the Bank of England, described a sequence of events in which such a credit shock could lead to a systemic crisis.[2] In brief, the process begins with losses in one sector that lead to the failure of one or more major financial intermediaries. If these failures, in turn, generate a crisis in the core

1. For a similar definition, see Kane (1992).
2. See Hewitt (1992).

banking and payments system, the credit shocks may have significantly harmful effects on the real economy.

Systemic risk might arise in several broad ways. The classic example is a run on many banks by their panicky depositors. If deposit accounts are not insured or depositors lack confidence in the insurer (as was the case with thrift depositors in Maryland and Ohio in the mid-1980s) or banks are unable to borrow quickly against their assets, the failure of one or more banks can prompt depositors at other solvent banks to demand an immediate return of their funds. Even though depositors may be confident that their banks are solvent under normal conditions, they may nonetheless fear that their banks have insufficient liquid funds available to pay back many depositors at the same time. If many depositors act the same way, simultaneously losing faith in the banking system and converting their deposits into cash, they can cause credit throughout the economy to contract and spending to fall. The bank runs of the early 1930s in the United States had such an effect. Although they did not cause the Great Depression, it is now understood that they made it significantly worse.[3]

Securities markets may also generate a contagious spread of losses. A sudden drop in securities prices may prompt further price drops if many market participants are highly leveraged, have purchased their assets on margin, and are forced by the initial price decline to sell their holdings. If, in turn, those who suffer losses cause one or more banks that are central to the payments system to fail, the resulting losses in liquidity may cause credit to contract and the level of real economic activity to fall. The stock market crash of 1929 provides perhaps the best illustration of such a sequence of events (although the October 1987 stock market crash did not have these effects).

Even in the absence of panicky behavior by depositors or investors, the contagious transmission of losses can occur if there is a significant disruption in the payments system or the mechanism through which transactions for goods, services, and assets are cleared and settled.[4] As we discuss in more detail later in this chapter, in modern economies, banks provide the principal means of payment through their deposits, which owners can draw on by check or electronic means. In turn, banks and securities exchanges have developed clearinghouses to sort

3. Bernanke (1983).
4. Central banks have emphasized this source of systemic risk. See, for example, Gilbert (1989).

out and transfer the ever-growing volume of transactions so that funds can be moved at the end of each clearing period, typically a day, on a wholesale basis between financial institutions rather than transaction by transaction. The clearinghouses perform another critically important function: they bear the risk that individual institutions will not be able to honor their obligations when it is time for the transactions to be settled. As a result, when one or more large institutions cannot pay, they can (under some institutional arrangements) expose the clearinghouses, their members, and thus the payments system as a whole to a breakdown. If banks cannot process payments, their customers cannot spend, and the economy will shrink.

The importance of these payments mechanisms cannot be overstated. The two major systems in the United States—Fedwire and the Clearing House Interbank Payments System (or CHIPS, owned by eleven larger New York banks)—transfer daily at least $1.7 trillion, an amount equal to about 40 percent of the annual GDP of the United States.

Panicky behavior by depositors or investors can cause interruptions to the payments system; conversely, payments interruptions may lead to panicky behavior by private participants. For this reason, the two sources of systemic risk may be intertwined.

Minimizing Systemic Risk

That financial activities and institutions may pose systemic risks does not necessarily mean that government should step in and regulate. If central banks prudently exercise their responsibilities as lenders of last resort, they can significantly reduce or even eliminate the threat of a systemic crisis.

Consider contagion risk. If the Federal Reserve in the 1930s had made credit liberally available to solvent banks to meet depositors' withdrawals, depositors would have had less reason to run. In the 1980s the Federal Reserve provided evidence that it had learned this lesson in a somewhat different context. Immediately after the October 1987 stock market crash, the Fed pressured major banks to continue their lending to securities firms, providing assurances that it would make liquidity available if necessary. More generally, the Fed immediately injected reserves into the banking system, bringing down interest rates. As a result, despite widespread fears at the time that the crash would trigger a recession, the economy expanded at a healthy rate in the final quarter of 1987.[5]

Governments have also used implicit or explicit guarantees to protect against systemic risk resulting from contagion. In 1933 the United States introduced deposit insurance for banks and later for savings and loans (or thrift institutions), a move that is widely credited for stopping the bank runs that were under way just before Franklin Roosevelt's inauguration. The insurance was originally provided only for deposits under $2,500, but the ceiling has been intermittently raised, the last time in 1980, when it was increased from $40,000 to $100,000. Table 3-2 shows that other major countries have since followed the United States, but generally have offered a lesser degree of protection to their bank depositors. In some of these countries, such as Germany, the insurance funds are operated by the banks themselves. Similarly, while all fifty states in the United States require insurers to participate in guarantee funds to protect policyholders when insurers fail, the funds are managed by the insurers. This is not the case, however, with deposit insurance for banks and thrifts in the United States, where the insurance funds are operated by an independent federal agency (the Federal Deposit Insurance Corporation) but are financed by assessments on the insured institutions.

In principle, deposit insurance is not necessary to protect against contagion as long as the monetary authorities faithfully carry out their lender-of-last-resort responsibilities. On the small chance that they do not, deposit insurance serves the same function.[6]

Central banks can also take the systemic risk out of the payments system by bearing the risk of nonpayment by participants. In the United States, for example, the Federal Reserve guarantees the funds transferred over the Fedwire system, which is reserved for large dollar transactions. Other countries provide similar guarantees for the large value transactions in their currencies.[7]

Private sector clearinghouses also have developed to handle large value payments transactions and securities trades. Since these private clearinghouses do not have sufficient resources to provide absolute

5. The Fed sent a similar signal that it was ready to provide liquidity again in October 1989 when equities markets suffered a substantial, but less severe, price decline.

6. For an extended discussion, see Guttentag and Herring (1987).

7. Borio and Van den Bergh (1993).

Table 3-2. *Illustrative List of Bank Deposit Insurance Systems*

Country	Year established	Insurance coverage limit	US $ equivalent (as of 7/1/93)	Premium pricing scheme
Canada	1967	C$ 60,000	46,806	0.1 percent of insured deposits
Denmark	1987	Dkr. 250,000	38,075	Max. 0.2 percent of total deposits; starting in 1989, total annual contributions of all members is kr. 700 million until fund reaches kr. 3 billion
France	1980	FF 400,000	69,512	Collected as needed; assessments based on deposits
Germany	1966	30 percent of the "liable capital of bank concerned per depositor"	N/A	0.03 percent of total deposits
Italy	1987	100 percent of first L 200 mil., 75 percent of next L 800 mil.	516,000	Unfunded arrangement
Japan	1971	¥ 10,000,000	93,370	0.012 percent of covered deposit balance
Norway	1961	Unlimited	Unlimited	0.015 percent of total assets
Switzerland	1984	SF 30,000	19,803	Unfunded arrangement
United Kingdom	1982	75 percent of deposit balance up to £ 20,000	22,373	Progressive levy with the effective rate not to exceed 0.3 percent of domestic sterling deposits
United States	1933	$100,000	100,000	0.23 percent of deposits (and higher depending on risk, up to 0.30 percent)

Source: Philip F. Bartholomew and Vicki A. Vanderhoff, "Foreign Deposit Insurance Systems: A Comparison," *Quarterly Report*, vol. 45 (Summer 1991).

guarantees, they instead use forms of private regulation to minimize default risks. Among other things, the clearinghouses typically set capital standards and limits on position risk, or the amounts by which one member can be in debt to any other member and to all other members collectively at any one time. In addition, the private clearing systems typically protect themselves against loss by setting performance bonds for their members (as is the case with U.S. futures markets) or collecting an assessment from members to build a loss reserve within the clearinghouse itself (as is the case with the Clearing House Interbank Payment System, CHIPS). Nevertheless, even private clearinghouses may be backstopped by the central bank. For example, had the Federal Reserve not taken the actions it did following the 1987 stock market crash, the futures and equities exchanges might have been forced to shut down, throwing the markets into chaos.[8]

If systemic risk can be so substantially reduced by the central bank, by government guarantees, and by private regulation practiced by the private clearinghouses, why should government regulation of financial markets and institutions be necessary? When the government provides a safety net, it also tempts private actors to pursue high-wire investment strategies at the expense of the government (and therefore taxpayers). Put another way, government safety nets help solve the systemic risk problem only by creating another problem: the danger that scarce funds available for investment will be diverted into socially unproductive endeavors or simply wasted. Regulation is necessary to counteract or constrain the effects of this moral hazard.

Consider deposit insurance. If depositors know that their funds are guaranteed by the government, they have no incentive to monitor the financial health of their banks. Although shareholders clearly have an incentive to do so in well-capitalized institutions, the incentive may diminish as the institutions' capital declines. When for any reason an insured depository loses all or a significant portion of its capital—perhaps because of a local or national recession that causes many borrowers to default—the fact that deposits are guaranteed may encourage the affected banks to attempt to grow out of their problems by attracting more funds and investing them in high-risk ventures. Such a strategy may be attractive since the managers and sharehold-

8. Bernanke (1990).

ers have very little to lose if the gambles do not work (most or all of the bank's capital already may be gone) and much to gain. The United States learned this simple lesson, at a cost of more than $150 billion, in the 1980s, when government regulators allowed, and indeed encouraged, the rapid growth of scores of economically insolvent savings and loans that were desperately attempting to dig themselves out of the hole generated by the 1981–82 recession and the high interest rate environment at that time.[9]

To be sure, many and perhaps most thrifts would not have been forced into insolvency by the double-digit interest rate of the early 1980s if policymakers had permitted the industry to invest in adjustable rate mortgages and other nonmortgage assets and to raise funds free of the interest rate ceilings that were in effect until 1982. But even though such policy mistakes had been made, much further damage could have been prevented if regulators had constrained the growth of insolvent or undercapitalized institutions so that only those institutions owned by shareholders with money to lose were allowed to grow. That this did not occur underscores the importance of sound capital standards in offsetting the moral hazard created by government safety nets for depositors or other creditors.

Indeed, if capital regulation were perfect—that is, if all financial intermediaries could be shut down and their creditors paid off just before the intermediaries became economically insolvent—other regulatory tools might not be necessary to protect an economy against the dangers of moral hazard. Moreover, deposit insurance would not even be necessary to prevent bank runs, although the central bank might still be required to lend to illiquid but solvent depositories.[10]

In practice, however, capital regulation may not and almost certainly does not achieve this ideal. For one thing, regulators may delay in taking appropriate action to constrain or to close insolvent institutions, either for fear of the public criticism they may endure for failing

9. As the commission officially charged with investigating the causes of the savings and loan crisis put it, deposit insurance was a "necessary," but not a sufficient condition for the S&L disaster. The most important additional causal factor was the failure of regulators to control the growth of many thrifts after the significant increase in interest rates in the early 1980s rendered virtually the entire industry economically insolvent and thus ideally positioned to take advantage of the heads I win, tails the government loses opportunities that deposit insurance allowed. See National Commission of Financial Institution Reform, Recovery and Enforcement (1993).

10. See Benston and Kaufman (1988).

to prevent the insolvencies or because they may be responding to political pressure to keep such institutions open. Equally, if not more important, regulators typically measure capital on the basis of the book values or the historical costs of the assets and liabilities of banks and insurance companies rather than on the basis of their market or economic values.[11] Since book valuations of firms in distress tend to exceed market valuations, the use of historical cost accounting for regulatory purposes (often distorted further by special regulatory accounting principles that hide losses) tends to reinforce any other pressures for delaying the closure of economically insolvent institutions. Regulatory forbearance can be especially dangerous when the institutions involved have access to government-guaranteed funds and thus can gamble for resurrection at taxpayers' expense.

Accordingly, other regulatory tools may be justified to backstop capital regulation, as illustrated in the first column in table 3-1. For example, banks typically are prevented from lending too heavily to any single borrower to limit their risk exposure. In addition, many countries limit the types of assets their banks and other financial intermediaries can purchase. The United States, for example, does not permit its banks to purchase corporate equities, while Japan prohibits its banks from owning more than five percent of the stock issued by any company. In a related vein, as shown in table 3-3, a few industrialized countries still limit the ability of their banks to affiliate with other types of enterprise, especially commercial companies, whose financial problems can infect the related banks and thus potentially stretch the safety net meant only for bank depositors to protect nonbank operations.

Disclosure requirements also may be used to prevent systemic risk, primarily by inhibiting the excesses that may lead to the crises that pose such risks. Since the 1930s, for example, the United States has required publicly owned U.S. corporations to register their securities and to provide appropriate and timely disclosures of their financial condition. These requirements are designed, in part, to help prevent uninformed speculation from bidding up asset prices to inflated

11. This is not the case for securities firms in major industrialized countries, where assets and liabilities are marked to market. Moreover, even under mark-to-market accounting, the balance sheet of a firm will not reflect the true economic value of the enterprise unless the asset side of the balance sheet includes some market-based estimate of the firm's franchise value or goodwill.

Table 3-3. *Permissible Activities for Banking Organizations in Various Financial Centers*

Country	Securities	Insurance	Real estate	Bank investments in industrial firms	Industrial firm investments in banks
Belgium	u	u	p	l	u
Canada	u	u	u	l	l
France	u	u	u	l	l[a]
Germany	u	u	l	l	u
Italy	u	l	p	p	l
Japan	l	p	p	l	l
Netherlands	u	u	u	l	l
Sweden	u	u	p	l	l[a]
Switzerland	u	u	u	u	l[a]
United Kingdom	u	u	u	l	l[a]
United States	l	p	p	l	l

Source: *Thompson's International Banking Regulator,* October 25, 1993, pp. 6–9. For details, see Appendix.

u = unlimited; l = limited; p = prohibited.

a. Not prohibited, but such investments are generally not made.

levels. That the securities laws have not fully succeeded in this endeavor—even informed investors can have wildly different outlooks about the performance of the economy and the individual companies within it—does not mean that the disclosure rules have been unhelpful in reducing stock price volatility and excessive speculation.

Disclosure of the financial condition of banks and other financial institutions can be especially important in discouraging their shareholders and managers from taking the excessive risks that may lead to failures of financial firms which, in turn, may give rise to systemic risk. To be effective in achieving this goal, however, disclosure must be meaningful, and the scope of government guarantees must be limited. Otherwise, investors and creditors will lack the ability and incentive to monitor the risk taking of financial intermediaries.

In this respect, two recent developments in the United States are of interest. One is the effort by the Financial Accounting Standards

Board (FASB)—the private-sector body to which the Securities and Exchange Commission has effectively delegated authority to set accounting rules—to encourage U.S. financial institutions to adopt market value accounting. With the exception about to be noted, the new rules, which became effective for large banks and other financial institutions in 1993, are meant at this point only to supplement existing book value statements. But they open the door to the possibility that mark-to-market accounting may eventually replace financial data based on historical costs. Even if no additional rules are adopted, the new FASB rules should enhance the ability of private parties to discipline wayward financial firms.

Nevertheless, the rules are not free from problems. This is because they also require banks to mark more of their securities to market than was the case previously, without at the same time marking the deposits that fund those investments to market. As a result, even if a bank has match-funded its assets—that is, matched the duration of its securities investments with the duration of the deposits funding them—movements in interest rates will cause the reported capital position of the bank to change even when the market value of the bank should not be affected. So-called partial mark-to-market accounting, therefore, is expected to lead U.S. banks to shorten the maturities of their securities investments.

The second development should provide stronger incentives for private parties to act on the new accounting information. Notwithstanding the formal features of their deposit insurance systems, illustrated in table 3-2, most countries have implicitly fully protected all their depositors by arranging for the merger of failing or failed banks with healthier partners, a practice that obviously weakens incentives of depositors and other creditors to monitor these institutions. In 1991, however, the United States adopted legislation that, among other things, may curtail the use of this practice. If this occurs, the Federal Reserve will have more responsibility for preventing systemic risk in the future, not by protecting the depositors at failing or insolvent banks, but instead through general open market operations of the kind that were used to flood the markets with liquidity after the October 1987 stock market crash. This should help restore some degree of market discipline for larger banks in particular.

One key challenge for financial regulators in all countries in the future is to find ways of making greater use of market forces to discipline financial institutions without at the same time exposing their economies to greater systemic risks. Just as markets process information about prices, tastes, and technologies more effectively than any single central bank or government body, market participants—provided they have access to all important relevant information—may be able to discipline financial activities in a more cost-effective manner than government regulators.

Unfortunately, certain regulatory tools may work at cross-purposes, tending to exacerbate rather than to reduce the danger of systemic risk. Restrictions against geographic diversification, commonly implemented through branching restrictions, prevent financial institutions from spreading their asset risk, thus exposing them to regional disturbances of the kind seen in the United States in New England and in the Southwest.[12] In the past decade the United States has gradually removed its restrictions against bank holding company expansion across state lines, and in 1994 Congress finally launched interstate branching. Thus the United States has now joined the nations of the European Union, which have largely removed their branching restrictions within countries and, with the advent of EU 1992, totally eliminated them for branching across national boundaries.[13]

In addition, a number of nations, notably Japan and many less developed countries, still maintain regulatory ceilings on interest that banks can pay their depositors, ostensibly to prevent excessive competition, which could weaken banks. However, deposit rate ceilings can be severely destabilizing, promoting systemic risk, as the United States has discovered. The reason, of course, is that when interest rates on unregulated investments rise above the deposit ceilings, depositors have strong incentives to run from their banks toward the alternative, higher-yielding investments. Ultimately, the United States

12. The president of the Federal Reserve Bank of Boston has noted that the New England economy would not have suffered as severe a "credit crunch" in the 1990s if many of the banks doing business in the region had a sizable presence elsewhere that would have cushioned the shock to their capital when real estate prices in New England collapsed. See testimony of Richard F. Syron before the Subcommittee of Financial Institutions Supervision, Regulation and Deposit Insurance of the Committee on Banking, Finance and Urban Affairs, U.S. House of Representatives, June 22, 1993, reprinted in the *Federal Reserve Bulletin*, vol. 79 (August 1993), pp. 777–87.

13. Organization for Economic Cooperation and Development (1992, p. 64).

was forced by double-digit market interest rates in the early 1980s to abandon its Regulation Q interest rate ceilings on bank and thrift deposits. The phase-out of interest rate ceilings has been more gradual in other countries, notably Japan, but by 1990 had been virtually completed within at least the countries of the Organization for Economic Cooperation and Development (OECD) and had been copied in many developing countries as well.[14]

Consumer Protection

A second important goal of financial regulation is to protect consumers against excessive prices or opportunistic behavior by providers of financial services or participants in financial markets. The concern with excessive prices, of course, is not peculiar to financial markets, but instead is manifested more generally through a commitment to antitrust enforcement in many countries. The United States was the first nation to adopt antitrust legislation (the Sherman Act of 1890) and since has had the most aggressive antitrust enforcement policy of any country in the world. Indeed, variations in the manner and intensity of antitrust enforcement between the United States, Japan, and the EU have been a growing source of friction, because the differences reflect fundamentally different valuations placed on consumer protection in these countries.

Protecting consumers from opportunistic behavior also has been an important objective of financial regulation, and here too the United States appears to have displayed the strongest interest. Opportunistic behavior can arise when one party to a transaction (typically the provider of the service or product) has better information than the other (typically the buyer). For example, until the United States made insider trading illegal, corporate officials and owners with better information about the fortunes of their companies could take advantage of noninsiders.[15] In addition, certain financial products—such as insurance policies and some types of securities—may be sufficiently

14. Organization for Economic Cooperation and Development (1992, pp. 40–41); and World Bank (1989, p. 122).

15. Until recently, insider trading was not prohibited in Germany nor effectively policed in Japan. However, this has changed with the adoption of the Insider Trading Directive of the European Economic Community and the disclosure of significant insider trading in Japan in the early 1990s.

complicated that without standardized disclosure rules, some buyers of those products could be misled into purchasing them.

Perhaps most important, without some type of regulation, providers of financial instruments with long or uncertain maturities may be in an especially advantageous position to benefit at the expense of unsuspecting customers. For example, individuals who purchase insurance expect their insurers to be able to pay claims when they are made. If insurers were not required to disclose their financial condition and to adhere to capital standards, unscrupulous operators could be tempted to take the money and run—to collect premiums at rock-bottom rates, to grant themselves high salaries and other perquisites, and then use the bankruptcy laws to shelter their gains when claims payments are called for many years later.[16] Similarly, workers covered by defined-benefit pension plans—for whom the plans may represent the major source of retirement income—count on their companies' being able to deliver on their promises many years into the future. Accordingly, it may be appropriate, as the United States has done since 1974, to require companies that provide these plans to set aside sufficient funds on a regular basis to fund them fully.[17]

Achieving Broader Social Objectives

Finally, because financial institutions and markets are so critical to the functioning of a modern economy and to facilitating all sorts of transactions, governments have been tempted to use financial regulation to pursue certain broader social objectives.

Perhaps the most common example is the allocation of credit to favored sectors of the economy, such as housing, which many countries have supported by chartering lenders who specialize in home

16. Although in the United States insurer-operated guarantee funds help protect policyholders against this kind of activity, the guarantees typically do not exceed $300,000 per claim, which can be well below actual claim amounts (especially for life insurance), so many policyholders still have strong reasons to be concerned about the health of their insurers.

17. The United States also has created the Pension Benefit Guaranty Corporation to backstop these requirements by insuring pension coverage up to approximately $30,000 a year for each worker. Yet just as deposit insurance has created a moral hazard for financial intermediaries to take excessive risks at the expense of the government insurer, the pension guarantees have had a similar effect among major U.S. companies. During the past several years, the U.S. Congress has considered legislation that would help offset the moral hazard embedded in the pension guarantee system by prohibiting firms from offering additional defined pension benefits without fully funding them in advance.

purchases. The United States has further promoted home ownership by extending implicit government guarantees to securities backed by housing mortgages and by allowing homeowners to deduct mortgage interest on their income taxes. In addition, until its interest rate ceilings were eliminated, the United States favored housing lenders by allowing them to pay their depositors a slightly higher interest rate (one quarter of a percentage point) than banks could pay their depositors, a policy that had the effect of enhancing the funds made available to finance housing.

Governments channel credit in other, more explicit ways. Most countries subsidize financing for exports in one fashion or another. Many countries also require their financial institutions to lend to certain regions or sectors. For example, under the Community Reinvestment Act (CRA) since 1977 the United States has required both its commercial banks and its thrift institutions to serve the credit needs of local communities, lower-income areas in particular. Meanwhile, governments in many less developed countries still own banks, which permits the direct allocation of credit on the basis of political rather than market criteria.[18]

In any event, governments should be concerned with the efficiency of financial markets because they provide a critical source of information that helps to coordinate decentralized decisions throughout the economy. Interest rates and equity prices are used by households in allocating income between consumption and savings and in allocating their stock of wealth. Firms also rely on financial markets for information about which investment projects to select and how such projects should be financed. Thus, the overall objective of government with regard to financial markets should be to ensure that they perform efficiently in helping to allocate and to transfer resources across time and space in an uncertain environment.

A second social objective of financial regulation, peculiar to the United States, is to prevent concentration of political and economic power within the financial sector, especially among banks. To accomplish this objective the United States until recently has restricted the ability of banking organizations to expand across state lines. Restrictions continue against bank participation in nonbanking activities,

---

18. For a survey of directed credit policies followed in less developed countries, see World Bank (1989, pp. 54–61).

however. Nevertheless, these restrictions have never been airtight, so institutions and their lawyers increasingly have found ways around them. For example, despite the limits on nonbank activity written into the Bank Holding Company Act, banking organizations have found ways to broker and to underwrite securities, to offer mutual funds, and to engage in various aspects of the insurance business. The fact that Congress has not stopped these efforts reflects the waning importance that federal policymakers attach to the once-strong concern about excessive concentration of power within the banking industry.

Moreover, market developments have made the concern itself obsolete (assuming it was ever valid). Since the end of World War II, banks' share of all financial assets held by financial institutions in the United States has plummeted, from 57 percent in 1964 to less than 30 percent in 1992.[19] While banks traditionally have been more important providers of credit in other industrialized countries, even there the importance of banks has been waning gradually while that of the securities markets has been growing.[20]

Third, because many illicit activities, such as the trade in drugs and organized crime, are facilitated by banks, a few governments have imposed reporting requirements on banks in an effort to combat money laundering. Again, regulation for this purpose is quite advanced in the United States, where banks are required to report all currency transactions of $10,000 or more. Historically, Switzerland has been most noted for protecting bank secrecy; its policy led to charges that it was a haven for criminals seeking bank services. But in the face of mounting international pressure, even this country relaxed its secrecy protections in 1992 (by eliminating anonymous bank accounts). In many countries, however, especially in Asia, where the drug trade historically has been quite strong, banks still are not subject to reporting requirements, nor are they required to establish a customer's true identity.

Financial Regulation in an International Environment

Financial activities, like trade, are not confined to national borders. In fact, driven by rapid reductions in the costs of communication and

19. Calculated from Board of Governors, Federal Reserve System, various issues.
20. See Litan (1991, pp. 42–43).

transportation, national economies, financial institutions, and financial markets are more linked today than ever before. Put another way, in an increasingly global marketplace, the financial sectors and indeed entire economies of individual nations are increasingly dependent on financial and economic developments in other countries.

Heightened openness leads to spillovers—effects felt in one country because of events or policy actions taken in other countries. Spillovers can be either positive or negative. For example, when one economy expands—especially a large one like the United States, Germany, or Japan—it ordinarily creates beneficial spillovers by attracting a larger volume of imports from other countries, encouraging growth in their economies. Conversely, macroeconomic difficulties experienced by one or more countries may force them to reduce their imports, widening the economic pain. In short, the presence of spillovers turns what once may have been purely domestic activities into international ones.

As a general rule, participants do not (nor can they be expected to) take into account spillover effects when deciding what to do, and as a result the sum of their collective actions will not produce an optimal outcome for society as a whole. For example, the industrial firm that faces no sanctions or penalties for exposing its neighbors to the harmful effects of pollution will produce more output and pollution than is socially desirable. Similarly, since firms often cannot capture all of the benefits of the new products or processes they may develop, they may invest too little in research and development.

Much of what governments do is to concern themselves with spillovers within their own borders—trying to prevent or minimize bad spillovers by taxing or prohibiting the activities that lead to them, or encouraging good spillovers by supporting the activities that generate them. Ideally, government action should be taken only where the spillovers are significant, since governments themselves can make mistakes and their programs and regulatory efforts may be expensive to administer.

The same guidelines apply when spillovers cross national boundaries. A central issue becomes whether the governments of individual nations should take action unilaterally or only by coordinating their activities in some way with other countries (and if so, which ones). This challenge cannot and should not be answered in an across-the-board fashion, but instead by weighing the costs and benefits of unilateral and coordinated action in each case, as later chapters will suggest.

Nevertheless, some generalizations at this point may be useful. Unilateral action has the advantage that it generally can be taken more quickly than if agreement with other countries is required. But in a world of increasingly mobile capital, unilateral regulations may be difficult to enforce because they may simply drive domestically based firms to move offshore or to engage in regulatory arbitrage. In addition, unilateral actions may balkanize commerce by raising the costs of doing business in multiple markets.

Multilateral actions avoid these pitfalls but have drawbacks of their own. They may take time to agree upon; in many cases, differences in outlooks and preferences between countries may prevent any agreement from being reached at all. For example, as Richard Cooper has pointed out in the context of disease control, given their many differences, nations are not likely to agree to cooperate unless they clearly recognize the importance of dealing with a problem and agree on its causes and solution (such as the provision of a vaccine to fight a disease).[21] In addition, to the extent that countries engage in multilateral regulatory action to level competitive fields, they may be disappointed to discover that while one set of rules may be harmonized, others that are not may become more important and may cause equal if not greater frictions.

Systemic Risk and the Payments System

We suggested earlier that financial activities conducted within countries can pose systemic risks because of possible contagion effects and disruptions in the payments system. In principle, the same is true when financial activities are conducted across national borders. But there is an important difference. Unlike domestic economies, which have their own central bank to provide liquidity in the event of systemic risk, there is no world central bank charged with providing liquidity to global financial markets should systemic risk be international in character. Central banks and other financial regulators from industrialized countries have been attempting to fill this void by

21. Cooper (1989). Similar conclusions hold in the realm of foreign affairs. The United Nations acted much more quickly to approve joint military action in response to Iraq's invasion of Kuwait, which was widely seen to pose broader geopolitical and economic risks, than in the case of the ethnic fighting in Bosnia, whose wider consequences were not and still are not generally agreed upon and where no politically acceptable solution was evident.

agreeing to solvency standards for internationally active banks. How-ever, the issue of which central bank or banks should be responsible for providing emergency liquidity to troubled international financial institutions, if that should be required, has to yet to be resolved.

Systemic risks can be transmitted across national boundaries in several ways. We consider them in order of increasing concern.

First, and most likely of lowest risk, is contagion by depositors—the possibility that bank runs by depositors in one country may spread to other countries. This is highly unlikely if the banks involved are doing business solely in other countries, but it is perhaps more plausible where a foreign bank that encounters trouble in its home market also has a branch or affiliate in a third country. In that event, depositors in the third country could become so nervous about their domestically owned banks that they mount a run on them. Neverthe-less, because depositors in the third country are likely either to be protected by insurance or to know that the central bank will faithfully discharge its responsibilities as a lender of last resort, such generalized runs are highly unlikely. For this reason, even if a deposit run should occur, it will result in a movement of funds not from banks to currency but instead from one or more troubled banks to any number of other healthy banks.

In fact, the world recently witnessed an international run by depos-itors on a bank—the Bank of Commerce and Credit International (BCCI)—but the run did not spread to other banks in the countries affected. In large part, this was because the smart international mon-ey had already left. In addition, the bank was relatively small by international (or even U.S. domestic) standards, with about $20 bil-lion in assets, and its failure did not have widespread implications for other institutions. Meanwhile, many depositors in different countries distinguished between the problems experienced by a foreign bank such as BCCI and their own domestic banks. They also must have been comforted by either explicit or implicit government protection of their accounts.

There is stronger evidence that contagion can spread across na-tional borders and affect securities markets. Nevertheless, it is far from clear whether such contagious behavior can have significantly damaging real economic effects. Thus, for example, the stock market crash of 1987 displayed clear evidence of herdlike behavior by actors throughout the world: the crash first occurred in the Japanese equities markets and then spread eastward to New York and eventually to London. In addition, for some time thereafter, movements in stock prices in different countries were significantly more correlated (moving in unison) than they were before the crash.[22] Nevertheless, the nearly uniform steep drop in stock prices around the world appeared to have a relatively small effect on economic output. Again, much credit goes to the central banks in the industrialized countries, which generally eased their monetary policies to ensure this result. But it also seems to be the case that businesses and consumers, although they had suffered huge losses in the market value of their equities holdings, did not significantly curtail their spending.

Looking to the future, regulators have expressed concern about the growing involvement of large banks, securities firms, and insurers in derivatives markets. A derivative instrument is a financial contract whose value is derived from the value of other assets usually traded in cash markets. Derivative instruments include forwards, futures, options, and swaps as well as complicated hybrids of these contracts, and are traded actively in global markets. Derivative instruments are used both to hedge risks and to generate revenues. As we showed in chapter 2, derivatives markets have grown very rapidly. Use of swaps, for example, has grown since their introduction in 1981.[23] At the end of 1992, the top fifty U.S. bank holding companies had swap contracts with combined loss exposure of $144 billion, 20 percent more than their combined capital.[24] An unknown, but surely sizable, fraction of this amount is an exposure to foreign counterparties.[25]

Regulators are concerned that the growth of derivatives activities may have exacerbated systemic risk. The main concern is credit risk, the possibility that the collapse of a large dealer in derivatives could cause heavy losses for other financial institutions and lead to a contagious loss of confidence that could jeopardize the financial system.

22. See Von Furstenberg and Jeon (1989).

23. A currency swap transaction between the World Bank and IBM in 1981 is usually cited as the first swap. See Smith, Smithson, and Wilford (1990, p. 48).

24. Put differently, the replacement cost of these derivatives was $144 billion. This may overstate credit exposure, however, since it does not account for the netting of obligations that may take place in the event of a default. See Group of Thirty (1993). The amounts are reported on page 59.

25. American International Group, Inc., the large insurance company, recently disclosed its maximum potential losses on its derivative positions classified by counterparty. Forty-one percent of its maximum potential losses were to banks headquartered outside the United States. For additional details see Maguire (1994).

This concern is heightened by the fact that trading within the derivatives markets is heavily concentrated among relatively few, large institutions that act as dealers. But derivatives transactions are fundamentally the same as other activities in which financial institutions take on credit risk. The risk of default by a borrower or counterparty is a fundamental feature of most financial transactions and, indeed, exposure to loss and concentration of credit risk is likely to be greater in banks' traditional lending activities or in settling international payments.

The first line of defense against credit risk in derivatives activities, as in other activities, is prudent management of credit exposures. This involves setting and monitoring counterparty credit limits and using other risk-reducing strategies such as netting of obligations and requiring collateral or other credit enhancements.

The authorities are concerned, however, that the sheer complexity and opacity of some derivative instruments and the speed with which market position may shift make it difficult for counterparties to evaluate whether market risks are being adequately managed and capitalized. If market risks are systematically underestimated, then counterparties may be exposed to greater credit risk than they are prepared to accept.

Finally, the authorities fear that in the event that regulatory intervention is deemed necessary to avert a systemic crisis, they will face substantial difficulties in winding down the affairs of a failed institution if it is deeply involved in derivatives markets. The immense complexity of some derivative instruments and the complicated trading strategies required to hedge some derivatives positions may present a formidable and potentially costly challenge to any entity that takes the responsibility for making an orderly liquidation of the failed institution. This is likely to be the case even if derivatives activities were not the source of the institution's problems.

Another aspect of derivatives trading raises concerns about macroprudential stability and the transmission of disturbances across markets. Options-based derivatives are often hedged dynamically by continuous adjustment of a portfolio that replicates the options contract. If an institution has written an option, then it may be buying the underlying asset when prices are rising and selling the underlying asset when prices are declining. This may amplify market price movements, exacerbating difficulties for other market participants. Moreover, the increased volatility may cause dealers in the underlying instrument to curtail their market-making activities, and markets may break down just when the writer of the option needs most to hedge. Alan Greenspan, chairman of the Federal Reserve Board, believes that the "price amplification effects of dynamic hedging may be significant only after large price shocks."[26] But in the event of large price shocks, intervention may require close cooperation among the relevant authorities in several countries if it is to be effective.

A related and potentially even more worrisome source of international systemic risk in the future relates to a potential breakdown of the international payments system, whether on account of insolvency or illiquidity of the participants.[27] Since bank accounts serve as money, virtually all payments made between parties that are not made in cash ultimately are made between banks. As explained earlier, settlement networks process these transfers, generally on a net basis. That is, at the end of each settlement period the systems net out all of the funds owed to and to be received by all banks on the system and then transfer the resulting net amounts between banks. But what happens when one or more parties on the settlement network have insufficient funds—either because they temporarily lack liquidity or because they are insolvent—to make these transfers?

Various countries and settlement systems handle this problem differently, but generally speaking, settlement systems operated by central banks assume the risk of nonpayment in their domestic currencies. Private clearing systems, having no ability to print money to cover any settlement shortfalls, use one or more techniques to manage this risk—supervising the capital strength and liquidity of their members, monitoring transactions over the settlement network in real time (not waiting until the end of the period to determine outstanding balances of the participants), limiting the bilateral and multilateral exposures of the participants, providing a pool of liquidity (financed by the members) to cover any shortfalls, and, if all other steps fail, prearranging for loss-sharing by participants in the clearinghouse. At present, three major clearinghouses, CHIPS and the two major settle-

26. See testimony by Alan Greenspan, chairman, Board of Governors of the Federal Reserve System, before the Subcommittee on Telecommunications and Finance of the Committee on Energy and Commerce, U.S. House of Representatives, May 25, 1994, p. 3.

27. One of the best treatments of this subject is Borio and Van den Bergh (1993). Before he left his position as president of the Federal Reserve Bank of New York, E. Gerald Corrigan was a prominent official spokesperson on issues relating to payments systems.

ment systems in Japan (Zengin and FEYSS), have such protections. Other settlement systems are open ended—that is, they do not have loss-sharing arrangements—and instead must delete (or unwind) the transactions involving nonsettling banks from all settlements at the end of the period and thus recalculate settlements without payments to and receipts from the nonsettling bank. Before 1990 CHIPS, the world's largest private dollar-clearing system, also was open ended, but it has since established both a liquidity reserve and loss-sharing arrangements.

As long as settlement systems handle only domestic transactions, any risks they entail also are wholly domestic in nature. But with the explosion in the volume of international transactions—payments between parties in different countries in different currencies—payment risks have become international. In practice this means that the failure of one or more major institutions in other countries to settle in a particular currency can transmit payment problems to the country that issues that currency.

If the settlement or clearing network has the resources to cover any shortfall, then the losses are shared only among the settling participants. But what if the losses are so great that they force the central bank responsible for the affected currency to rescue the settlement process? In that event, financial events abroad can cause the domestic central bank to bear losses. Accordingly, financial institutions and activities around the world entail risks of spillovers or externalities across national boundaries that must be borne by central banks and the economies they help manage.

Central banks and bank regulators from at least the industrialized countries have recognized the dangers of payments-related systemic effects that may cross national boundaries. In particular, they have responded by agreeing on minimum capital standards for banks and by attempting to reach a similar agreement on such standards for securities firms. Capital standards ensure that institutions have a cushion to absorb losses, whether from credit losses (failures to pay by borrowers and other counterparties), trading losses, or losses from interest rate fluctuations. In the process they help protect against systemic problems related to solvency risks.

Capital standards do not, however, directly address systemic risks arising from interruptions in payments systems, which may be caused by any temporary disruption in liquidity available to participants in the system. Instead, threats to the payments system in each currency now must be handled and the costs borne by the central bank responsible for that currency. There are no explicit loss-sharing arrangements for central banks that are analogous to the loss-sharing arrangements of the private settlement networks that have created them (such as CHIPS, Zengin, and FEYSS).

Systemic Risk and Securities Firms

Large securities houses that take large positions in financial assets are also subject to some of the same perceived interconnections that can lead to a contagious loss of confidence in depository institutions. For example, if a large securities firm were to fail, other securities houses that do business with and have claims against it could be severely harmed, possibly to the point of bankruptcy. Can such a domino effect entail sufficiently large systemic risks, both domestically and internationally, to pose the same kinds of dangers posed by failures of large banks? At least four distinctions between depositories and securities firms suggest that the best answer is no.

First, the nature of the customer relationships of banks and securities firms differs significantly. Unlike bank depositors, whose funds are commingled with those of bank shareholders, customers of securities firms typically have their funds held in accounts that are segregated from the institution's own assets. As a result, although the failure of the securities firm may cause losses to investors in the firm, it generally will not cause losses to its customers.

Second, investment managers do not offer debt contracts that guarantee rates of return and are redeemable at par, as is the case with bank deposits. Accordingly, securities customers have little to gain from scrambling to be first in line to redeem their claims if their securities firm is threatened with failure.

Third, the portfolio of a securities house typically consists of marketable securities that can be easily evaluated and transferred to other firms with minimal disruptions to customers in the event of failure.

Fourth, in many countries securities firms play a much less crucial role than they do in the United States in intermediating funds from savers to investors. As a result, any damage to the securities industries in these other countries is less likely to cause significant harm to their economies.

Notwithstanding these key distinctions between banks and securities firms, there are sound reasons why regulators in many countries require their securities houses to meet capital requirements similar to those imposed on depositories. In the event of a steep decline in asset prices, capital requirements help ensure that securities firms can remain viable and thus avoid undermining confidence in the functioning of the markets. Indeed, it is noteworthy that even the 1,000-point drop in the Dow Jones average during the fall of 1987 did not trigger the failure of more than a few securities firms; and no large firm failed.[28]

Even the failure of Drexel Burnham Lambert in 1990—one of the largest securities firms in the United States at the time—did not produce a significant disruption in the markets.[29] This may, of course, provide evidence that the regulatory authorities and market participants intervened adroitly to prevent a crisis or that the capital requirements and other regulations then in place were adequate to absorb even the extraordinary shocks to the securities markets experienced during October 1987. But it may also indicate that the contagious transmission of shocks among securities houses is a less serious concern than the contagious transmission of shocks among depository institutions.

Systemic Risk and the Insurance Market

Finally, domestic insurance markets are exposed to a variation of international systemic risk by virtue of the fact that many domestic primary reinsurers depend on foreign reinsurers to assume excess or catastrophic risks. When these reinsurers become reluctant to extend insurance in any particular line, their actions can force their primary insurance customers to raise rates or to cut back the availability of insurance in domestic markets. To be sure, it would be inappropriate to classify small changes in the willingness of reinsurers to provide their services as a source of systemic risk. But if many or all reinsurers

28. See Loehnis (1990).
29. On the day of the Drexel failure (February 13, 1990), the Dow Jones average actually finished the day above its previous close.

run for the door simultaneously, the effects on primary insurers and their customers could be immediate and significant.

Fortunately, the major shocks experienced in insurance markets, while significant in their effect, have not entailed what we would call systemic risk. Thus when foreign reinsurers withdrew from portions of the commercial liability market in the mid-1980s, U.S. insurance markets experienced a liability crisis marked by significant increases in liability insurance rates and cutbacks in coverage. But insurance was still broadly available. Similarly, recent natural disasters in the United States, such as Hurricane Andrew in August 1992 and the Los Angeles earthquake in January 1994, also have prompted foreign reinsurers to be more reluctant about providing coverage to U.S. insurers, a reaction that in turn has made U.S. insurers less willing to provide property coverage in the affected areas. But here, too, insurance markets have not collapsed. The results may not be so benign, however, in the event of more substantial natural disasters, such as an even larger earthquake in California or the much-feared large earthquake that could strike Japan.

Consumer Protection

In general, the preferences of different countries relating to consumer protection do not have significant spillovers across national boundaries, provided that countries accord foreign financial institutions national treatment. That is, the United States can decide, if it wants, to impose a more elaborate set of disclosure standards than other countries and to pursue a more aggressive antitrust policy with respect to all financial institution doing business within its borders. But as long as foreign financial institutions from other countries abide by U.S. rules while doing business in the United States, they should not be affected. Nor should the fact that consumers abroad may be less well protected against abuses and financial losses affecting consumers or their financial service providers at home.

There are at least two important qualifications, however. First, disclosure rules may be costly, thus increasing the cost to borrowers or reducing the interest that financial institutions may be willing to pay their depositors. If customers can easily obtain the same financial services from providers outside the home country—for example, the Eurodollar market—burdensome consumer protection regulation that consumers are not willing to pay for can generate spillovers by driving customers to other markets.

The second, more important qualification has to do with deposit insurance or, more broadly, government safety nets (including central bank lender-of-last-resort assistance) that may back bank deposits and other investments. Although, as shown earlier, there are differences in the degree of formal government protection provided to bank deposits, in practice the governments or central banks of virtually all industrialized countries (and perhaps many more countries than that) stand behind all such deposits, so consumers have little reason to choose among depositories of different nationalities based solely on the amount of insurance coverage available. However, as illustrated in table 3-2, banks in different countries pay different amounts for their insurance. While these differences are relatively small for most countries, there is a wide disparity—at least fifteen basis points, if not more—between the bank insurance premiums paid by U.S. banks and those paid by banks from the other countries listed.[30] To this degree, therefore, U.S. banks suffer from a competitive disadvantage relative to foreign banks, one that may be only partially reflected in the deposit rates provided to their customers (the rest being reflected in the profits of the banks). That is, other factors being equal, foreign banks are in a position to raise deposits more cheaply than U.S. banks and ultimately to lend them out to U.S. borrowers because of this deposit insurance premium differential. U.S. banks can avoid the deposit insurance tax by raising their funds outside the country, but to attract those funds they may still have to pay somewhat more than they might otherwise have to if they were not subject to a deposit insurance tax.

In short, while countries may not differ in the degree of protection they provide bank deposits, they do differ in the extent to which they charge the institutions—and ultimately their customers—for this protection. This can lead to an unlevel playing field, about which some banks have complained. Of course, the field could be made more level if U.S. bank regulators and policymakers found a way to lower the cost of bank failures and thus the premiums paid by banks for deposit

30. On the surface, a fifteen-basis-point differential—or 0.15 of 1 percent—may not appear wide. But in normal times, U.S. banks earn about eighty basis points on their assets; against this figure fifteen basis points is much more significant. Barth, Brumbaugh, and Litan (1992, table A-5).

insurance. Recent trends indicate that this may be likely, but not for several years.[31] Until then, it could be said that U.S. banks will continue to operate at a competitive disadvantage both because public policy mistakes in the past allowed higher rates of bank failure here than in other countries and because other countries may deliberately decide not to charge the banks for the failures in their industry.

Other Social Objectives

We discussed earlier how financial institutions and markets have been regulated for domestic purposes to achieve certain social objectives, such as the allocation of credit to favored sectors, regions, or purposes; to prevent the concentration of political and economic power; and to inhibit illegal activities, such as the marketing of illicit drugs and organized crime, that may be conducted through or facilitated by financial institutions. We make no claims either way as to the advisability of regulating for these purposes. The question we take up here is to what extent, if any, the cross-border nature of financial activities and transactions involves spillovers that could affect any of these objectives. Similarly, and perhaps more important, to what extent do the regulatory efforts of individual countries to achieve domestic objectives entail or induce spillovers?

Consider first the desire to allocate credit. If countries decide to do so for domestic reasons, they are likely to apply the principle of national treatment to demand that foreign institutions doing business within their borders satisfy the same requirements in this regard as domestically owned institutions. A prime example is compliance with the CRA provisions in the United States, which apply to all banks doing business in the country. To a small extent, such requirements may work to the disadvantage of foreign banks, which tend to concentrate more heavily in wholesale than in retail activities, and which may be unfamiliar with the specialized credit needs of local communities in the United States. But many U.S.-owned institutions may suffer from the same disadvantage, which in any event can be overcome over

31. In March 1993, the Federal Deposit Insurance Corporation (FDIC) officially revised downward its forecast of future bank failures, such that the insurer was then projecting the possibility of lowering the bank deposit insurance premium beginning in 2002 rather than in 2006, as had been previously forecast. See Rehm (1993a). However, more recent, unofficial forecasts by the agency indicate that deposit insurance premiums could be cut even sooner. See Rehm (1993b).

time, as is true for other types of regulation. In short, there is no inherent reason why, in pursuing domestic credit allocation objectives, the governments of individual countries will generate significant spillover effects in other countries.

This conclusion can change, however, when countries get together to harmonize certain aspects of financial regulation, specifically for the purpose of leveling the playing field for their financial institutions. The parties to the Basel Accord have agreed to require banks in their countries to meet risk-based capital standards. In designing these standards, the regulators from the various countries allowed banks to back their residential mortgage loans with only half the capital (per dollar or currency unit of the loan) that is required for most other loans. This decision amounts to an agreement to permit all members of the Basel Committee to favor their housing sectors to the same degree. If they had not done so—more specifically, if they had permitted individual countries to set their own risk weights—then a principal objective of the Basel Accord, the elimination of different capital standards as a source of potential competitive advantage for a nation's banks, would not have been achieved. Put another way, the attempt to level playing fields truly becomes a slippery slope. Once countries specifically want to level a playing field in one respect, other differences in domestic regulatory regimes as well as in methods and levels of taxation may also have to be harmonized to achieve the level playing field objective.

Countries also may deem it desirable to allocate credit across national boundaries as well, for reasons similar to those that motivate domestic regulation to achieve this purpose. In particular, left to its own devices, the international capital market may undersupply less-developed countries with funds to enable their economies to grow and thus to serve as larger markets for the exports of goods and services from the developed world. This may be especially true for public infrastructure projects, education, and medical care, whose benefits cannot be easily captured by any single private investor, inside or outside the country. But rather than requiring financial institutions from their own countries to make credit available for this purpose, countries instead have decided to help capitalize specialized development banks such as the World Bank to pursue this objective. In general, we believe this approach to addressing market failures in the capital markets is better than imposing regulatory requirements (or taxes) on private financial institutions (the CRA model in the United States), which may not even share in any benefits generated by such credit allocation.

A second domestic regulatory objective, pursued more intensively in the United States than elsewhere, has been to prevent specific financial institutions—especially banks—from accruing an undue amount of economic and political power. Again, there is no reason why policies aimed at achieving this objective, such as limitations on bank powers, should have any significant spillover effects across borders, provided they are applied on a national treatment basis.

However, some countries have not provided foreign financial institutions with national treatment, but instead have restricted access to their markets, whether by limiting the degree of foreign ownership of those institutions or by prohibiting foreign-based institutions from even entering the market. Such policies are motivated by the fear that foreign-owned institutions will acquire excessive power over the domestic economy. In addition, governments may impose restrictions against the entry of foreign institutions in order to bestow benefits on those that are domestically owned.

Clearly, therefore, restrictions on access can and do have spillover effects on other countries by harming the owners of their financial institutions. They are analogous to the at-the-border restrictions on foreign trade, and for this reason it is not surprising that they have been a central subject of the Uruguay Round of GATT negotiations, which we discuss in chapter 4. Indeed, just as countries benefit themselves (and not just other countries seeking to export) when removing their own trade restrictions—by encouraging their domestic firms to become more efficient and giving their consumers access to cheaper and often higher-quality goods from abroad—countries can also benefit by eliminating their restrictions against entry by foreign financial institutions and other service providers. As an illustration, during the early 1990s when commercial lending by domestically owned banks fell, U.S. borrowers and the economy as a whole certainly benefited from the willingness of foreign-owned banks, especially those in Europe, to expand their lending.

Finally, it is hardly a secret that criminal activities (and illegal products, such as drugs) cross national borders almost as easily as do financial services. And so it should be clear that differences in regulating financial institutions for the purpose of inhibiting crime or catching criminals can have spillover effects on other countries. In particular, countries that rigorously protect bank secrecy, largely to make banking in their jurisdictions more attractive, also at the same time reduce the costs of engaging in criminal enterprise everywhere, not just in the countries where the banks may be located. As criminal activities have flourished, these spillovers have become increasingly noticeable, driving countries to increase their efforts to cooperate in combating crime by removing the secrecy protection given to bank customers.

The Appropriate Size of the Supervisory and Regulatory Domain

A clear challenge for policymakers at all levels of government—local, national, and international—is how to deal with activities whose consequences spill across jurisdictional boundaries. This is no less true in the financial arena, where spillover effects can be substantial.

In the concluding section of this chapter, we outline several views of the appropriate regulatory and supervisory domain. Some of these views suggest that regulatory and supervisory domains for certain purposes should be global. Other views indicate that domains for other purposes should be much smaller. But to be useful, analysis should not ignore the legacy of history. Regulation has been largely a national function. Indeed, it has been regarded as an essential element of sovereignty even within countries that have federal systems of government. Thus an evaluation of the appropriate size of supervisory and regulatory domains needs to be supplemented with a consideration of the circumstances under which national regulatory authorities are likely to be willing to cooperate.

The Public Interest View

As Kenneth Scott has observed, the traditional, public-interest view is that financial regulation "is intended to promote the public good by requiring individuals and firms to change their preferred behavior in ways that will benefit others."[32] Much of the argument advanced so far in this chapter is consistent with this view.

32. Scott (1988).

Given the public interest rationale for financial regulation, what should be the appropriate regulatory and supervisory domain? Jerry L. Mashaw and Susan Rose-Ackerman have asked this question with regard to the choice between state and federal regulation.[33] The four factors they list are equally applicable to the international arena.

The first factor is the extent of externalities. If regulation is to be effective in correcting externalities, then the jurisdictional boundaries of the regulatory authority should "be conterminous with the extent of the external effects."[34] International financial integration has clearly expanded the geographic range over which the negative externality of a financial collapse can be transmitted.[35] The enormous international interbank market and the huge volume of international payments has made the quality of bank regulation and supervision in each of the major countries a matter of international concern. Moreover, virtually every country views protection against systemic risk as a fundamental role of financial regulation. Thus there may be a case for international cooperation to deal with systemic risks.[36]

Whether such cooperation need involve all countries, however, is doubtful. Integration and the potential for harmful spillover effects is most extensive among the Group of Ten or the OECD countries. In the light of the problems of negotiating agreements among large, heterogeneous groups, it may be useful to foster cooperation first among the advanced, industrial countries and then widen the scope for cooperation as the institutional framework develops and integration proceeds.

The second factor is the scope for prisoner's dilemmas in which one regulatory jurisdiction tries to manipulate its regulations to gain at the expense of other jurisdictions even though all jurisdictions would be better off if they collaborated. Chapter 2 documented instances of international regulatory competition, showing that regu-

33. See Mashaw and Rose-Ackerman (1984).

34. Mashaw and Rose-Ackerman (1984, p. 116).

35. Benston argues that with "most countries now offering most depositors de jure or de facto deposit insurance, a multiple collapse of the money supply cannot happen now unless the central bank allows or causes it." Moreover, international banking and fund flows do not alter this conclusion. Nonetheless, the failure of a major bank in one country can cause the failure of banks in other countries, and a financial collapse in one country can have international repercussions. Benston (1993, p. 12).

36. Benston argues that systemic risk does not warrant harmonization of national regulations, but he does not address the usefulness of less ambitious forms of international cooperation. Benston (1993, p. 13).

latory arbitrage had undermined attempts to impose taxes on financial transactions.

This rationale for expanding the regulatory domain in the financial context is more problematic. It is undoubtedly true that international financial integration has undermined the capacity of individual countries to tax financial transactions, to demand arbitrarily high levels of consumer protection, and to allocate credit to preferred borrowers. But it does not follow that all countries would be better off if they agreed to harmonize such regulations, even if one adopts the view that regulation reflects the public interest. Preferences among countries may differ with regard to levels of taxation and ways of administering taxes. Similarly, countries will not necessarily agree on the degree of consumer protection that they consider necessary or desirable, much less on how consumers should be protected. And many countries regard credit allocation as a distinctly second-best way of meeting the needs of deserving borrowers. Thus, even though regulatory arbitrage is a powerful feature of the contemporary international financial system, there may be relatively few genuine prisoner's dilemmas since the national regulatory prisoners would not voluntarily choose to cooperate.

The most important exception to this general conclusion would arise if regulatory arbitrage inhibited policies that protected the basic safety and soundness of the financial system. But regulations that enhance safety and soundness provide benefits for which users of financial services may be willing to pay, so it is not inevitable that regulatory competition will lead to a degradation of prudential standards or to a race to the bottom. The obvious historical exception to this assertion occurred during the 1980s in the United States, when state regulators of thrift institutions competed in laxity of regulation. But this was a special case, because depositors were able to rely on the same quality of federal insurance regardless of the state regulatory jurisdiction they chose in placing a deposit. National deposit insurance undermined the incentive for depositors to monitor the quality of prudential supervision and the safety and soundness of the institutions with which they placed deposits. In an international context depositors would be obliged to consider international differences in the quality of insurance and prudential supervision. The Cayman Islands, for example, could not credibly compete.

The third factor relates to collective action problems in formulating and implementing regulations. Collective action is less likely the larger and more heterogeneous the group.[37] The time required to reach a consensus and the transaction costs in negotiating regulations also tend to increase as the size of the group expands. Just as negotiating an agreement is more difficult, so is renegotiating and amending an agreement in response to changing circumstances. These considerations argue in favor of relatively small regulatory domains, such as the countries represented on the Basel Committee, which are likely to be more sensitive to changing circumstances.

Regulation and supervision require the production and transmission of information. The international scope of financial institutions means that at least some of this information must be collected beyond national regulatory domains. This will require some degree of international cooperation and argues for a larger regulatory domain. But this consideration is offset to some extent by the fact that the quality of information is likely to deteriorate if it must be "transmitted up a long bureaucratic chain."[38] Moreover, the risk that data will be misinterpreted increases in proportion to the bureaucratic distance between where the data are collected and where they are used.

The fourth consideration is the substantive, net benefit of variety and uniformity. Uniform international regulations reduce regulatory compliance costs for international institutions. Moreover, uniform regulations are likely to generate more predictable outcomes when problems are taken to court. But against these advantages must be weighed the possibility that the wrong regulations will be harmonized across countries. This is an especially troubling possibility if there is reason to doubt the public interest view of regulation. At least two alternative views of regulation and one overriding feature of the financial system suggest that there may be a compelling case for some degree of regulatory diversity.

Public Choice Theory

An alternative rationale for regulation is derived from public choice theory. This theory is particularly pertinent in situations where regulations do not appear to be generated in response to plausible evi-

37. Olson (1982, pp. 24–31).
38. Mashaw and Rose-Ackerman (1984, p. 118).

dence of market failure. Examples may include interest rate ceilings, fixed commissions, and some barriers to entry. Public choice theory views regulation as the outcome of the efforts of interest groups, politicians, and bureaucrats to use the political process for their own personal benefit.[39] If regulatory agencies are to some extent captured by their regulatees, diversity among regulators is useful.[40] Competition among regulators will undermine attempts to establish a regulatory cartel. Moreover, the possibility for users of financial services to shift among differently regulated firms and the opportunity for regulated firms to shift among regulators provides a useful protection against arbitrary or excessively burdensome regulation and is likely to result in more efficient regulation. Competition also stimulates innovation. In an era of rapid technological advance and financial change, competition among regulators is more likely to lead to a dynamically efficient regulatory framework in which regulated institutions can adjust flexibly to the changing needs of their clients.

Industrial Organization Theory

Competition and diversity among suppliers of regulatory services are equally important in the industrial organization view of financial regulation as developed by Edward Kane.[41] For Kane, financial regulation exists as a response to the demand of financial service firms and their clients for certification of soundness and facilitation of the clearing and settlement of transactions. In his view, government suppliers can dominate private suppliers of regulatory services because governments can offer hidden subsidies and have reputational capital that makes it hard to force their exit when they are operating inefficiently.[42] Kane argues, "Duplicative regulatory functions and overlapping administrative boundaries that may seem inefficient from a purely static point of view provide dynamic opportunities for struc-

39. Scott (1988).
40. Scott (1988).
41. Kane (1988).
42. Kane defines financial regulatory services as "efforts to monitor, discipline, or coordinate the behavior of individual financial service firms to achieve some greater good." He observes that many private entities provide regulatory services, including independent financial analysts, auditors, credit-rating agencies, self-regulatory bodies, accounting standards boards, and trade associations. Kane (1988, pp. 346–47).

tural arbitrage . . . [that] disciplines poor regulators and rewards good ones."[43]

Accommodating Socially Useful Financial Innovations

Advances in technology and financial theory have led to a rapid increase in the pace of financial innovation. Such change can be viewed as the result of attempts by the private sector to respond to opportunities that exist in the marketplace. Robert C. Merton has identified several forces driving the innovation process.[44]

First, innovations have responded to market demands for risk sharing, risk pooling, hedging, and intertemporal or spatial transfers of resources that are not currently available. Second, innovations have satisfied continuing needs for lower transactions costs or increased liquidity. Third, innovations have reduced asymmetric information between trading parties and improved the monitoring of the performance of agents by principals who ultimately bear the risk of bad outcomes. Fourth, innovations have enhanced the ability of investors to influence the allocation and disposition of corporate assets. Fifth, innovations have facilitated the avoidance of taxes and regulatory and accounting constraints.

Private sector entrepreneurs generally introduce financial innovations, but in some important instances governments have successfully taken an active role in the innovation process. For example, the U.S. government played a leading part in securitizing mortgages so that what had been a very segmented set of local markets became a highly integrated national market. And the United Kingdom made an important contribution to the array of investment opportunities by issuing indexed bonds, thus providing investors with a hedge against the risk of general inflation, which no private party could credibly supply. This role of government within the financial system is often neglected, but it offers important potential benefits. Encouragement of financial innovations can add substantial value to both the financial sector and the broader economy. Indeed, it is an important dimension in which national governments can compete. Successful innovations

43. Kane emphasizes an important qualification: regulatory profits must be properly measured and monitored. He is concerned that governments tend to conceal regulatory subsidies and underreport contingent liabilities. Kane (1988, p. 361).

44. Merton (1989).

developed in one national market are likely to be quickly adopted and adapted in other national and international markets.

Summary

The literature on federalism and regulation suggests a number of factors that should be considered in the identification of appropriate regulatory domains—the extent of externalities, the existence of prisoner's dilemmas among regulators, collective action problems, economies of scale in administration, and the trade-off between the values of uniformity and diversity. These considerations imply that the size of the appropriate regulatory domain may vary with motives for regulation and the characteristics of the activity and firms to be regulated.

Consider, then, the various motives for regulation set forth earlier in this chapter. A global perspective eventually may be the appropriate regulatory domain to deal with systemic risk since the externalities may be global in scope. But a global regulatory domain is not necessary to achieve national consumer protection. Indeed, harmonization may be counterproductive, since countries are likely to differ with regard to the degree of consumer protection they desire and the means they wish to use to achieve the desired degree of protection. Similarly, a global regulatory domain is not appropriate for the purpose of allocating credit to preferred borrowers. Although any one country may be able to achieve its preferred allocation more effectively if regulations are harmonized internationally, other countries may well disagree about whether or how they wish to subsidize particular participants in the financial system. A decentralized, international regulatory system is more responsive to differences in national preferences. Finally, concerns over concentration of power within each country argue against centralization of regulatory power across countries. Competition among national regulators is likely to enhance competition among financial institutions and facilitate socially useful innovations, precluding the possibility that barriers to entry will protect monopoly profits for incumbent institutions.

Chapter 4

International Efforts in Financial Regulation to Date

*I*N CHAPTER 3 we outlined two types of spillovers that can be generated by financial institutions and their activities: those that largely affect entire economies (or major parts thereof) and those that primarily affect specific industries and firms. At the same time, we highlighted the fact that in attempting to address the first type of spillover countries may be forced, by either domestic political considerations or international pressures, to avoid the second.

In this chapter we describe the various efforts that have been undertaken so far by different groups of countries to coordinate and harmonize the regulation of financial institutions and markets, whether to address international spillovers, to level the playing field, or to do both. The principal efforts include the Uruguay Round of GATT negotiations; the various directives of the European Union; the recently completed North American Free Trade Agreement (NAFTA); past efforts by central banks from industrialized countries to coordinate emergency liquidity assistance; past and continuing efforts by the Basel Committee to coordinate bank supervision and to define bank capital standards; and the negotiations by the International Organization of Securities Commissions (IOSCO) to establish capital standards for securities firms. As shown in table 4-1, these initiatives cover different parts of the financial services industry, address different regulatory objectives, are premised on different regulatory principles, and have involved different sets of countries. Once access for financial service firms is ensured, however, the critical questions are whose rules apply to the firms that are permitted to compete, and who is designated to enforce those rules?

Table 4-1. *International Financial Regulatory Initiatives*

Initiative	Dates	Financial industries affected	Regulatory objective	Principle	Countries involved
Basel capital and supervisory standards	1980s to present	Banking	Solvency	Harmonization of rules; coordination of supervision	G-10 plus Luxembourg
EU	1992 to present	All	Solvency; rights of access	Harmonization and mutual recognition of rules; home country supervision	EU
GATT	Negotiations abandoned, 1993	All	Rights of access	National treatment	GATT members
IOSCO	Being negotiated	Securities	Solvency	Harmonized rules	Most industrial countries
NAFTA	1994	All	Rights of access	National treatment	Canada, Mexico, United States

In principle, countries can answer these questions in several ways without walling themselves off entirely from international financial activity:

—They can impose and enforce their own rules on foreign firms doing business within their borders. That is, they can adopt a host country regulatory policy. This preserves national autonomy but may not be effective because of regulatory arbitrage.

—They can maintain host country rules but coordinate their supervision with other countries. This preserves national autonomy while attempting to limit the costs of regulatory arbitrage and specifically the movement of local firms to countries with lax regulation, which then export services back to their home countries.

—They can agree on minimum standards but then adopt more restrictive versions to take account of host country concerns not believed to be fully reflected in the international minimum.

—They can accept both the rules and the supervisory judgments of the foreign governments in countries where foreign firms are headquartered. Such a policy of mutual recognition, which effectively delegates regulatory responsibilities to home countries, is likely to be adopted only where host countries have close political relations with home countries and where some agreement on minimum standards has been obtained first, as is the case with European Union financial standards.

—They can harmonize their rules in the pursuit of establishing a level playing field. Yet even with harmonized rules, the host or home countries can decide separately how they should be enforced: through coordination with regulators from other countries or through delegation of enforcement to a centralized body.

The various international initiatives to date have followed different approaches in different contexts, although none has yet created an international enforcement agency.

Rights of Access

The abolition of external restrictions may be sufficient to permit free trade in goods. But services often must be delivered in person or through establishments located in other markets. For example, it is impossible for a Frenchman to give a haircut to an American living in

New York unless the French barber provides the service in New York. Similarly, it was once thought that banks, insurance companies, and securities firms generally could not serve the needs of their customers unless they had a physical presence—an office and individuals who work there—in the countries where their customers are located.

As we demonstrated in chapter 2, however, advances in communication and technology have substantially eroded this requirement, at least for so-called wholesale financial services, or investments, funds transfers, and other services sold to large companies. These customers increasingly can obtain loans from or make deposits to banks abroad, simply by calling them up or faxing or mailing them the required information.[1]

It is more expensive for customers of retail services—primarily individuals and small businesses—to shop in different countries. Here preferences for local providers, or foreign providers with a local presence, still govern the purchase of most financial services. One does not see, for example, many individuals living in Iowa placing their funds in banks located outside this country or purchasing insurance from insurers operating out of foreign offices. To be sure, this may, and probably will, change as advances in telecommunications expand horizons and markets, just as individuals today increasingly are shopping by mail or faxing across state lines and in the future will do so through interactive television. But that day has not yet arrived, at least with respect to retail financial services in an international context.

As a result, the right to establish a financial service business—subject to the same solvency, consumer protection, and other regulations applicable to domestically owned institutions—is an issue of threshold importance for providers and their governments. Without it, competitors have difficulty getting on the field (although with modern communications they may still be able to compete to some extent from distant fields).

There are at least four basic ways nations can treat foreign service firms, in particular with respect to access and more generally with regard to conditions of doing business. The standard toward which most countries aspire is national treatment or nondiscrimination: foreign residents are to be given at least the same chance to establish

1. See also O'Brien (1992, pp. 52–54).

a business as domestic residents. At the same time, however, countries may decide to follow policies of reciprocity as to which foreign firms are admitted. But national treatment would dictate that any firms so admitted must then be treated just like domestic firms.

A potentially more lenient approach is one of mutual recognition, treating operatives of foreign countries in the host country as they would be treated in their home country. For example, such a policy would permit foreign banks with unlimited branching rights at home to have the same freedom abroad, even in countries with a more limited branching policy (as the United States has had in the past). As suggested above, mutual recognition requires a strong degree of trust between jurisdictions and agreement on minimum standards, as is the case with the European Union (EU).[2]

A more restrictive but often tactically useful policy is one of reciprocity: not allowing entry by foreign firms unless their governments allow entry to the residents of one's own country. Reciprocity discriminates among firms based in different foreign countries and has a strong fairness appeal. "If other countries are not fair to us, then why should we be fair to them?" the argument runs. By the same token, because reciprocity promises better treatment to foreign firms if their governments remove barriers to access, it is a tempting tool for policymakers to use to pry open foreign markets, even though it explicitly recognizes a right to discriminate against firms from some countries. As noted above, reciprocity regarding access may still be consistent with national treatment, which applies to firms once they are admitted (under whatever principle).

The most restrictive policy is one that is discriminatory against foreigners for no clear tactical reason, except on nationalist grounds, opposing undue foreign influence or protecting domestic cartels. Such a policy may limit the extent of ownership of financial and other firms, as is true for banks in many less developed countries and in some industrialized countries (including Canada, Finland, Iceland, and Norway), or may simply prohibit foreign ownership altogether.[3]

Interestingly, some countries—the United States is a notable example—have not even provided for the most liberal of these three

2. For an extensive discussion of mutual recognition practiced by the EC, see Key (1989).

3. For a survey of the entry restrictions prevailing in OECD countries, see OECD (1992, pp. 66–68).

policies, mutual recognition, for domestic residents within their own borders. Thus in this country most states have required some form of reciprocity with other states before allowing out-of-state bank holding companies to enter. More important, until the 1994 interstate banking legislation preempted their doing so, virtually all states prevented out-of-state banks from setting up branches in their jurisdictions. In contrast, states do not discriminate against insurance and securities firms headquartered in other states.

We are concerned in this book, however, with international regulatory issues and in this section in particular on the rights of access to firms from different countries. Three major international initiatives, two regional and one multilateral, have either already liberalized or are attempting to liberalize restrictions on entry by financial service firms into other markets.

NAFTA

The narrowest regional forum is the recently completed negotiation of the North American Free Trade Agreement (NAFTA), which extends to Mexico many of the provisions that Canada and the United States agreed to in their Free Trade Agreement (FTA) of 1988. In both cases, since the United States has long provided for national treatment for foreign financial institutions, the principal object of the negotiations, at least with respect to financial services, has been to remove the entry restrictions maintained by the other two countries.

For example, in the FTA, Canada agreed to exempt U.S. financial service firms from the Canadian limitation that foreigners own no more than 25 percent of the equity of any regulated financial institution.[4] In addition, U.S. banks were exempted from Canada's ceiling on the aggregate amount of foreign ownership of Canada's banking sector. Apart from a reaffirmation of its commitment to extending national treatment to Canadian financial institutions, the only major concession provided by the United States was to permit both domestic and Canadian banks (and their holding companies) to deal in, underwrite, and purchase Canadian government bonds (both federal

4. Both U.S. and Canadian investors, however, were still subjected to Canada's limitation that no individual investor own any more than 10 percent of the equity of any regulated financial institution.

and provincial); such permission had previously applied only to U.S. government securities.

NAFTA extends all these provisions to Mexico. In turn, Mexico has agreed to open up its highly restricted market gradually to financial institutions from the United States and Canada. Nevertheless, even after the transition period is complete—for most industries, after 2004—Mexico will limit the market share of banks that acquired their position by acquisition rather than by de novo entry.[5]

Although all parties to the NAFTA provisions on financial services would benefit, Mexico and the United States stand to reap the largest gains because of their already extensive trade and investment and their geographical proximity. U.S. financial institutions can be expected to make major inroads into the Mexican financial services market, which has been long protected from foreign competition and where profits are recognized to be high. At the same time, the added competition in Mexico should lower the costs of financial services for Mexican residents while encouraging Mexican-owned financial institutions to become more efficient.

EU Initiatives

The most far-reaching international agreements relating to access by financial services firms to date, of course, have been made by members of the European Union. Through a series of directives, the EU countries have gone far down the road toward harmonizing their regulatory systems.

With respect to access, the EU has essentially removed all barriers to cross-border branching for financial services firms within the community by providing what has been referred to as a single passport. Thus, under the Second Banking Directive, adopted in 1989, once a firm obtains a license to engage in the banking, securities, or insurance business in one EU country, it gains the right to open branches that engage in the same business in other EU member states. Moreover, the EU allows European financial institutions to become universal banks—that is, for banks not only to accept deposits and make loans, but also to issue, underwrite, and hold corporate securities, thus allowing securities and banking firms to enter each other's busi-

5. For a summary of the key provisions of NAFTA on financial services, see Hufbauer and Schott (1993, pp. 61–65).

ness in each of the EU countries.[6] In no other international forum have countries addressed this controversial question of bank powers, which outside the EU remains subject to different country-specific rules.

The EU's single passport policy also applies to non-EU financial service firms. Thus, once an American bank obtains a license from one EU member state to open a subsidiary or affiliate, it can do business through that office in all other EU member states. Nevertheless, the EU commission will continue periodically to assess whether non-EU countries are discriminating against EU firms (in the sense of failing to grant national treatment). If so, the commission has the power, as a last resort, to retaliate—that is, to demand reciprocity.

GATT

The most ambitious international initiative designed to remove current restrictions on access by financial service firms, and indeed by firms engaged in services generally, was undertaken in the Uruguay Round of GATT negotiations. The proposed GATT provisions would have instituted a policy of national treatment for financial institutions and in the process removed the entry restrictions maintained in this area by many countries, less developed countries in particular. Individual countries would still have had the freedom to set their own rules governing the operation of financial institutions, but they would have had to apply those rules evenhandedly to domestic and foreign firms. Because negotiators were unable to reach formal agreement, financial services issues were omitted from the final Uruguay Round pact.

The Threat of Reciprocity

Despite the foregoing initiatives aimed at widening access to foreign markets, various countries still reserve the right to or are threatening to adopt a policy of reciprocity with respect to access by foreign financial institutions. Thus the EU already has announced that it has

6. Alliances between banks and insurance companies, however, remain subject to the laws of individual EU states under a system of national treatment. That is, a German bank may be affiliated with an insurance company and conduct such joint activities within Germany, but those activities may not be pursued jointly in other EU countries if those countries do not permit such affiliations in their countries.

a reciprocity stick in the closet should other countries discriminate against financial services firms based in the EU. In addition, despite the long-standing U.S. policy favoring national treatment of foreign financial institutions, the Senate of the United States has seriously considered legislation to adopt a policy of reciprocity instead. The most recent example was the Fair Trade in Financial Services Act proposed by Senators Donald W. Riegle, Jr., and Jake Garn in the early 1990s. After initially opposing the proposal, the Treasury Department during the Bush administration eventually embraced it, provided it gave regulators ample discretion to deny licenses to foreign firms from countries that did not, in the language of the bill, give "effective market access" to U.S.-based institutions. The objective of the Riegle-Garn legislation was to help open the Japanese financial market in particular to American financial firms. The Clinton administration also endorsed the legislation, but it was dropped from the interstate banking bill Congress adopted in 1994.

Understandably, the Japanese government has strongly opposed financial services reciprocity. Japan argues that its markets are formally open to all foreign institutions; indeed, in some respects foreign financial institutions benefit from not only national treatment but ultranational treatment.[7] For example, until the Japanese government permitted its own banks to engage in securities underwriting activities (through subsidiaries), foreign banks were so authorized even though Japanese banks were not.

Critics respond that despite the absence of formal barriers to foreign financial firms, the Japanese *keiretsu* system—the close affiliations between banks and nonbanks—nevertheless has the effect of preventing foreign banks and securities firms from financing Japanese economic activity. Japanese manufacturers that are owned in part by Japanese banks and securities houses quite naturally channel their banking and securities business to those *keiretsu* affiliates. Japanese policymakers and firms defend the *keiretsu* system as a useful means of ensuring a ready supply of patient capital to Japanese companies It is conceivable that Japan may modify the *keiretsu* system in coordination with other countries.[8] If it does not, access to the Japanese market is likely to become a growing source of friction among Japan, the United States, and Europe, not just in the financial arena but in other

7. Semkow (1992, pp. 331–414).
8. For a discussion of the prospects of this outcome, see Fukao (forthcoming).

sectors as well. And if that happens, threats of reciprocity may become more frequent and may be more vigorously pressed.

Systemic Risk and Solvency

Although international agreement on rights of access would appear to be of threshold importance in resolving frictions between countries regarding financial services, in fact the Group of Ten has devoted more effort to addressing the potentially most significant spillover problem in financial markets: systemic risk.[9] These initiatives have evolved over the past two decades, triggered by the failure in 1974 of three internationally active banks, Bankhaus Herstatt of Cologne, the British-Israel Bank of London, and the Franklin National Bank of New York.

At least four lessons can be learned from all these efforts. One is that countries do not make the effort to coordinate or to harmonize their activities unless a crisis already has alerted them to the need for action, or the countries perceive that a crisis is imminent. Second, multilateral efforts take time, often a lot of time, to bear fruit. Third, in the process of addressing systemic risk or other important international policy objectives, governments inevitably are drawn into adopting policies that also level the playing field so that the firms owned by their domestic residents will not be put at a competitive disadvantage relative to foreign-owned firms. Fourth, once international institutions are created to address certain problems, they can take on a life of their own, as countries look to them to resolve new frictions and to address new issues.

Banking Crises of 1974

The world economy experienced a traumatic year in 1974. The sharp increase in oil prices caused major economic dislocations, exacerbated inflationary pressures, and intensified exchange rate volatility. Of the three internationally active banks that failed, the closure

---

9. The Group of Ten includes the ten leading capitalist countries—Belgium, Canada, France, Germany, Holland, Italy, Japan, Sweden, the United Kingdom, and the United States. Luxembourg and Switzerland also participate in the group. The governors of the central banks of the Group of Ten meet regularly at the Bank for International Settlements in Basel, Switzerland.

of Herstatt had by far the most significant effect on the rest of the world.

Herstatt had been notorious for overtrading, taking foreign exchange transactions that were very large relative to its capital.[10] When the German authorities discovered that Herstatt had fraudulently concealed losses that exceeded half the book value of its assets, they closed the bank on June 26, 1974, at the close of business (4:00 p.m.). This was the end of the business day in Germany, but still morning in New York. The closure of Herstatt aborted the settlement of millions of dollars of foreign exchange contracts. Banks that had paid European currencies to Herstatt earlier in the day in the expectation that they would receive dollars at the close of the business day in New York suffered losses. When Herstatt's New York correspondent received word of the closure, the bank declined to honor $620 million in claims on Herstatt's account. This abrogation of foreign exchange contracts caused a prolonged disruption in foreign exchange trading.

Lack of information regarding the allocation of spot transaction losses and the anticipation of prospective losses on forward transactions with Herstatt also led to dislocations in the international interbank sector of the Eurocurrency market. Although market participants believed that the magnitude of defaulted foreign exchange contracts was great, they did not know the identity of the counterparties who would sustain losses. In the absence of reliable information, market participants took precautions against the worst outcome. They withdrew lines of credit from banks that were judged least able to sustain the losses if they were, in fact, counterparties to Herstatt's foreign exchange contracts. Many banks that had relied on their ability to borrow at the London Interbank Offer Rate were obliged to pay a substantial premium above that benchmark rate. Some were unable to borrow at all.

Emergency Liquidity Assistance for International Banks

The disproportionately large spillover effects from the closure of Herstatt, a relatively small, privately held German bank, focused official attention on the growing interdependence of the international banking system. The incident also raised the troubling question of whether emergency liquidity assistance would be available to banks

10. For a thorough discussion of the Herstatt affair, see Dale (1984).

that were active in the international interbank market. Which (if any) central bank would offer emergency liquidity assistance to particular banks and banking offices? In what amount? Under what conditions?[11]

Central banks have been unwilling to provide clear answers to these questions. Just as the Bank of England in the era of Walter Bagehot was reluctant to announce the policies it would pursue in the event of a crisis, so the central banks of the major industrial countries have been intentionally vague about arrangements to provide emergency liquidity assistance. Such a policy of calculated ambiguity has been defended as necessary to promote market discipline of banks.

The disruption of international markets was so great in the wake of the collapse of Herstatt, however, that the central bank governors of the Group of Ten made an official announcement recognizing that while it was not "practical to lay down in advance detailed rules and procedures for the provision of temporary liquidity," the means were available for that purpose and would be "used if and when necessary."[12] This policy has since been reaffirmed by central bankers in several leading countries.

The reaction by the Group of Ten illustrates that policymakers from a relatively small group of countries can successfully coordinate their actions to respond to a financial crisis. In addition, the regular monthly meetings in Basel provided a strong institutional infrastructure for decisionmaking that facilitated this degree of cooperation.

Nevertheless, announcing that necessary liquidity is available without specifying the circumstances under which that will be the case can be criticized. While uncertainty over whether the lender of last resort (LLR) will act may intensify market discipline over some banks, it can also be destabilizing, precipitating the systemic crisis central banks most fear and try so hard to avoid. Conversely, to the extent that market participants expect the central banks to come to the rescue, market discipline is weakened.

---

11. The value to a bank of access to emergency liquidity assistance is higher the greater the certainty that the lender of last resort will act and the broader the range of circumstances in which it will act. A Group of Thirty survey identified uncertainty over lender-of-last resort arrangements as one of the chief concerns of bankers regarding risks in international banking. See Group of Thirty (1982) and our discussion of this issue in chapter 5.

12. Johnson and Abrams (1983, p. 34).

In short, calculated ambiguity may be unable to achieve the two objectives for which it is ostensibly designed: ensuring market discipline, but also reducing systemic risk. In addition, in an increasingly integrated financial system, central banks and their governments may be forced to bear excessive costs of emergency assistance to the extent that rules are not agreed on in advance for allocating financial responsibility for rescuing the depositors or creditors of foreign-based financial institutions operating outside their home countries. Chapter 5 proposes an international mechanism that would help avoid these problems.

Coordination of Supervision

In addition to stimulating a policy pronouncement on emergency liquidity assistance, the disproportionately large spillover effects from the closure of Herstatt also raised the question of whether banking supervision had kept pace with the expansion of international banking. After the collapse of Herstatt in 1974, the governors of the Group of Ten established the Standing Committee on Banking Regulations and Supervisory Practices, composed of representatives of the supervisory authorities and central banks of the Group of Ten countries plus Switzerland and Luxembourg.[13] When the Basel Committee was formed, banks headquartered in these twelve countries accounted for roughly 90 percent of international banking activity.[14] Thus a relatively small group could plausibly address global problems.

The Basel Committee met for the first time in February 1975.[15] For most bank supervisors, this was their first opportunity to meet

13. While descriptive, the formal name of the committee proved so cumbersome that it was seldom used. Initially, most references to the committee used the name of the chairman—first the "Blunden Committee," then the "Cooke Committee." In order to discourage this practice the Committee shortened its name to "The Basel Committee on Banking Supervision." For still greater brevity, we refer to it as the "Basel Committee."

14. Other international groups of bank supervisors include the Contact Group of EU Supervisory Authorities, the EU Banking Advisory Committee, the Banking Supervisory Sub-committee of EU Governors, the Offshore Group of Banking Supervisors, the Commission of Latin American and Caribbean Banking Supervisory and Inspection Organizations, the SEANZA Forum of Banking Supervisors, the GCC Committee of Banking Supervisors, the Group of Banking Supervision Officials in Arab Countries, the Group of Banking Supervisors from Central and Eastern European Countries, and the Caribbean Banking Supervisors Group. For additional information about these groups, see Basel Committee on Banking Supervision (1992, pp. 108–39).

15. The formal charge to the committee included: the establishment of broad principles for international coordination of banking supervision with which all supervisory sys-

their foreign counterparts. Unlike central bank governors, bank supervisory authorities traditionally have had an exclusively domestic focus.

The Concordat, an agreement reached on September 26, 1975, was the first major accomplishment of the Basel Committee.[16] In the Concordat the committee agreed that the basic aim of international cooperation should be to ensure that no foreign banking establishment escaped adequate supervision, and to achieve that end it outlined an allocation of supervisory responsibilities.

In particular, while the committee recognized that supervision was the joint responsibility of the host and parent supervisory authorities, it allocated primary responsibility for supervision of solvency to the supervisor of the parent bank. This is the obvious solution for a foreign branch because the solvency of the foreign branch is inextricably related to that of the parent. The role of the host supervisory authority is more important in the case of a subsidiary or joint venture, but the Basel Committee stressed that even when the foreign entity was separately incorporated, the parent bank should recognize a "moral commitment" to support faltering corporate children even though limited liability excuses the parent bank from the legal obligation to provide additional resources. Consequently the parent supervisory authority should monitor the insolvency exposure of the parent bank arising from the activities of its foreign subsidiaries and joint ventures.[17]

To facilitate cooperation between parent and host authorities, transfers of information were essential. This raised immediate difficulties. Many of the members of the Basel Committee were constrained by bank secrecy laws that prohibited exchanges of information relevant to judging the solvency of a banking entity. Over time the Basel

---

tems might conform; the identification of gaps in the supervisory coverage of international banking; and the provision of opportunities for supervisors to exchange information and discuss best supervisory practices.

16. The Concordat was not officially disseminated until March 1981, when Peter Cooke, then chairman of the committee, made public a report to the governors by the Basel Committee. See Bank for International Settlements (1982, p. 2).

17. The Concordat also allocated primary responsibility for supervision of liquidity to the host authority. The host authority was assumed to have a better capacity to judge the foreign bank's liquidity position in local currency transactions and a better incentive to ensure its compliance with local monetary regulations. With regard to the management of liquidity in foreign currencies, the comparative advantage of the host authority was less clear.

Committee has made some progress in modifying secrecy laws to ease the flow of information among supervisory authorities.

In 1978 the Basel Committee recommended adoption of the principle of consolidation—that banks' international business should be monitored on a consolidated basis—to improve the quality of information on international bank activities. Cooke emphasized that this was a natural extension of the Concordat: consolidated supervision "is an invaluable aid to parent supervisors in enabling them to fulfill in practice their responsibilities under the Concordat for the supervision of the solvency of their banks' foreign affiliates."[18]

The principle of consolidation is difficult to implement, however. Problems arise when the parent's ownership of a foreign entity is partial or if the entity engages in additional, nonbanking business. Differences in national accounting practices also impede meaningful consolidation.

The principle of consolidated supervision is not a panacea even if properly implemented. For example, claims on affiliated banks are not legally binding claims on the parent bank. No host supervisor routinely insists that foreign parent banks fully guarantee the liabilities of their affiliates, and the comfort letters required by some host authorities have doubtful legal standing. Since parent banks are not legally responsible for claims on separately incorporated foreign affiliates, the host country supervisor must be concerned about the solvency of resident foreign banking entities. Considered apart from the rest of the banking family with which it is affiliated, each entity must be solvent. Consolidated supervision thus offers little assistance to the host supervisory authorities unless they have complete confidence that the parent bank will honor the liabilities of the local affiliate without limit and that the parent supervisory authority is monitoring the solvency of the consolidated banking group effectively.

For different reasons, the principle of consolidated supervision also is of limited value to the home country authority. Local bankruptcy

18. Cooke (1981, p. 238). This principle was noncontroversial in most member countries. Indeed, some countries had practiced consolidated supervision for several years. But in Germany adoption of the principle of consolidated supervision entailed a major debate and required legislation. German banking law was amended to permit consolidated banking supervision in accord with the EU's directive on consolidation. For additional information, see Basel Committee on Banking Supervision (1985, pp. 51–52).

laws often discriminate in favor of local creditors, even if the entity in question is a foreign branch.[19] Thus the parent supervisory authority must be sure that the parent bank is solvent in its own right and on a consolidated basis. It must recognize that, in the event of trouble, assets in a foreign office may not be available to cover deficits in other parts of the banking family. As the Concordat recognizes, the solvency of a foreign banking entity is intrinsically a mutual concern of both the parent and host supervisory authorities.

The Limitations of Coordinated Supervision

Just as the Basel Committee was created in response to a crisis, the Concordat has been revised several times in response to crises it was not able to prevent. The first crisis occurred when a prominent Italian bank, Banco Ambrosiano SpA, failed in 1983. Banco Ambrosiano SpA controlled a Luxembourg holding company, Banco Ambrosiano Holdings (BAH), that had been carefully situated in a gap in the international supervisory system (see figure 4-1). BAH was chartered in Luxembourg as a financial holding company, not a bank, and thus it was not subject to bank regulation in Luxembourg. Meanwhile, because Luxembourg's rigorous secrecy laws protected holding companies from foreign scrutiny, the Bank of Italy was unable to supervise BAH, notwithstanding the fact that it was deeply engaged in a banking business.[20]

Although the activities of BAH were shrouded in secrecy, it was able to borrow more than half a billion dollars from 250 international banks. Clearly these interbank placements were not made on the basis of rigorous credit analysis, because even now, with the benefit of a decade of hindsight, little is known about what BAH actually did with the money. It seems likely that the banks that made deposits with BAH relied heavily on the evident connection of BAH with Italy's largest privately owned bank, Banco Ambrosiano SpA, and on the

19. For example, for the purposes of French bankruptcy law the BCCI branches in France are considered to be a separate legal entity just as if they had been incorporated in France.

20. In particular, BAH owned Banco Ambrosiano Overseas Ltd., then one of the largest banks in Nassau (a jurisdiction well known for the rigor of its secrecy laws but not for the quality of its supervision of foreign banks), and Banco Ambrosiano Andino in Peru (a jurisdiction in which foreign banks may not have been subject to any supervision whatsoever). Campbell-Smith (1982) and "The Skippers" (1984).

Figure 4-1. *The Corporate Structure of Banco Ambrosiano*

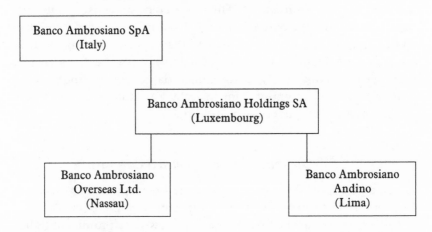

Source: Campbell-Smith (1982, p. 16).

presumption that the Italian authorities would recognize a moral commitment to protect creditors of the foreign subsidiary.

Although spillover effects from the collapse of Banco Ambrosiano were limited mainly to six other Italian banks with similar organizational structures, market participants learned an important lesson from its collapse: corporate structure matters. Although all the creditors of Banco Ambrosiano SpA were repaid promptly, creditors of BAH received only partial repayment after considerable delay.[21] Disregarding the question of whether official supervision prevents bank failures, sophisticated market participants inferred that in the event of trouble, governments are unlikely to assist entities for which they do not have primary supervisory responsibility.

The Basel Committee responded in May 1983 to Banco Ambrosiano with the first major revision of the Concordat. The revision reaffirmed the previous provisions of the Concordat but amended the document in several key respects.[22]

First, the committee recommended that if the entity is not classified as a bank by the host supervisory authority, the parent super-

21. At least one bank rating agency provides two ratings for each bank: one based on the financial condition of the bank and a second based on the likelihood that the bank will receive official support.

22. Basel Committee on Banking Regulations and Supervisory Practices (1983, p. 1). The principles are reprinted in Dale (1984).

visory authority should either supervise it or demand that it be closed. In the context of the Banco Ambrosiano case, this implies that since Luxembourg did not classify BAH as a bank, the Bank of Italy should have demanded the right to supervise BAH or should have required the parent to shut it down.

Second, the committee suggested that if the host supervisory authority thinks that supervision by the parent authority is inadequate, it should either prohibit operations of the local entity or place stringent prudential restrictions on its operations. In the context of the Banco Ambrosiano case, this implies that if Luxembourg suspected that banking activity was being conducted by BAH and that supervision by the Bank of Italy was inadequate, it should have closed BAH or placed stringent conditions on its operations.

Third, the committee recommended that if the parent entity is a holding company, supervisors of separate subsidiary banks should cooperate to supervise the holding company. In the context of the Banco Ambrosiano case, this has the highly impractical implication that the Bahamas and Peru should have cooperated in supervising the holding company protected by Luxembourg secrecy laws.

Fourth, the committee recommended that if the holding company is a subsidiary, the parent supervisor should supervise the holding company and its subsidiaries or close it. This appeared to be a direct criticism of the behavior of the Bank of Italy. When the Bank of Italy found that it could not supervise BAH, it should have demanded that Banco Ambrosiano SpA close BAH.

While the 1983 revisions to the Concordat appeared to be motivated by the collapse of Banco Ambrosiano, a participant in the meetings of the Basel Committee stated that the committee was also concerned at the time about another international bank that was not subject to consolidated supervision—the rapidly growing BCCI. Ironically, BCCI constituted the second failure of coordinated supervision.

The history of the failure of BCCI and its ramifications around the world—especially in the developing world, where most of its depositors live—are well known. So are many of the events relating to the investigation of U.S. individuals connected with the bank. Here we summarize only the implications for international bank supervision.[23]

23. For an extended discussion of the BCCI affair, see Herring (1993).

BCCI was founded in 1972 with the objective of financing trade with the third world. Although many important managerial decisions were made in Pakistan, the bank was initially based in Abu Dhabi and incorporated in Luxembourg. Later the Bank of America greatly facilitated the international expansion of BCCI by investing $2.5 million in exchange for a 25 percent equity stake in the start-up bank. BCCI's association with what was then the largest bank in the world gave it an aura of respectability that it could not otherwise have achieved so quickly. In return the Bank of America hoped to gain a stronger foothold in the Arab world through its association with BCCI.

Over time the Bank of America became frustrated and concerned about the reluctance of BCCI to provide it with adequate information. Late in 1977 it began to sell its stake in BCCI. Over the next two years the founders of the bank obtained additional capital from Saudi Arabian sources. Shares were purchased by the bank's employee benefit fund as well. By this time BCCI had gained entry into nearly seventy countries. Indeed, by the mid-1970s it had more retail branches in the United Kingdom than any other foreign bank.

The founders of the bank carefully structured the organization to avoid consolidated supervision in all the countries in which it did business. The nonbank holding company was established in Luxembourg, and subsidiary banks were chartered in countries with well-established secrecy laws: Luxembourg and the Cayman Islands. Nevertheless, most managerial decisions were made in London and in Pakistan. This complex corporate structure virtually precluded consolidated supervision of the activities of BCCI. To further fragment external scrutiny of the bank, separate auditing firms were hired for each bank.

As a result, no supervisory authority was in a position to anticipate clearly the bank's downfall until it happened in 1991. Moreover, neither Luxembourg nor the Cayman Islands had the resources to oversee BCCI's worldwide operations, and the Bank of England did not want the burden of supervising the global operations of a bank it did not charter.

What of the Revised Concordat? Why did the members of the Basel Committee not accept their obligation to see that a sizable international bank with total book value of roughly $20 billion was adequately supervised?

First, the Revised Concordat is a code of best practices, not an enforceable set of rules. Second, BCCI had already entered most major markets before the revision of the Concordat in 1983. When a foreign bank seeks entry to a country, the local supervisory authorities have significant leverage in applying fit and proper tests. But once the foreign bank has received a license to conduct a banking business, most supervisory authorities must have evidence that it has committed serious violations of local laws or is insolvent before the license can be revoked. Such evidence is difficult to compile.

Third, supervisory authorities are always reluctant to take actions that diminish the prospects that depositors will be repaid. Public disciplinary action against BCCI would almost certainly have caused a run on the bank and inflicted losses on depositors.[24]

Quite clearly the BCCI affair demonstrated the limitations of international bank supervision when confronted by unscrupulous operators intent on exploiting the gaps in national bank supervisory systems, even when supervisors from different countries attempt to coordinate their activities, as was the case with BCCI.[25] Although the failure of BCCI inflicted heavy losses on an estimated 530,000 unsophisticated depositors around the world (many in less developed countries), the bank's collapse had no spillover effects on the international financial system.[26] The institutions that play a critical role in the functioning of interbank markets had virtually quarantined the bank because of its unsavory reputation.

Since BCCI's collapse, the Basel Committee has again revisited its supervision guidelines, this time adding a provision authorizing supervisors in the host country to impose restrictive measures if they are uncomfortable with the quality of the home country supervision of a local banking establishment. Such measures may include setting a deadline for the bank and its home supervisory authority to meet acceptable standards, obliging the banking establishment to be restructured as a separately capitalized subsidiary, or closing the bank-

24. This view weighs the interests of current depositors more heavily than those of future depositors. But, since the authorities lacked objectively verifiable evidence that BCCI was insolvent, forbearance seemed a defensible (and attractive) option.

25. In 1987 the supervisory authorities from Britain, the Cayman Islands, France, Luxembourg, Spain, and Switzerland formed a regulatory college to share information about the operations of BCCI. This sharing of information was consistent with the Revised Concordat, but it proved entirely inadequate.

26. Jack and Hill (1993, p. 4).

ing establishment. This emphasis implicitly recognizes the difficulties of harmonizing supervisory standards in a world where countries differ greatly in their supervisory traditions and in their capacities to monitor global financial institutions.

If these standards had been applied to BCCI, Luxembourg should have exercised consolidated supervision over BCCI because it chartered the parent of the banking group. If other countries were not satisfied with the quality of Luxembourg's supervision of BCCI, they should have taken restrictive measures against local offices. This example, however, points out a significant impediment in implementing the new guideline. Since Luxembourg is a member of the European Union, the Second Banking Directive prohibits other member states from discriminating against branches of Luxembourg banks. Moreover, restrictive measures are inherently easier to apply to banks seeking entry than to banks that may have altered their structure or conduct of business.

Given the gaps in even these revisions, if countries truly want to insulate themselves and their citizens against BCCI-type problems in the future, they will have to take supervisory matters into their own hands. That is what the United States has done and the United Kingdom has proposed.

For example, in addition to the restrictive measures incorporated in the newly issued Concordat, the Bank of England wants to be able to withdraw authorization from a bank if it subsequently sets up branches in countries lacking an effective supervisor and if the nature of a bank's business changes, even though its ownership structure is unaltered. Such measures, if applied to a member of the European Union, would clash with the EU's fundamental principle of mutual recognition. But they would address the difficult problem of dealing with a foreign bank after it has gained entry.

Meanwhile, as part of the Foreign Bank Supervision Enhancement Act of 1991 (a subsection of the Federal Deposit Insurance Corporation Improvement Act of 1991), the U.S. Congress has mandated that the Federal Reserve take similar measures toward the establishment and termination of foreign bank offices in the United States. The 1991 act applies not only to branches and subsidiaries of foreign banks, but also to agencies and loan production offices. Under the law the Federal Reserve assumes primary supervisory responsibility for all foreign banking entities even if they hold a state charter and must determine whether home country supervision is adequate with regard to five standards. The act provides a process to control the entry of foreign banks into the United States and to strengthen the authority of the Fed to regulate, supervise, and terminate foreign bank offices.

Nevertheless, the new regulations adopted by the Fed to implement this legislation would not necessarily have prevented BCCI from gaining control of First American Bankshares, the U.S. subsidiary of BCCI. Even though the Fed strongly suspected that BCCI was seeking to gain control of First American Bankshares and made extensive investigations of the ownership structure of the holding company, it was unable to thwart BCCI. Even under the new regulations, the Fed will continue to have difficulty determining who is really buying an American bank if the purchaser is intent on concealing its true identity.[27]

Common Bank Capital Standards: The Basel Accord

The Basel Committee has done more than just attempt to coordinate supervisory authorities. From its inception, the committee was concerned that the diversity of national systems of capital measurement impeded comparisons of the capital adequacy of banks in different countries and gave rise to competitive pressures to weaken capital standards.

During the global recession in the early 1980s, governments in the major industrial countries became increasingly uneasy about a general decline in the capital strength of their banks and about the exposure of several large international banks to the debt of less developed countries in particular. In the United States these concerns led Congress to enact the International Lending Act of 1983, which instructs the federal supervisory agencies to "establish examination and supervisory procedures to assure that factors such as foreign currency exposure and transfer risk are taken into account in evaluating the adequacy of the capital of banking institutions."[28] In addition, the act required the chairman of the board of governors of the Federal Reserve System to "encourage governments, central banks, and regu-

27. The requirement of effective, consolidated supervision by the home country, however, may have had an effect.
28. 12 U.S.C. 3903 (b).

latory authorities of other major banking countries to work toward maintaining and, where appropriate, strengthening the capital bases of banking institutions involved in international lending."[29]

In 1984 governors from the Group of Ten charged the Basel Committee with recommending a framework for assessing the comparability of different measures of capital adequacy used by member countries and with developing minimum international bank capital standards. This initiative reflected concerns not only over the risks to the banking system posed by troubled debt in less-developed countries, but also about the rising volume of off–balance sheet activity, such as letters of credit, loan guarantees, and transactions in derivative instruments, which was not well captured by traditional leverage ratios or requirements based on assets reported on the balance sheet.

The Basel Committee responded by developing a framework for measuring capital.[30] International negotiations on implementing a common framework proved cumbersome, however. And frustration over the slow pace of progress led the banking authorities from the United States and the United Kingdom to negotiate a bilateral accord that the two countries applied just to the banks within their jurisdictions.[31] The U.K.-U.S. accord defined capital for regulatory purposes and established risk weights for on–balance sheet assets and off–balance sheet commitments. The risk weights emphasized credit risk.[32]

The bilateral initiative prompted the Basel Committee to develop and announce its own Accord on capital adequacy in July 1988. The Basel provisions were subsequently incorporated into the national regulatory systems of each member country, becoming effective on an interim basis during 1991 and on a final basis in 1993.

The risk-based capital standards required banks to maintain shareholders' capital equal to four percent of their risk-weighted assets, including measures of their off–balance sheet activity; and to maintain

29. 12 U.S.C. 3907 (b)(3)(c).

30. See Committee on Banking Regulations and Supervisory Practices (1985, pp. 8–15).

31. The U.S. version was published in a joint news release by the three federal banking regulatory agencies—Comptroller of the Currency, Federal Deposit Insurance Corporation, Federal Reserve Board—on January 8, 1987.

32. The Anglo-American accord also made a crude attempt to take account of transfer risk and interest rate risk. The former was taken up in the Basel Accord with modifications and became the key distinction between countries inside and outside the OECD. The interest rate risk proposal was dropped and only recently readdressed in the April 1993 proposal.

a total capital ratio (counting loan loss reserves and subordinated, or long-term uninsured, debt among other items) equal to 8 percent. Different risk weights applied to individual asset categories but did not take account of portfolio risk or the risk enhancement or reduction associated with the correlation of risks among assets. At one extreme, safe assets such as government bonds were assigned a zero risk weight, while at the other extreme, traditional loans were assigned a 100 percent risk weight, thus requiring the full 8 percent total capital support.

Although technically the Basel Accord sets forth minimum standards, in practice it represents a significant move toward harmonized standards. The existing national differences, such as those reflected in the Capital Adequacy Directive (CAD) of the EU, are relatively minor.[33] The United States also deviated in several ways that strengthen the requirement. For example, although the Accord formally applies only to large "international banks," U.S. bank regulators have imposed the requirements on all its banks. In addition, the United States now maintains a separate, and for many banks more stringent, set of capital standards calculated on the basis of unweighted assets (the so-called leverage ratio).

Nevertheless, the degree to which bank capital standards were harmonized is a striking feature of the Basel Accord. It reflects the observation we made earlier that once countries agree to address a potential spillover, such as systemic risk, they may be impelled by domestic political forces to accomplish the objective in a way that attempts to level the playing field. The 50 percent risk weight assigned to mortgages in the Accord is an excellent example, since it reflects a strong preference by several of the Basel signatories to tilt bank finance toward housing. Other countries went along so as not to penalize their banks. Of greater importance, banks in Europe and North America initially were very supportive of the Basel efforts to harmonize bank capital rules since they viewed them primarily as a way to constrain the growth of Japanese banks, which Japanese regulators allowed to operate with greater leverage than other banks. In this regard, the Basel standards appear to have been successful—again, from the standpoint of banks in Europe and North America—since the growth

---

33. For a summary, see Friedland (forthcoming), based on an unpublished manuscript, May 4, 1993.

of Japanese banks has slowed significantly since 1990.[34] More generally, the Basel standards have helped make disclosure of the financial
condition of banks around the world more uniform, a result that has
enhanced the effectiveness of market discipline (by facilitating comparisons of banks by depositors, creditors, and shareholders).[35]

Nevertheless, the Basel Accord has significant limitations, which
were recognized even by the members of the committee. Not only do
the standards ignore portfolio risk, but they also fail to take account
of trading risk, interest rate risk, market risk, operational risks, and
some counterparty risks. In addition, the Basel countries form an
exclusive club; the agreement does not apply to many industrialized
countries are not represented, and no less-developed countries belong. This has become a particularly sensitive issue for the less-developed countries, since the risk weights give preferential treatment
(20 percent) to bonds issued by governments in countries belonging
to the Organization of Economic Cooperation and Development
(OECD) relative to bonds issued by other governments (100 percent). Such a scheme obviously discourages banks from investing in
bonds from outside the OECD.

Meanwhile, the initial standards themselves have been targets of
criticism, especially because the major industrial economies experienced sluggish growth and recession followed by slow growth as the
Accord was implemented. Although the standards have been ap-
plauded for forcing weak banks to increase their capital ratios and
reduce their risk taking, the risk weighting system continues to be a
target of controversy. The much higher risk weights assigned to conventional lending than to government bonds would seem to encourage banks to tilt their asset portfolios toward bonds, thus contributing
to a reduction in the supply of credit to private-sector borrowers. In
fact, U.S. banks clearly have reallocated their portfolios in favor of
government bonds since 1990.

Defenders of the risk weights respond by noting that depository
institutions not subject to the Basel standards, such as credit unions,
also shifted their portfolios toward government bonds, suggesting that

34. To a significant degree, market participants would have forced Japanese banks with
lending problems and asset losses to slow their growth or to shrink even in the absence of
the Basel standards. But the standards probably had some independent effect as well.

35. This point was emphasized during the discussion of our initial draft by Lawrence
Promisel of the Federal Reserve Board.

banks may have been responding to weak loan demand. In addition, they note that both banks that were not constrained by capital requirements and banks that were so constrained moved toward bonds, suggesting that the Basel Accord had nothing to do with the portfolio shift.[36] Critics, however, respond that, at least in the United States, the Basel standards were binding for weak banks and that these institutions did in fact invest more heavily in government bonds than their healthier counterparts, behavior that is consistent with the incentives created by the standards.[37] The fact that this debate continues indicates that portions of the standards remain controversial.

The Basel Committee has attempted to address some of the shortcomings of the initial standards by proposing supplemental rules governing market, interest rate, and counterparty risks.[38] The proposals are elaborate, highly technical, and complicated documents that attempt to refine the amounts of capital that banks must maintain against each of these various forms of risk.

The market risk proposal is modeled after the 1993 Capital Adequacy Directive, which became final in 1993.[39] Specifically, it would require banks to maintain a third tier of capital consisting of subordinated debt (limited to 250 percent of tier 1 capital, or shareholders' equity) to back their holdings of debt and equity securities.

The market risk proposal also contains mechanisms for measuring exposures based on the market values of the derivative instruments or contracts, not on their notional amounts. In addition, the proposal would permit netting of securities exposures in the same currencies with the same institutions—so-called bilateral netting—but would only permit multilateral netting (across parties) where member institutions are dealing with a clearinghouse, so that the exposures of the institutions would be to the clearinghouse and not to each other. Such clearinghouses are not in place now primarily because swaps and certain other derivatives differ in their legal structure and so cannot be readily offset against each other. Indeed, the legal basis for enforc-

---

36. For a sample of this line of defense, see Mullins (1993).

37. See Haubrich and Wachtel (1993).

38. The proposals were set forth in April 1993 in three separate documents: "The Supervisory Recognition of Netting for Capital Adequacy Purposes," "The Prudential Supervision of Netting, Market Risks, and Interest Rate Risks," and "Measurement of Banks' Exposure to Interest Rate Risk."

39. Council Directive 93/6/EEC, published in *Official Journal of the European Community* No. L 141.

ing these contracts remains in doubt in some key industrial countries.[40] It is conceivable, if not likely, that international efforts now under way to standardize the legal provisions of these instruments will overcome this problem, and if that happens, clearinghouses almost certainly will be formed. But until that occurs, banks covered by the proposed Basel provisions will not be able to net their derivatives exposures across institutions and thus would need to maintain more capital under the proposal than they would if clearinghouses existed.

Finally, the interest rate proposal would allow each country to measure the exposures of their banks to changes in interest rates, within certain guidelines. The guidelines spell out how instruments of various maturities and of different types (floating or fixed rates) should be treated.

As we suggested in chapter 3, concerns have grown that banks are not the only institutions whose activities pose systemic risks. There are fears that the failure of a large securities firm, especially one with extensive exposure to banks and other counterparties, domestic and foreign, could have similar consequences. Specifically, the failing firm may not honor its commitments to counterparties, including clearinghouses, which in turn could trigger a chain reaction of liquidity problems at other institutions.[41]

We maintained in chapter 3 that such fears are overstated. They nevertheless account for the growing interest within the International Organization of Securities Commissions (IOSCO) in developing minimum capital standards for securities firms analogous to those developed for banks by the Basel Committee.[42] In January 1992, IOSCO's technical committee on capital standards held its first joint meeting with the Basel Committee in an effort to coordinate a common minimum capital standard for debt and equity securities in particular. The search for commonality was motivated by the desire to ensure a level playing field, not just between securities firms in different countries, but between banks and securities firms, both of which compete

40. See the recent Group of Thirty report evaluating the legal enforceability of derivatives, which highlights areas in which legislative change is desirable in nine countries. Group of Thirty (1993).

41. See Organization for Economic Cooperation and Development (1991, pp. 35–36).

42. As of 1992, IOSCO had 101 members. Since 1975 it has been engaged in efforts to exchange information about the enforcement of securities laws and, where possible, to harmonize accounting and disclosure requirements, clearing and settlement procedures, and, most recently, capital standards for securities firms.

in the same kind of business.[43] Some progress toward agreement was reached: the technical committee supported the building block approach pioneered by the Basel Accord, whereby separate standards are established for different types of risk (such as credit risk and market risk), provided that countries can continue to apply single or comprehensive capital standards covering all types of risk when those standards are at least as high as those implied by the building block approach. Nevertheless, the IOSCO and Basel committees—largely because of differences between the United States and the EU—continue to differ on other key issues, notably on the amounts of capital that must back derivatives instruments.

If these disagreements are resolved, it is likely that capital standards for banks and securities firms will converge. Historically they have differed in the degree to which they have rested on market valuations of assets and liabilities. Unlike banks, which hold much of their assets in illiquid form (loans), securities firms hold virtually all of their assets in liquid securities. Understandably, therefore, regulators generally have insisted that securities firms, but not banks, comply with marked-to-market accounting principles. But as we noted in chapter 3, the distinctions between bank and securities accounting practices are eroding as both types of firms hold the same or similar assets and as banks, in particular, securitize much of their balance sheets. As a result, the United States is moving its bank accounting standards toward market value accounting. Denmark already requires its banks to state all of their assets and liabilities at market value. We expect stronger moves toward marked-to-market accounting in other countries in the future.

Consumer Protection

In regulating the solvency of their financial institutions, governments are engaging in what may be the most important act of consumer protection of all: ensuring that the contracts customers make with their institutions are fully performed. And as we have just indicated, there has been substantial international coordination of solvency regulation of at least banks to date.

43. The pressure to level the playing field is especially intense in countries where securities activities are conducted mainly by universal banks.

But consumers may also be harmed in other ways in their dealings with financial institutions. Countries differ in the degree to which they attempt to regulate institutions or markets to prevent such harm. Some countries still regulate the interest rates that banks may charge retail customers, but this perverse type of regulation is waning. Most countries in the developed world, however, punish insider trading of securities. And as securities trading increasingly crosses national boundaries, pressures have grown for regulators to share information and to coordinate their enforcement of fraudulent practices and insider trading activities.

IOSCO has responded with several resolutions urging such information sharing by all member countries, even where the matters under investigation may not violate the laws of the country from which information is being requested. In addition, IOSCO has issued guidelines for countries to follow in negotiating bilateral or multilateral Memoranda of Understanding (MOU) on information sharing. At a 1991 IOSCO conference, U.S. regulators signed three such MOUs: the Securities and Exchange Commission (SEC) with its counterparts in the EU and Norway; and both the SEC and the Commodities Futures Trading Commission (CFTC) with their counterparts in Great Britain.[44]

IOSCO also has a working group devoted to harmonizing disclosure requirements and procedures of issuers of securities to facilitate investing by customers in markets of different countries. In 1989 the organization recommended that regulators use common disclosure documents. The EU has moved furthest in this direction.

A key issue that has not yet been resolved, however, is the extent to which accounting standards in different countries should be harmonized. The case for some harmonization is strong. Markets cannot function efficiently without timely disclosure of relevant information to investors. Differences in accounting rules throw sand into the gears of the market, complicating comparisons of the performance of firms doing business in different countries.

An international body devoted to the harmonization of accounting rules, the International Auditing Practices Committee (IAPC) of the International Federation of Accountants, has made some progress toward this objective. In 1992 that committee adopted a resolution

44. See Doty (1992, p. 80).

urging IOSCO to recognize the IAPC's core group of international standards as a basis for cross-border transactions. However, domestic firms in each country remain bound by the accounting rules applicable in those countries.

In the meantime—that is, until nations agree on common accounting rules—differences in the rules are becoming more important sources of contention between countries and their securities markets. A central question has become whether the exchanges will accept for listing only those foreign companies that comply with host country accounting rules, or whether the exchanges will practice mutual recognition and list some or all foreign companies that comply with their home country rules even though they do not comply with host country rules. The SEC in this country thus far has insisted on a host country policy. But this seems unduly rigid, at least for large, well-recognized foreign firms whose financial condition is generally well known to institutional investors worldwide. If the SEC continues to insist on a host country accounting policy for such companies in a world of increasingly globalized trading, it will simply cost U.S. exchanges trading business with few apparent benefits to investors.[45]

In the long run, it is conceivable that accounting policies may be harmonized without government intervention, which would render disputes of this kind moot. The reason is that institutional investors may demand greater uniformity as they seek to diversify the geographical composition of their investment portfolios. As we suggest in chapter 5, that outcome may be made more likely by improved efforts at coordinating measurement and information exchange concerning the dealings of financial market participants. But it is not necessarily an outcome that should be brought about by governmental negotiation, which can have the unwelcome effects of frustrating continued financial innovation if the "wrong" standards are agreed on.

Other Objectives

In chapter 3 we identified several other objectives that financial regulators have pursued in different countries, including the alloca-

---

45. To avoid this problem, the New York Stock Exchange has suggested that "world class" foreign company shares be listed in a separate table or identified with an asterisk to alert investors to the fact that they comply with different accounting rules. See Freund (1993, p. A6).

tion of credit toward favored uses or regions, prevention of concentration of economic and political power, and prevention of crime. Of these three objectives, we suggested that only the third had significant international dimensions. Nevertheless, before we describe international efforts made thus far to combat international criminal activity through regulation of financial institutions, we digress briefly to address some international issues related to regulatory efforts to limit concentration.

Financial Structure and Concentration

As we noted in chapter 3, countries differ in the way in which they permit their financial institutions to be structured, and specifically in the extent to which they allow banks to own, to be affiliated with, or to be owned by nonbanking and even commercial enterprises. Loosely speaking, among the developed countries, the EU countries and Canada have moved furthest in the direction of allowing some common affiliations between bank and nonbank activity, with Germany at one extreme allowing its banks not only to engage in securities activities but to own large equity positions in nonbanking corporations. Other European countries have agreed to permit universal banking—the mixing of banking and securities underwriting—but continue to differ over whether banks can take equity positions in nonbank operations. In addition, differences remain over the extent to which EU banks may be owned by nonbanking operations.

At the other extreme, the United States has taken the most restrictive attitude toward the mixing of banking with other activities. This is reflected in the limitations on bank involvement in securities activities under the Glass-Steagall Act and the proscriptions on bank holding company involvement in activities not closely related to banking. Japan has been somewhere in the middle between the United States and the EU. Before World War II, Japan freely allowed the mingling of banks and nonbanks in *zaibatsu*. These alliances were formally banned by the United States after the war, which transplanted its Glass-Steagall restrictions on the mixing of banking with securities and other nonbanking activities. Japanese banks were permitted, however, to take limited equity positions in nonbank companies (up to five percent of their stock). This led to the creation of *keiretsu* relationships between banks and their borrowers.

In short, while significant differences in banking structure have existed at least among the countries of the industrialized world, most countries have maintained some restrictions on the affiliations of banks with other types of enterprise.[46] Why?

One reason is that governments and their citizens have feared that banks could exert undue control over economic activity. Ironically, this fear has been greatest in the United States, where banks have played the smallest role in intermediating the funds of savers to investors. A second reason for the restrictions is that all governments, by providing a safety net for bank depositors, implicitly subsidize their banks and, at least potentially, weaken market discipline of banks (for which capital regulation and supervision are necessary substitutes).

The increasing internationalization of finance, however, has been weakening the economic and political power of domestically owned financial institutions and thus should be allaying concerns about concentration. At least that has been the case in the United States, where regulators, at the prodding of banks, have been able to exploit various crevices in the Glass-Steagall Act to permit banks to engage in most of the securities-related activities from which that act was thought to bar them (including brokerage, underwriting, and the sale of mutual funds). Similarly, as it has seen the United States weaken its own restrictions, Japan has allowed its banks to own securities subsidiaries (and conversely, securities firm to own banks). Both countries, in short, have been converging toward the EU's universal banking model without explicit international coordination. That they have done so is a testament to the market developments that have been driving the countries in similar directions.

Still, it is doubtful that all countries will permit the same type of financial structure in the near future. Policymakers in the United States, in particular, remain concerned about the extension of the federal safety net to affiliates of banks. In addition, some have been concerned that customers of bank affiliates can be confused or misled into believing that their dealings with the nonbank affiliates are protected by deposit insurance despite the best efforts of regulators and banks to persuade them otherwise. In chapter 5 we offer one straightforward way of addressing these concerns that admittedly is not now

46. For a comprehensive review of the relevant restrictions in at least the OECD countries, see Organization for Economic Cooperation and Development (1992, pp. 92–113).

followed in any country but that at some point could form a basis of agreement.

•

Money Laundering

Finally, because financial institutions may (unknowingly) facilitate criminal activities conducted across national borders, nations most affected by these activities have recently recognized the importance of jointly regulating financial institutions and transactions in order to frustrate criminal enterprise.[47] The broadest effort to date is a 1988 United Nations convention, signed by forty-four countries, on illicit drug traffic. The convention requires participating states to punish the production and trading of narcotic drugs when "committed internationally" as criminal offenses under their domestic laws. Among other things, the convention defines as a punishable offense the "organization, management or financing" of activity related to narcotic drugs. This means that banks and other financial institutions that knowingly accept the proceeds of international drug trafficking would be in violation of the convention. In addition, the convention requires member states to assist each other in the investigation and prosecution of parties that may be engaged in international drug-related enterprise and specifically states that countries should not decline to render assistance on the basis of bank secrecy.[48]

The Basel Committee has gone one step further toward international cooperation in attacking money laundering. In 1989 it issued a Statement of Principles, which urges banks in the Group of Ten countries to "make reasonable efforts" to determine the true identity of all customers and then to disassociate themselves from transactions relating to money laundering. Unlike the UN convention, which merely sanctions institutions that have actual knowledge that their customers are engaging in illicit activities, the Basel statement affirmatively requires banks to make efforts to avoid dealing with such customers.

47. Our discussion of this topic draws on Spencer (1990) and Sproule and St.-Denis (1989).

48. Ending bank secrecy can be economically painful. In 1993 South Korea required accounts at financial institutions to be registered in the holder's real name, a move that is widely believed to have slowed the growth of the economy given the earlier reliance by small and medium-sized businesses on money deposited in "phony-name" accounts. See Blustein (1993, p. D9).

Also during 1989, as an outgrowth of the G-7 summit, fifteen nations set up a Financial Assets Task Force, which has agreed on a series of recommendations to eradicate international money laundering. Although the task force's recommendations are not binding on the banks of member states, a bank's refusal to cooperate taints its reputation, making it more difficult for that bank to deal with institutions in other countries.

While the international efforts at controlling money laundering have made some progress, they have stopped short of dealing fully with the problem. It is one thing for countries to say they are going to punish money laundering, but it is quite another for countries to facilitate the prosecution of this activity. One important impediment to effective prosecution, of course, is bank secrecy legislation, which some countries still maintain. As countries without such legislation tighten their efforts to combat money laundering, drug traffickers will increasingly shift their financial business to the few remaining countries that continue to shelter the identity of bank customers.

But even countries that do not protect the confidentiality of bank customer identity cannot effectively prosecute money laundering unless banks are required to report transactions of certain sizes, as they are in the United States. The UN Convention and other international agreements would be more effective if such reporting requirements were added.

Chapter 5

Prospects for International Cooperation in the Regulation and Supervision of Financial Services

*T*HUS FAR we have described only those international initiatives that are already under way. As a preface to our discussion of a future international regulatory agenda, we briefly summarize what international negotiations have not accomplished.

First, there appears to be unfinished business from the current initiatives. For example, members of the GATT failed to agree on provisions to liberalize cross-border trade in financial services in the Uruguay Round negotiations. The Basel Committee continues to wrestle with the bank risks that were not addressed in the 1988 accord. In addition, implementation of the Basel Concordat has been uneven among members of the Basel Committee (as the BCCI scandal revealed); other major banking centers have not adopted, much less implemented the principles. Meanwhile, regulators have yet to come to any agreement on capital standards for the securities industry. And international control of money laundering through the banking system remains highly imperfect.

Second, some potential financial spillovers have not yet received adequate international treatment. Although negotiators have made significant progress toward harmonizing rules relating to the *solvency* of individual banks that are internationally active, much less attention has been paid to potential threats to the international payments system that may arise from *illiquidity* of individual banks. Central banks of host countries are responsible for supervising liquidity, but the agreements (if any) for coordination of emergency liquidity assistance are murky at best.

Perhaps the most important issues affecting future financial spillovers relate to accounting standards for financial institutions. Market discipline can be even more effective than government supervision and regulation in restraining risks in the financial marketplace. Yet market participants cannot perform their role with maximum effectiveness unless they have access to timely, comparable, reliable information about the health of financial institutions.

Finally, the authorities will continue to experience pressures to harmonize rules to level the international financial playing field. Perhaps the most controversial differences in rules relate to differences in financial structure among countries, often referred to as differences in bank powers. In particular, while the rest of the industrialized world appears to be moving in the direction of universal banking, the United States maintains high, but steadily eroding, walls between its banks and other financial institutions, as well as between banks and commercial enterprises. In addition, countries also maintain different premiums for deposit insurance, different bank reserve requirements, different tax rates, and different bankruptcy laws—all of which perpetuate an unlevel playing field.

The very persistence of these variations in financial structure, taxes, and subsidies implies that countries currently enjoy some scope for regulatory diversity, but technological advances are likely to increase the strength of regulatory arbitrage. The existing diversity suggests that attempts to negotiate international harmonization will be difficult. In many instances it may also be inappropriate.

In this chapter, we discuss five key items on the unfinished agenda: emergency liquidity assistance for internationally active banks; extensions of the Basel Accord and the Concordat; development of harmonized standards for securities firms; regulation and supervision of international financial conglomerates; and the role of market discipline.

The Willingness to Cooperate

Under what circumstances is international cooperation likely to occur? More specifically, under what circumstances are sovereign nations likely to cooperate to achieve regulatory and supervisory objectives?

One way to answer these questions is to observe the conditions that have produced perhaps the most successful effort in international cooperation, which occurred in the area of public health. As we noted in chapter 3, international cooperation in this area is so advanced and the gains from international cooperation are so obvious that it is difficult to imagine a time in which cooperation on health matters did not take place. Yet, as Richard Cooper has pointed out, it took nearly a century to achieve fully effective international cooperation in the control of the spread of contagious diseases. The factors that at first inhibited international cooperation and finally made it possible have interesting implications for the scope of international financial regulation.

Much of our language for describing financial crises is based on the metaphor of the contagious spread of disease. Edward Kane, for example, has used the language of epidemiology to analyze systemic risk.[1] He argues that the global financial system may be regarded as a system of linked subsystems like the human body. The linked subsystems of the international financial system together channel funds and financial instruments among different kinds of transactors whose accounts are often located in different countries. Kane argues that systemic risk has two related meanings: the danger that one or more component subsystems of the organism may fail (subsystem failure risk) and the danger that the coordinating structure may break apart (disintegration risk). International financial integration may increase systemic risk by exposing financial firms in one country to the contagious spread of losses from foreign financial firms.[2]

Cooper concludes that international cooperation in public health depended on a complicated interaction of "epidemics of disease, public actions in response to them, diplomacy, commercial and other economic interests, and the advance of both scientific and practical knowledge."[3] All countries shared the objective of containment of disease, and the outbreak of disease often led to a public call for greater regulation, but this shared objective was not sufficient to

1. Kane (1992, pp. 257–58).

2. Extending the metaphor, Kane argues that this concern reflects a misunderstanding of the theory of vaccination. Although international financial integration unquestionably exposes financial institutions to "additional pathogens," whether vulnerability to disease also increases depends on what happens to the immune system. Kane argues that heightened market discipline has strengthened the financial system's immune system, in part because it reduces the autonomy and control of national regulators. Kane (1992, p. 258).

3. Cooper (1989, p. 180).

achieve joint international action. Cooperation took place in stages. It began with exchanges of information on the propagation of diseases and preventive measures and with attempts to standardize quarantine regulations. Frequent attempts were made to agree on classifications of diseases and reporting systems to monitor outbreaks. The most difficult stage was reaching agreement on cooperative action in the event of an outbreak. As long as countries disagreed about the likely consequences of alternative courses of action, joint decisionmaking was not feasible. Cooper observes that "societies are reluctant to undertake costly or even merely inconvenient actions on the basis of contending theories of uncertain merit."[4]

The development of an international public health system depended on international consensus about how diseases were transmitted and what action could be taken to prevent contagious transmission. Thus joint action depended critically on the advance of scientific and clinical knowledge. Once countries agreed on how to act, the extent of cooperation advanced to the point of establishing an international agency and jointly financing international action to control and to attempt to eradicate contagious diseases.

Political scientists have also tried to identify institutional factors that facilitate cooperation among nations.[5] Three insights may have particular relevance to international cooperation in financial regulation and supervision. First, the prospects for cooperation diminish as the number of players increases.[6] Second, international regimes—defined as sets of norms, principles, rules, or decision-making procedures—facilitate cooperation by aiding in the decentralized enforcement of agreements.[7] Keohane suggests a related rationale, "Clustering of issues under a regime facilitates side-payments among these issues: more potential *quids* are available for the *quo*."[8] Alternatively, a dominant power that adjusts its own policies and attempts to

---

4. Cooper (1989, pp. 180–81).

5. For a recent survey article, see Milner (1992). See also Haggard and Simmons (1987).

6. Milner notes that this hypothesis may be undercut by other considerations. For example, "Concerns over relative losses can be attenuated in a multilateral setting." (1992, p. 474).

7. Milner (1992, p. 475).

8. Keohane (1984, p. 91).

realize mutual gains may serve as the functional equivalent of a regime.

Third, an international community of experts—defined as "a professional group that believes in the same cause-and-effect relationships . . . [and] shares common values"—advances cooperation.[9] This is consistent with Cooper's emphasis on the importance of practical and scientific knowledge in the achievement of international cooperation in public health. Milner notes that, in addition, communities of experts may often have domestic political influence that facilitates international agreement. Cooperative agreements are strengthened by the power of these experts in their own governments.[10]

Taken together, these considerations suggest that international cooperation is more likely:

—the smaller the group of countries that must agree;

—the broader the international consensus on policy objectives and the potential gains from cooperation;

—the deeper the international agreement on the probable consequences of policy alternatives;

—the stronger the international institutional infrastructure for decisionmaking; and

—the greater the domestic influence of experts who share a common understanding of a problem and its solution.

These considerations help explain why international cooperation began first and has advanced furthest among international bank supervisors in the Basel Committee. First, banks headquartered in the Group of Ten countries (plus Luxembourg and Switzerland) control a very large proportion of cross-border banking transactions; thus cooperation among a relatively small group of countries could have a major effect. Second, bank supervisory authorities in all major countries share a concern with financial stability. This concern was heightened by a series of events, starting with the collapse of Herstatt in 1974, that emphasized that international spillovers in banking crises are potentially an important source of instability that international supervisory cooperation could diminish.

Third, international agreement on the role of bank capital in minimizing international systemic risk was so extensive that it led

9. Haas terms this an "epistemic community." Haas (1990, p. 55).
10. Milner (1992, p. 479).

to efforts to harmonize capital adequacy requirements. Although regulatory regimes differ widely among the countries participating in the Basel Committee, each country regulated bank capital. Each country also shared an implicit view that capital requirements provide an important buffer against bank failures and that bank failures could threaten financial stability. This provided a foundation for negotiation of common minimum capital adequacy standards.

The procedures of the Basel Committee are designed to facilitate consensus building.[11] The regular, confidential, off-the-record exchanges of views, identification of best practices, and drafting of policy papers helps the authorities find common ground without the distractions of external pressures. Moreover, banking supervision is a relatively arcane subject, and so bank supervisory authorities probably have considerable scope for autonomous decisionmaking. Many agreements negotiated by the Basel Committee could be implemented directly without amending domestic legislation. Finally, the Basel Committee benefited from the institutional infrastructure developed by the central bank governors of the Group of Ten, who have met monthly in Basel for many decades.

These considerations also help explain why cooperation among regulators of insurance and securities firms has lagged behind cooperation among bank supervisory authorities. In both cases the number of policymakers that must be consulted is substantially larger and more diverse and includes official and self-regulatory bodies and financial exchanges. There is less agreement on potential gains from international harmonization of regulation (or the costs from failing to harmonize), perhaps because the world economy has been spared serious crises that are directly attributable to international spillovers from the collapse of securities or insurance firms. The tradition of international cooperation is much less deep and less well-established among securities regulators, although the International Organization of Securities Commissions (IOSCO) is building an international infrastructure for decisionmaking. Most key insurance regulators have not even met their counterparts in other leading countries. In neither case can international cooperation build on a long tradition of central bank collaboration.

11. Cooke (1990, pp. 310–35); and Hayward (1990, pp. 787–88).

Emergency Liquidity Assistance for Internationally Active Banks

The lender-of-last-resort problem was one of the first international issues to be addressed jointly by the regulatory authorities. The response has been to adopt a policy of calculated ambiguity in order to preserve at least some market discipline. That policy has two major defects, however.

Defects of a Policy of Ambiguity

Ex ante, calculated ambiguity provides a wholly unwarranted competitive advantage to the largest banks. Since the lender of last resort (LLR) cannot make a credible commitment to behave randomly, market participants will proceed on the basis of expectations about how the LLR is likely to behave and which institutions are most likely to receive LLR assistance. (Indeed, several private rating firms provide assessments of the likelihood that a bank will receive official assistance along with an evaluation of its creditworthiness.)

It is very easy to identify the banks most likely to receive assistance. The ad hoc cost-benefit analysis that central banks customarily undertake includes many factors—the condition of the bank, why the bank is in trouble, the bank's prospects for recovery, and the state of the economy—but the overriding consideration is the potential spillover cost if support is not forthcoming. Market participants logically conclude that creditors are most likely to be protected at a large bank because failure of a large bank is likely to cause a greater drop in aggregate demand, interrupt more credit relationships, and pose greater threats to the payments system than the failure of a small bank. Even more important, the failure of a large bank is more likely to undermine confidence in the banking system generally and to lead to runs on other banks. Reliance on discretionary LLR assistance gives these banks an unwarranted funding advantage vis-à-vis smaller banks, which are less likely to receive assistance. Moreover, it weakens market discipline on precisely those institutions that, by virtue of their size, pose the greatest potential threat to the stability of the banking system.

Calculated ambiguity is also defective ex post—that is, in the event a run actually occurs. Implicit commitments are not sufficient to prevent runs. In the event of a liquidity shock, the precise nature of the implicit commitment falls into question. Does the LLR merely promise that it will not close a major bank precipitately, or does it offer creditors complete assurance against loss? If the former, for how long is the commitment extended? If the latter, precisely which categories of creditors are covered? Ambiguity regarding answers to such questions is fatal to the maintenance of confidence. Uncertainty provides an incentive to run, and maturing liabilities provide the opportunity. The collapse of Continental Illinois in 1984 illustrates the consequences of not making commitments explicit in advance of trouble. Nine days after the run on Continental began, the U.S. authorities took the unprecedented step of explicitly guaranteeing the bank's depositors and creditors. Nonetheless, the run continued.[12] After Continental's solvency was in question and doubts had arisen regarding the response of the authorities, even the announcement of an explicit guarantee did not restore confidence.

In sum, a policy of ambiguity is defective both before a liquidity shock occurs and after it has happened. A policy of ambiguity is tantamount to a policy of implicit guarantees for large banks, which encourages depositors to place deposits with these banks on the basis of cursory credit evaluations. However, it offers no real protection against a liquidity shock if some event raises questions about the bank's solvency.

A Case for Explicit Commitments

As we have demonstrated, implicit guarantees offered to large banks under the policy of ambiguity undermine ex ante discipline. The freedom of action that central bankers seem to prize so greatly, therefore, is largely illusory. As Corrigan has shown, the banking authorities in most industrial countries have taken measures to protect all depositors from losses resulting from bank failures in most circumstances.[13]

12. Joint Press Release by the office of the Comptroller of the Currency, the Federal Deposit Insurance Corporation and the Federal Reserve Board, May 17, 1984.

13. The proposal outlined in this section was first made by Guttentag and Herring. This section draws heavily from that work, which contains a much more extended discussion. Guttentag and Herring (1987, pp. 150–86). Corrigan (1990). Herstatt and BCCI are the most notable counterexamples in the post–World War II era.

If, in fact, the authorities would never allow a major bank to close precipitately, much would be gained if they committed themselves in advance. A policy of explicit commitment, assuming the LLR has the means to make it credible, would prevent runs on major banks. Such a policy would not eliminate the unwarranted funding advantage possessed by these banks, but at least society would garner the benefit of greater financial stability to set off against this cost.

Such a commitment would not and should not represent a commitment to protect *shareholders* against loss, to continue the bank as a separate entity, to maintain the existing management if the bank is continued, or to protect creditors of a parent or affiliates of the bank. The only commitment would be to avoid termination of the bank's operations so that depositors and borrowers would be able to continue business as usual.

To be sure, such a precommitment policy faces two objections. First, any market discipline now imposed on major banks by depositors might be diminished. This objection does not seem overwhelming, however, because depositors exercise only limited discipline against large banks in practice and because holders of publicly traded subordinated debt (who cannot run and would not be protected by the commitment) are a preferable means of focusing market discipline on large banks.

A second, more important objection is that runs on major banks may sometimes serve a useful purpose. If regulatory controls are so weak that the authorities cannot prevent a major bank from operating imprudently, a run may provide the authorities with the leverage they need to exact changes in policies and management; LLR assistance can be made the quid pro quo for such changes. In some countries this may be the best means available to regulators for disciplining a bank. Even where regulators have the powers necessary to discipline a bank, furthermore, they may not do so for fear of political repercussions, because of bureaucratic inertia, or because they are simply unaware of the seriousness of a bank's problems. In such cases, a run is an effective spur to action.

For this reason, we do not advocate that LLRs forswear the option of closing a major bank precipitately. Rather we argue for a more modest and logically prior step—that LLRs explicitly acknowledge *all* the specific banks for which they recognize responsibility, without committing themselves to any course of action in an emergency. This first step would allow markets to identify banks that have no LLR while clarifying responsibilities toward some other banks for which existing lines of responsibility are uncertain.

Our proposal has two major objectives. The first is to increase market discipline over banks that do not have access to emergency liquidity assistance by identifying them. Because the policy of calculated ambiguity can undermine market discipline in instances where confidence in the availability of emergency assistance is completely misplaced, there is a compelling case for indicating which banks do not have access to an LLR.[14] If, for example, the market had been fully aware that Banco Ambrosiano Holdings and, more recently, BCCI did not have access to emergency liquidity assistance, each bank would likely have faced much stronger constraints on its growth much earlier.[15]

The second objective is to clarify responsibility among central banks for those banks that do have access to emergency liquidity assistance. When responsibility is not clearly allocated, there is a risk that a crisis will be exacerbated by delays in the provision of assistance. Delays may arise because of misunderstandings and disputes among LLRs regarding which central bank is responsible for a given bank and because an LLR that had not assumed that it was responsible before the need for action arose may not have made previous arrangements for evaluating and perfecting claims to collateral and for obtaining information on a bank's condition.

The Group of Ten central banks may have already made an explicit allocation of responsibilities. (This is one possible interpretation of the 1974 communique.) If so, the apportionment of responsibilities should be disclosed to the market. An explicit apportionment of responsibilities need not undermine market discipline since each LLR will continue to make the availability of assistance dependent on the costs and benefits under the conditions prevailing at the time. The objective of enhancing market discipline does not provide a rationale

14. LLRs should, however, resist the temptation to exaggerate the number of banks that would not have access to emergency liquidity assistance. If important banks headquartered in the LLR's country are capriciously excluded, the list will lack credibility, and the market will rely on implicit commitments.

15. Looking back still further, Bankhaus Herstatt might not have been able to engage in "overtrading" if potential counterparties had known that Herstatt would not have access to emergency liquidity assistance.

for a policy of ambiguity regarding the apportionment of responsibilities. If, on the other hand, the LLRs disagree about the apportionment of responsibilities, it is misleading and potentially dangerous to encourage the market to believe that they have agreed on an allocation.

In sum, the proposal is for each LLR to publish a list of banks for which it acknowledges sole or shared responsibility. By implication, the market would be placed on warning that any bank that does not have an acknowledged LLR will not have access to emergency liquidity assistance.

The best approach to generating such lists would be through agreement among central banks.[16] The Concordat's approach to allocating responsibility for the supervision of solvency provides a useful model because it ensures that the LLR is in the same country as the supervisory authority with primary responsibility for monitoring the bank's solvency, which is also likely to be the country of the authority (usually the chartering authority or deposit insurance agency) responsible for disposing of the bank should it fail.[17]

If all LLRs adopted these principles, banks without access to emergency liquidity assistance would include banks headquartered in countries that do not have an LLR and their foreign branches and

16. Such an agreement need not cover all central banks. Except where cross-border cooperation is called for, the principles could be adopted by a single LLR. Multilateral agreement might, indeed, be the end of an incremental process rather than the starting point.

17. Such an allocation of responsibility for providing emergency liquidity assistance might proceed as follows:

—The LLR in the parent country will give offshore branches of banks chartered in the parent country the same access to emergency liquidity assistance as the parent bank.

—The host country LLR will not provide emergency liquidity assistance to branches of foreign banks except as a conduit for the parent country LLR, at the latter's risk; however, it may cooperate with the parent country LLR in providing emergency liquidity assistance. Such cooperation may take the form of providing information to the parent country LLR or helping the parent country perfect a claim to the bank's assets in order to arrange a collateralized loan.

—Foreign subsidiaries and affiliates of banks chartered in the parent country will not have direct access to emergency liquidity assistance from the LLR in the parent country. They may have indirect access to the extent that they are supported by the parent bank and the parent bank requires assistance, but the LLR in the parent country is free to deny assistance to the parent bank in such a case.

—Host LLRs may grant foreign-owned banks access to emergency liquidity assistance on equal terms with other locally chartered banks or they may discriminate against them.

foreign-owned banks chartered in countries that have no LLR or do not offer emergency liquidity assistance to foreign-owned banks. These banks would be the focus of market discipline along with banks located in countries that do not adopt the principles. With an explicit apportionment of LLR responsibilities, furthermore, the market would tend to evaluate the capacity of an LLR to deliver. LLRs can usually provide completely credible commitments in their own currency, but an LLR's credibility in making commitments in foreign currencies depends on its country's foreign exchange reserves.

With an explicit allocation of LLR responsibilities, entry might be difficult for banks not on the list. A policy of ambiguity, however, discriminates against banks that are presumed not to be guaranteed—a category that surely includes most potential new entrants. It is likely, moreover, that if LLRs choose to be explicit, they will experience political pressures to develop objective, equitable criteria that do not discriminate capriciously against new entrants.

A similar issue arises with regard to removing a bank from the list. Would not the announcement undermine confidence in the bank and destabilize the banking system? This is plausible, but it is not obvious that an ambiguous policy is preferable. If the alternative to explicitly withdrawing access is withdrawing access secretly, without informing the market, it is not clear that the ultimate result will be more favorable. If the market falsely believes that an institution has access to emergency liquidity assistance, market discipline will be unduly slack, and in the event access to emergency liquidity assistance becomes necessary, the blow to confidence in the system will be greater.

Being on the list undoubtedly conveys a valuable benefit to a bank, but the list also gives the supervisory authorities powerful bargaining leverage that can be used to induce a bank to agree to more effective prudential supervision. Moreover, since the quality of the LLR matters, the list may give banks an incentive to shift their charters over time to better-supervised centers that have a more credible capacity to provide emergency liquidity assistance.

What about market discipline for large banks? Later in the chapter we outline a suggestion for supplying such discipline through means that do not pose the systemic risks that deposits entail.

Refinements and Extensions of the Basel Concordat and Accord

The Basel Committee has focused on two fundamental functions: supervision and rule making for internationally active banks. The attempt to coordinate and to improve the effectiveness of international supervision has led to several revisions of the Concordat.

The Basel Committee process has been more important, however, than any single, substantive agreement. The regular exchange of information, discussion of emerging problems, identification of best supervisory practices, and development of close personal relationships among bank supervisors has strengthened the international financial system in ways that outsiders will never be able to measure. This has been a major achievement in light of the fact that before 1974 most bank supervisors did not know their counterparts in other leading financial centers. The network of relationships established at the Basel Committee undoubtedly facilitates the flow of information in the event of a crisis and helps minimize spillovers.

The Basel Committee continues to wrestle with its original charge to make sure that no internationally active bank eludes effective supervision. The collapse of BCCI highlighted some continuing problems. First, it underlined the difficulty that supervisors face in dealing with a bank that changes its structure or conduct of business after it gains entry to a market. Inevitably, the supervisory authorities have more leverage over an institution before it is authorized to do business. Once an institution has gained entry, the burden of proof shifts to the host supervisory authorities. The standards for continuation of business are more difficult to enforce than standards for entry. It is seldom sufficient to know that an institution has become unsound;. it is necessary to prove it beyond reasonable doubt, because such decisions are inevitably challenged in court.

Second, the liquidation of BCCI has exposed conflicts in national bankruptcy laws that rest uncomfortably with the concept of consolidated supervision. Major countries such as France and the United States insist on ring fencing (or giving local residents first claim on) local assets of a failed institution, while some other countries such as the United Kingdom press for a global solvency standard that is more consistent with consolidated supervision.

Third, the collapse of BCCI discredited the polite fiction that countries are alike in their supervisory capacities and objectives. And it raised the question of how to accommodate international differences in the quality of banking supervision.

The latest revision of the Concordat, with its emphasis on minimum acceptable standards, marks a step away from the traditional Basel Committee emphasis on convergence. The United States has gone even further in implementing a unilateral approach in the Federal Deposit Insurance Corporation Improvement Act, which prevents foreign banks from doing business in the United States unless U.S. regulatory authorities have satisfied themselves that the banks are effectively regulated and supervised in their home countries. In the process, the United States has effectively exported its own supervisory standards to the rest of the world, a result that places a potentially much heavier regulatory burden on banks seeking to enter or to expand in the United States.

These developments suggest that banking supervisors should in the future consider cooperating, at least for internationally active banks, on three issues. First, if host countries insist on satisfying themselves about the quality of the parent country supervision, it may be possible to reduce compliance costs for these banks at least by harmonizing information requirements among countries. Second, it may be useful to develop an internationally coordinated procedure for supervising and certifying the quality of supervision. Third, the Basel Committee should encourage the harmonization of bankruptcy laws for unwinding the affairs of insolvent international banks.

What about further attempts to harmonize bank capital standards themselves? As we explained in chapter 4, the Basel Committee appears to be very intent on pursuing this goal, working to refine the initial standards so that they take account of the various risks that were essentially ignored in that first endeavor. We are more skeptical about the usefulness of this agenda.

There is no doubt that the initial Basel Accord represented a triumph of international financial diplomacy. The Accord also made a significant contribution toward improving disclosure. Important bank counterparties, such as corporate customers and other banks, have begun to focus on tier one capital ratios as a way of comparing the strength of internationally active banks. Moreover, in order to get the best possible price for new issues of equity and subordinated debt, some banks have voluntarily disclosed more information and information of better quality. And security analysts and ratings agencies continue to press for better disclosure. All of this has enhanced market discipline over the capital adequacy of internationally active banks.

But it is one thing to improve disclosure. It is quite another to expect that financial regulators from different countries can measure the myriad risks that banks face and attempt to impose uniform capital standards applicable to banks in all participating countries that reflect the various risks without distorting bank behavior. For example, concern over the growth of derivatives activity has intensified pressure for the regulatory authorities to extend the Accord to take account of market risk. The April 1993 proposal on market risks takes a very complicated and detailed approach to assigning risk weights that not only moves much further in the direction of micromanagement than the original Accord, but does so in a suboptimal way.[18] Although this regulatory initiative is motivated by concern that bank involvement in derivatives may exacerbate systemic risk, the outcome may be perverse. Inefficient regulation that stifles the development of derivatives may exacerbate systemic risk by impeding the ability of firms to hedge against adverse price movements in volatile markets. And it imposes extra costs on sophisticated firms, which are obliged to maintain two information systems, one to monitor the market risk defined by the regulators, the other to monitor the institution's actual risk exposure.

More fundamentally, however, we question the wisdom of further efforts to refine the initial Basel standards. Regulators are always trying to catch up with rapidly changing market practices. Internationally negotiated regulation will inevitably be even slower. International regulatory agreements are cumbersome to negotiate, implement, and revise. While it is easy to be enthusiastic about harmonizing the *right* rules, in a rapidly changing financial system there is a very real danger that the *wrong* rules will be harmonized, or that rules that may be *right* for the moment will become *wrong* after they are implemented. The complexity of international negotiations means that international agreements are very difficult to fine-tune after they are made because all parties are likely to find it costly to

18. For a critique of the proposal by a group of leading international banks see Institute of International Finance (1993).

reopen negotiations. This does not mean that national regulators should ignore market risks. Rather it means that efforts to develop internationally harmonized regulations may not be the best approach.

The first maxim of regulators should be: "Do no harm." But this dictum is often very difficult to live by. International harmonization of capital requirements for market risk may be premature because we simply do not know enough about how to quantify such risks and how market participants are likely to respond to alternative regulations.[19] This may be a case where there is value in regulatory diversity.

There are some indications that the Basel Committee may be retreating from its detailed April 1993 proposal for applying capital requirements to market risk. The Basel Committee may be willing to let banks use their own internal risk assessment models to assess the amount of capital needed to cover market risk.[20] Rather than specifying detailed risk weights, the regulators would specify the magnitude of the market shock that they expect banks to be able to withstand.[21] Banks would then simulate the impact of the shock on the market value of their positions. Banks would be required to maintain adequate capital to withstand the declines in market value produced by the specified market shocks. Examiners would assess the adequacy of the bank's simulation models and internal controls to ensure that they exceed minimum standards specified by the regulatory authorities.[22]

Because of uncertainty about the correct risk weights and how market participants may respond to new risk weights, we question the

19. The analogy to cooperation in fighting diseases is again instructive. Cooperation in that instance was achievable, in large part, because the participants had agreed on the likely consequences of alternative courses of action. In fast-moving financial markets, agreement has proven elusive.

20. Both Federal Reserve Governor Susan Phillips and Danièle Nouy, director of surveillance in the French Banking Commission, have commented that the Basel Committee is leaning toward accepting the banks' internal models as a way to assess market risks. See Acworth (1994, p. 2).

21. Guttentag and Herring advocated this approach to prudential supervision in Guttentag and Herring (1987, pp. 602–33).

22. Alan Greenspan suggests a way in which such an approach could be used to make sure that dynamic hedging strategies are prudently implemented, a supervisory concern noted in Chapter Three. "Some of the market shocks that regulators would specify would be instantaneous and, therefore, would generate large simulated losses on dynamically hedged options positions. The need to maintain capital to support these losses would strongly discourage undue reliance on dynamic hedging." See Testimony by Alan Greenspan (1994, p. 12).

usefulness of further extension of the rule-making function of the Basel Committee. Instead we believe the Committee should continue to place primary emphasis on its role as a forum in which supervisory authorities can exchange views about how best to measure and to control various sorts of risks. The July 1994 paper "Risk Management Guidelines for Derivatives" is a particularly good example of this approach.[23] In this paper, the Basel Committee describes best practice for sound management of derivatives activities for use by supervisory authorities and banks. Simultaneously, a parallel paper was issued by the International Organization of Securities Commissions (IOSCO), to securities regulators and securities firms.

Now that at least some minimum capital standards are in place, we would recommend that individual countries be given considerable discretion about how to set additional standards, if any, for other types of risk not yet covered by the Accord. We recognize, of course, that such a policy will not level the playing field across countries. But this was an illusory goal to begin with. Banks and other types of institutions are affected by too many other regulatory, tax, and cultural factors that differ between countries.[24] Attempts to defy this reality are likely to be self-defeating. Thus, even if bank capital standards could be truly harmonized, given the differences in supervisory attitudes toward asset valuation, countries can and almost certainly would continue to generate offsetting differences along other lines.

Some may argue that it would be ideal to move beyond the traditional Basel Committee process and to centralize supervision in some supranational regulatory agency with full powers to implement consolidated supervision. The political obstacles to this option are overwhelming. Members of the Basel Committee still experience impediments in simply sharing information. The prospect of surrendering sovereignty to some supranational entity is virtually unimagin-

23. Basel Committee on Banking Supervision (1994).

24. Hal Scott and Shinsaku Iwahara have undertaken a careful study of how the Basel Accord affected the competitive position of Japanese banks relative to U.S. banks. Scott and Iwahara (1994). In general they conclude that competitive advantages between banks in two countries are not primarily caused by differences in capital ratios, but by differences in other factors, especially by differences in implicit subsidies from official safety nets. Specifically they conclude that the Accord did not level the competitive playing field between Japanese and U.S. banks because it did not address other, more important sources of competitive advantage and it failed to deal with differences in accounting rules, balance sheet regulations, legal regimes, capital markets, and the enforcement of capital requirements.

able. Certainly a policy of greater autonomy is not without cost. But given the flawed alternatives of complete harmonization and the unrealistic prospect of a single international financial supervisory and regulatory authority, a minimum standards approach that provides greater national autonomy seems preferable.

In fact, such a policy may—and probably would—allow greater room for market discipline rather than regulation. We would welcome a greater emphasis on market discipline.

Rules for Securities Firms

For similar reasons, we are skeptical about the merits of extending the accord to encompass securities firms. While failures of securities firms may pose payments risks, they do so primarily because of their linkages with banks. But in this respect, securities firms do not differ from many other types of financial and nonfinancial institutions to which banks are exposed. We see no compelling case why the Accord should be extended to these other types of firms and believe the same logic applies to those firms involved in the securities business.

Although pleas for competitive equity create pressures for extending the same rules to all players, it is not clear that there is a compelling systemic risk rationale for doing so. If banks and securities firms pose different systemic threats to the international financial system, they need not be subject to the same rules. Consider an example from another sphere of government regulation. Suppose that a government has decided to impose a tax to control pollution and that it is considering how the tax should apply to two electric power plants—one that generates electricity from coal and emits substantial amounts of sulphur-dioxide and one that generates electricity from solar power. Some would argue that the same tax should apply to both producers to level the competitive playing field, but clearly this approach makes no sense if the objective is to control pollution.[25]

Securities firms differ from depository institutions in four important respects, as described in chapter 3. Nonetheless, regulators in many countries impose on securities firms capital requirements that vary directly with the open positions in financial claims assumed by securities firms. Moreover, IOSCO is attempting to harmonize these

25. See Schaefer (1992) for a similar argument.

requirements. The rationale is that in the event of a shock, such as the October 1987 worldwide stock market crash, institutions should be capitalized adequately to avert undermining confidence in the efficient functioning of markets.

Although the sharp drop in securities prices during October 1987 spread with alarming rapidity across national securities markets, few securities houses failed, and none of the failures was large enough to jeopardize other firms.[26] Moreover, when a major securities house, Drexel Burnham Lambert, collapsed in 1990, disruptions to the market were minimal.[27] This may, of course, be evidence that the regulatory authorities and market participants intervened adroitly to prevent a crisis or that the capital requirements and other regulations in place were adequate to absorb even the extraordinary shocks to the securities markets experienced during October 1987. But it may also indicate that the contagious transmission of shocks among securities houses is a less serious concern than the contagious transmission of shocks among depository institutions. Although we are skeptical about the merits of harmonized capital standards for securities firms, some may argue that there is a role for international—although not necessarily intergovernmental—action to deal with certain aspects of the securities business.

Clearing and Settlement

The possibility that a counterparty may fail before a transaction is settled means that participants must evaluate not only the security they wish to buy, but also the creditworthiness of the counterparty and the reliability of the clearing and settlement mechanism. Concern over the integrity of the clearing and settlement process can distort the prices of securities and disrupt the flows of funds.

Governments clearly have an interest in maintaining the integrity of both domestic and foreign clearing and settlement systems, playing a useful role in improving the clearing and settlements mechanism, as did the U.S. government, for example, when it developed the book-entry system for clearing and settling U.S. government securities. However, it should be noted that a private organization, the Group of

26. Loehnis (1990).

27. When the firm failed, the anticipated flight to quality in the government securities market was slight and quickly reversed, and the Dow Jones average actually finished the day (February 13, 1990) above the previous close.

Thirty, has taken the lead in pressing for improvements in the clearing and settlement process in national securities markets. The Group of Thirty has urged that private exchanges and governments reduce the time for matching and settlement of trades. The ultimate aim is the establishment of delivery-against-payment systems for settling financial transactions and the use of depositories, netting mechanisms, and standardized numbering systems to facilitate international transfers. The Basel Group of Experts on Payments Systems has also conducted useful studies identifying weaknesses in international clearing, settlement, and payments systems and suggesting remedies. This is clearly an area where the interests of governments and market participants overlap.

The integrity of clearing and settlement arrangements may well be the most significant potential source of negative externalities. This is an area in which there is broad international consensus on policy objectives and there are significant potential gains from cooperation.

Protection of Customers from Better-Informed Securities Firms

Central to the efficient operation of the financial markets is confidence in the financial information on which decisions are made.[28] Confidence that financial markets operate according to rules and procedures that are fair and transparent and that place the interests of investors first is a public good. It increases flows through financial markets and the effectiveness with which financial markets allocate resources across time and space. However, this public good is likely to be underproduced because the private return to securities firms that adhere to strict codes of conduct is likely to be less than the social return. Unethical firms may be able to ride free on the reputation established by ethical firms and take advantage of the relative ignorance of clients.

Small customers in particular may find it very difficult to evaluate the quality of financial information and services provided to them for their investment decisions. Indeed, even after a decision is made and financial results are announced, it is difficult to determine whether an unfavorable outcome was the result of bad luck, even though good advice was competently and honestly rendered, or the result of in-

28. This and the following sections draw heavily on Santomero, Herring, and Viotti (1991).

competence or dishonesty. Because it is so difficult to evaluate the quality of many financial services, customers are vulnerable to both adverse selection and moral hazard. Adverse selection is the possibility that customers will choose an incompetent or dishonest firm for investment or agent for execution of a transaction. Moral hazard is the possibility that firms or agents will put their own interests or the interests of one customer above those of another customer, or even engage in fraud. In short, uninformed customers are vulnerable to incompetence, negligence, and fraud.

The expectation of repetitive transactions with a client will give owners of some firms reason to be concerned about their reputations. This will reduce the risks to uninformed customers of adverse selection or moral hazard except when the expected gain from taking advantage of a client is very large or when the interests of a firm's employees differ from those of the owners. But primary reliance on a firm's concern about its reputation is not an entirely satisfactory solution to the problem of asymmetric information. Since it takes time to build a reputation for honest dealing, primary reliance on reputation to establish the quality of securities firms tends to restrict entry into the securities business. This may result in higher transactions costs than would prevail in a perfectly competitive market. For this reason it may be useful for regulators to establish fit and proper tests to provide an alternative way for securities firms to affirm their quality ex ante.

Ex post, strict enforcement of codes of conduct with civil and criminal sanctions will help maintain confidence in securities markets, instruments, and firms. It also provides securities firms with incentives to adopt administrative procedures that ensure that clients are competently and honestly served and that employees will behave in a way that upholds the firm's reputation. But different countries may apply different methods to achieving these objectives. We see no compelling evidence of undesirable spillovers across national boundaries from any differences in these approaches and therefore see no reason why they should be harmonized.

Protection of Investors from Better-Informed Issuers of Securities

Investors are often at an informational disadvantage with respect to issuers of securities. This too is a disadvantage that varies with the resources of the investor. Very large investors often have the leverage to compel an issuer to disclose relevant data and the expertise to analyze such data. Small investors may lack both the leverage and the expertise. For this reason it may be useful to standardize accounting practices, require the regular disclosure of data relevant to a firm's financial prospects, and encourage the development of rating agencies that enable even small investors to take advantage of economies of scale in gathering and analyzing data.

In most developed countries there has been a pronounced trend toward the institutionalization of savings: more and more money is being managed by fewer and fewer decisionmakers. Individuals increasingly place their savings with insurance companies, pension funds, or mutual funds rather than dealing directly in markets themselves. Because large institutions have the resources and the incentives to monitor securities firms and issuers carefully, problems associated with asymmetries in information are, perhaps, less important than they once were. Nonetheless, confidence in the integrity of financial markets—confidence that relevant information is available to all investors in a timely fashion and that securities houses place the interests of their customers first—is an important asset to a domestic financial market in the world competition for funds. Consumer protection measures differ widely among countries, reflecting differences in history, institutions, and social preferences. These issues, too, do not belong on the harmonization agenda.

Inefficient Regulation of Securities Markets

Not only may harmonized standards for securities be unnecessary, but ineptly applied regulations may produce perverse results. Capital requirements may be set higher than necessary to prevent systemic contagion and may serve as a barrier to entry that raises costs to users of financial services and generates supernormal profits for large firms. Similarly, fit and proper tests may be used to limit competition rather than to give assurances that all competitors are competent to perform services offered. Codes of conduct may be useful in protecting unsophisticated customers, but excessive monitoring and compliance costs may unnecessarily raise costs to users of financial services. The possibility that the wrong set of rules may be harmonized internationally, or that internationally harmonized rules may be especially difficult to change in response to dynamic market developments, provides a strong argument against international harmonization.

The costs of inefficient regulation are obviously of concern to providers of financial services, but they should also be of concern to users of financial services and to the public at large. Excessive regulatory costs may destroy the very markets they are intended to safeguard. Investors will face a truncated domestic menu of assets, firms may be unable to obtain cost-effective domestic financing, and domestic investment may diminish, thereby reducing a country's economic growth and undermining its international competitiveness. Regulatory diversity is especially valuable in this sphere. International competition among national regulators may provide a useful escape from repressive financial regulations.

Dealing with Financial Conglomerates

Whatever the choice of corporate structure, financial conglomerates that perform a basic banking function will inevitably be regulated in an attempt to mitigate potential social costs from bank failures, which were discussed in chapter 3. This is made even more likely by the perception of investors that the regulatory authorities will attempt to mitigate the effect of an abrupt bank failure. This undermines market discipline on bank risk taking. However, the form this regulation should take in a complex and competitive international market is unclear. Just as there are several different models for organizing a financial firm, there are several different approaches to regulating the financial industry or the activities that it conducts. How should regulation be organized in the global financial market, taking into account the benefits that the financial sector provides and the costs and benefits of regulation itself? This is still an open question.[29]

Two basic approaches are predominant in world markets: institutional regulation and functional regulation. In continental Europe, any institution that performs some of the functions of a banking firm is likely to be subject to bank regulation. This approach may be termed institutional regulation. In the United Kingdom, in contrast, the way any particular component of a financial services institution is regulated generally depends on the kind of business it does. This

29. Herring and Santomero (1990); and Herring (1993b).

approach may be termed functional regulation. Since Japan and the United States have not yet officially accepted the universal banking model, most commercial and investment banking functions are performed in separately incorporated entities, which are separately regulated. In these countries institutional regulation has been broadly congruent with functional regulation, but regulatory conflicts emerge as traditional functional distinctions blur.

These contrasting approaches to regulation give rise to a complex international regulatory framework. Within the current international regulatory maze, institutions are regulated differently even when they undertake the same kind of business.[30] These contrasting regulatory approaches create substantial competitive tensions, giving rise to demands for international harmonization of regulation to level the international playing field.

It is by no means clear how to harmonize the regulation of financial conglomerates if, indeed, that should be the goal. Both the functional and institutional approach have their merits.

Because functional regulation is more specialized, it is generally viewed as more sensitive to the particular features of a specific kind of business and is likely to pose lower barriers to entry by new firms. Since new entrants are often an important source of innovation, this may contribute to the dynamic efficiency of the financial system. Moreover, if the functions performed by institutions vary substantially over time, functional regulation may adapt more readily to changing market conditions. Functional regulation may provide a more stable regulatory framework than institutional regulation.[31]

When special-purpose firms take on multiple functions, however, the functional approach becomes increasingly awkward. In addition, functional supervision of a financial conglomerate tends to fragment prudential supervision and may enable a financial conglomerate to avoid regulation for some activities. If the soundness of the conglomerate as a whole (not just the conduct of particular functions by the

---

30. Four regulatory categories may be identified: (1) special-purpose firms, which are functionally regulated; (2) universal banks, which are institutionally regulated; (3) centrally managed groups of special-purpose institutions, which are subject to both institutional and functional regulation; and (4) centrally managed groups of special-purpose institutions, which are subject to functional regulation with regard to some activities but are free from regulation for most of their activities.

31. Merton (1989, pp. 225–61).

conglomerate) is of policy concern, this fragmentation may jeopardize the stability of the system.

Moreover, the functional approach risks disagreements among functional supervisors regarding the sharing of supervisory responsibilities and the level of capital adequacy each prefers. It also gives rise to the possibility of counterproductive disputes among regulators over enforcement prerogatives and a scramble for assets in the event that the conglomerate experiences financial difficulties. In order to avoid such problems functional supervisory authorities sometimes pressure a financial conglomerate to cordon off the particular functions they monitor and place them in a separately incorporated subsidiary, perhaps insulated from the rest of the conglomerate by fire walls. In effect, corporate structure tends to be dictated by regulatory convenience but at the social cost of some loss in efficiency.

In principle many of these problems could be mitigated by having only one regulator or designating one functional regulator to be a lead regulator charged with responsibility for overseeing the solvency of the financial conglomerate. The lead regulator would facilitate communication among different functional regulators and coordinate responses in the event of trouble. The lead regulator, in effect, would adopt an institutional view.

The United Kingdom has developed the lead regulator approach to harmonize the efforts of the numerous functional regulatory bodies that have emerged under its Financial Services Act.[32] Sweden is moving toward a single regulator approach by merging the Bank Inspection Board with the Insurance Supervisor. Both these approaches reduce the gaps and inconsistencies that may occur when functional regulation is applied to a conglomerate institution. Applying prudential supervision to the institution as a whole, however, may convey an impression to the market that the institution will receive official support in the event of difficulties. This weakens market discipline and may place specialized institutions at a competitive disadvantage.

Is it essential that the lead regulator supervise the safety and soundness of *all* activities of the conglomerate? Or can the lead regulator focus solely on the core banking businesses, which have traditionally been regarded as their fundamental charge? Should the

---

32. The United States faces an additional problem of harmonizing the activities of multiple regulators who supervise the same function.

conglomerate be subjected to prudential supervision on a consolidated basis even though there is no legal obligation to amalgamate the resources of the separately incorporated entities in the event of trouble? To some extent this depends on a judgment about whether a subsidiary of a financial conglomerate can fail without bringing down the rest of the conglomerate and undermining confidence in the financial system.

If the market can be convinced that legal separateness is meaningful—that subsidiaries or affiliates may be permitted to fail without precipitating the collapse of the parent or sister institutions—then prudential supervision may be quite selective and full consolidation will be unnecessary. This may also be the case if critical functions can be protected within a failing group. If, on the other hand, the market views the financial firm as indissoluble and the insulation provided by operational and legal separateness as illusory, then prudential supervision must take place on a consolidated basis. Otherwise the collapse of the firm may become contagious, undermining market confidence. Indeed, to the extent that fire walls inhibit the transfer of funds within the firm, the lead prudential supervisor of the financial conglomerate may seek to dismantle them because they jeopardize the safety and soundness of the conglomerate.

Gerald Corrigan, former president of the New York Federal Reserve Bank, has argued that expanding the allowable activity of banks requires that the authorities expand their regulatory net to include all activities of diversified financial institutions as well as all other institutions engaging in these activities. We are concerned that such an approach may undermine the efficiency of international financial markets. Moreover, in view of the evident difficulties that the authorities have experienced in supervising simpler institutions, it is difficult to be optimistic about their capacity to undertake such an ambitious task. We believe that concentrating regulatory attention on the basic banking function is likely to be more productive than broadening the focus to include the entire financial conglomerate. Accordingly, we favor regulating functions, not institutions, and confining the safety net to a limited menu of basic banking functions.

If the principal source of risk is the threat of a disruption of the payments system, then a minimalist strategy may be possible. If all transactionable accounts are collateralized and the collateral is marked to market daily, it may be possible to regulate strictly on a functional

basis. That is, requiring financial conglomerates to place their transactions activities in a narrow bank—either a separately chartered
subsidiary or a collateralized part of a conventional bank—would
permit those organizations to be freely involved in a wide range of
other kinds of activities, financial and nonfinancial, without threatening disruption of the payments system.

Such a narrow bank option has attracted increasing interest and
support in the United States.[33] We recognize that the concept has not
received careful study outside the United States, and for this reason
alone it could take many years for it to receive serious consideration
in the international regulatory community. Although we do not believe the idea has an imminent likelihood of acceptance, the narrow
bank concept neatly solves concerns regarding risks to the payments
system posed by financial conglomerates.

Finally, we take note of the fact that the Basel Committee recently
formed a group of securities regulators, insurance regulators, and
banking regulators to study problems in supervising global financial
conglomerates. The study group clearly faces a challenging agenda.
Regulatory traditions differ sharply among bank, securities, and insurance regulators. Relative to bank regulators, securities regulators
tend to be much more diverse. They include not only government
officials, but also organized exchanges and self-regulatory groups.
Unlike bank regulators or insurance regulators, securities regulators
tend to emphasize mark-to-market accounting and the liquidity of
assets. Securities regulators are happy to permit short-term instruments to count as capital. Their emphasis is on prompt and orderly
liquidation of a faltering institution more than on sustenance and
restoration. Securities regulators do not always perceive a need for
consolidated supervision, the central feature of the Basel Committee
approach.

Insurance regulators are still more heterogeneous than bank regulators or securities regulators. Indeed, there are profound differences
in approach between regulators of life insurance and regulators of
property and casualty insurance. Like bank regulators, insurance

33. For a sample of the literature, see Litan (1987); Herring and Santomero (1990);
Restructuring America's Financial Institutions: Report of a Task Force (1989); and Pierce
(1991). In addition, in 1992 a presidential-congressional commission on the causes of the
savings and loan crisis was the first official body to recommend narrow banking. See
National Commission on Financial Institution Reform, Recovery and Enforcement (1993).

regulators tend to take the long view rather than emphasizing the orderly unwinding of positions. In contrast to bank regulators, they tend to assess capital adequacy by looking at the liability side of regulated institutions rather than the asset side. Like securities regulators, they tend to discount the necessity of consolidated supervision.

The extension of the Basel process of identifying potential problems and best supervisory practices to this broader group of regulators is likely to improve the resiliency of the system. And regular meetings of functional regulatory authorities will undoubtedly foster personal relationships that will facilitate crisis management should it become necessary. But we hope that the committee will stop short of formulating rules to harmonize financial structure.

It should be expected that different countries will arrive at different conclusions regarding the appropriate corporate structure for financial conglomerates. For historical reasons, the Swiss view on the appropriate corporate structure of a financial conglomerate, for example, is unlikely to converge with the American view. We see no compelling prudential reason to force convergence.

Market Alternatives to Regulatory Harmonization

No matter what degree of international cooperation the authorities ultimately achieve, effective supervision faces severe limits, especially in an age of rapid financial innovation and increasing financial integration. Supervisors inevitably have much poorer information than the managers of the institutions they supervise. Moreover, they get that information with a time lag that is compounded by processing delays inherent in any bureaucratic structure. In most cases, if the managers of an institution want a particular risk profile, supervision and regulation cannot effectively keep them from attaining their objective. Moreover, the substantial difficulty in negotiating harmonization of bank regulations and supervisory practices suggests that it may be useful to place greater emphasis on harnessing market forces to help monitor safety and soundness.

In principle, impersonal market forces, unencumbered by the complex bargaining that is intrinsic to any international bureaucratic process, should be able to monitor the insolvency risk of banks more efficiently and discipline banks that take excessive risks. In practice two difficulties arise. First, depositors and creditors who feel protected by the safety net will lack the incentive to acquire and evaluate the appropriate information. This leaves only equity holders with the responsibility for monitoring the riskiness of their institutions. Can monitoring by shareholders compensate for slack monitoring by depositors and creditors? Shareholders do indeed have a strong interest in monitoring the expected profitability of banks, but their risk preferences will often diverge from those of depositors, creditors, and the supervisory authorities. The exposure of shareholders to downside risks is limited by their equity stake, but their potential upside gain includes all returns that exceed the amount promised to depositors and creditors. In contrast, depositors and creditors, including the official institutions that implicitly back up large institutions, must be concerned about the possibility of large losses that exceed the equity of shareholders. Moreover, they will not benefit from any potentially offsetting large gains. The upshot is that shareholders will generally prefer riskier portfolios than creditors, depositors, and the supervisory authorities, and this conflict of interest will worsen as the equity position of shareholders declines.

In the absence of a financial safety net, creditors and depositors will have an incentive to monitor managers to make sure that they are not taking risks that benefit shareholders at their expense. But if depositors and creditors feel protected by the financial safety net, shareholders are likely to take greater risks in order to take advantage of slack monitoring by depositors and creditors. This is one of the principal rationales for prudential supervision and official regulation of capital ratios: capital adequacy requirements counteract to some extent the pernicious moral hazard of the safety net. It also underlies our concern for greater clarity regarding lender-of-last-resort arrangements.

Second, many important international banks do not publicly disclose much information that is pertinent to evaluating safety and soundness. An indication of this problem is that in every country banks disclose much more information to the banking authorities than to the general public. The limited information they do disclose is generally not comparable across banks within the country, much less across banks in different countries. This may be a useful area for public policy intervention, but international harmonization of accounting standards and disclosure policy would involve most of the difficulties that have impeded harmonization of meaningful, risk-adjusted capital-asset ratios. It is not clear that efforts to harmonize disclosure would be more successful.

Nonetheless, pressure from the Basel Committee to raise capital adequacy ratios has led indirectly to some improvements in disclosure. In order to get the best possible price for new issues of equity and subordinated debt, some banks have voluntarily disclosed their hidden reserves. And security analysts continue to exert pressure for more and better-quality disclosure as they attempt to compare the profitability of firms based in different countries. Rating agencies are also becoming an important force for improving disclosure practices as banks attempt to tap sources of capital outside their domestic markets. Market participants increasingly focus on Tier I and Tier II capital ratios in evaluating internationally active banks.

Market discipline also could be increased by providing incentives for market participants to exercise closer scrutiny of financial institutions. The key incentive is fear of loss. As noted above, however, the safety net reduces the perceived vulnerability of creditors to loss. Changing this perception requires a clear change in regulatory behavior. Regulators must abolish the perception of guarantees for all creditors. This may be accomplished either by explicitly exempting some creditors from the protection of the safety net or requiring private third-party guarantees in addition to existing government support.

Formally withdrawing the safety net and publicly announcing that financial institutions will no longer benefit from implicit or explicit guarantees is the approach taken in New Zealand. Such a policy has proved easier to proclaim than to enforce, however.[34] The government must be willing to permit a failure and to sustain the consequences. As we noted earlier, governments have found it difficult to follow through on their announced intentions in the past. Thus market participants usually view such official proclamations with skepticism. They know too well that political pressure generally triumphs over principle in time of public crisis.

Another method of instilling discipline is to impose the de jure system of seniority that already exists between senior and subordinated debt. Faced with the prospect of loss, holders of subordinated

34. Guttentag and Herring (1987, pp. 150–218); and Herring (1991).

debt would have a strong incentive to monitor performance and to impose discipline. Indeed, their loss exposure and hence their perspective is like that of the deposit insurer.[35]

Moreover, discipline by subordinated debt holders is likely to be less destabilizing than discipline by depositors. Depositors tend to discipline banks largely by redeeming deposits for cash when concerns arise about the solvency of the institution. This kind of "quantity" discipline is like an on-off switch; it is very abrupt and may cause liquidity costs that make the expectation of an incipient insolvency a self-fulfilling prophecy. In contrast, holders of subordinated debt tend to discipline banks largely through the price at which they are willing to hold the outstanding stock of debt. Their opinions are registered moment by moment in secondary market prices. This kind of "price" discipline is more like a rheostat; the degree of discipline can be modulated to match the perceived risk.

If subordinated debt were assigned a repayment priority equal to that of deposit insurance, official prudential supervision would be usefully augmented by private market discipline. If, in addition, internationally active banks were obliged to roll over a proportion of their subordinated debt each quarter, then they would be obliged to face the continuing scrutiny of at least one category of creditors with a strong incentive to monitor insolvency risk carefully.

Finally, the regulatory authority may require that banks partially insure their deposits with private insurance companies. Although private insurance companies could not provide complete, fully credible deposit insurance against systemic risks, they could nonetheless reduce vulnerability to systemic problems by monitoring insolvency risk and setting appropriate risk premiums for the banks for which they provide reinsurance. Of all these proposals, we believe that a subordinated debt requirement for large banks would be the most fruitful to pursue at the international level. The Basel Accord already allows banks to meet one of their capital requirements (the Tier II standard) through subordinated debt. It would be a small, but highly useful step to make such a requirement mandatory. This would provide a healthy, stable source of market discipline instead of poten-

---

35. Horvitz (1983) first discussed the benefits of discipline by holders of subordinated debt.

tially destabilizing runs on deposits, which our proposed LLR pre-commitment policy would address.

Competitive Equity

Competitive equity has been a fundamental part of the rhetoric of international regulatory cooperation, but does it deserve an important place on the agenda? We believe the supervisory authorities should focus on systemic soundness, not on the attainment of a level playing field. Although economists may be sympathetic to this proposition, politicians and bankers tend to argue that the primary objective of international supervisory cooperation should be the creation of a level international playing field to enhance the international competitiveness of national financial institutions. Changes in the competitiveness of national financial institutions clearly affect the profitability of the institutions involved, but are there social gains that correspond to these private gains? Should it matter which shareholders own the efficient financial institutions so long as such institutions do not have market power and national residents have access to high-quality services at minimum cost?

In principle it is possible to separate the issue of fairness from the issue of competition. Competitive markets may be demonstrably unfair to particular institutions, but competitors may be injured without damaging competition. Pleas for competitive equity are often better regarded as requests for governmental assistance in reallocating wealth from one set of shareholders to another rather than as proposals to improve the efficiency of markets. When one set of shareholders is mainly foreign and the other domestic, moreover, national governments are likely to respond even though efficiency is not at stake.

In some instances, however, questions of competitive equity appear to have a direct bearing on efficiency. Most such instances involve the identification of some sort of interference by the domestic or foreign government, which may be interpreted as giving foreign competitors an artificial advantage. Examples include tax policy, accounting requirements, disclosure laws, implicit deposit guarantees, social overhead expenditures, employment restrictions, and any number of other policies. Domestic competitors argue that in the absence of such governmental interference they would gain market share. Government action is urged to offset or to terminate the artificial advantage enjoyed by foreign competitors. Similar arguments for fair trade have long been common in the manufacturing sector, but as international competition intensifies among international financial institutions, pleas for competitive equity are cropping up with increasing frequency in the financial services sector, too.

It is undoubtedly naive to expect that cosmopolitan public interest will motivate efforts to coordinate international supervision. Most research about why we have regulations and why regulations change suggests that regulatory agencies will inevitably be responsive to national interest; indeed, regulatory agencies will often be especially responsive to the interests of those institutions they regulate. Nonetheless, it should be emphasized that charging the supervisory authorities with the objective of creating a level international playing field will inevitably project them onto some very slippery slopes. The danger is that in attempting to move toward a level playing field, international cooperative efforts may slide away from the goal of enhancing the safety and soundness of the international financial system.

Comments

Yasuhiro Maehara

Richard Herring and Robert Litan have provided a comprehensive overview of financial regulation in the global economy and of the prospects for international cooperation. They cover a variety of important issues confronting financial regulators and central banks, offering a number of stimulating concepts for future discussion. First I would like to discuss the conceptual framework underlying, in my interpretation, their analysis of financial regulation, and then comment on the "future international regulatory agenda" described in chapter 5.

It appears that Herring and Litan base their analysis on the following three premises: first, regulators always lag behind market developments; second, regulations tend to create distortion in the efficient allocation of resources; and third, to maintain the safety and soundness of the international financial system without damaging the strength of financial innovation, market discipline should be used to the maximum extent possible.

I cannot agree more with the premise that the market mechanism is a better way to "monitor the insolvency risk of banks more efficiently and discipline banks that take excessive risks," as the authors argue. It can never be overemphasized, as the authors point out, that the central challenge for financial regulators is "to minimize systemic

Yasuhiro Maehara is chief representative, Bank of Japan, Washington office. The views expressed here are those of the author and do not necessarily represent those of the Bank of Japan.

risks without dampening useful innovation or encouraging counter-productive innovation." In this light, the role of the authorities is to implement prudential policy with a view to the better functioning of the market mechanism. As Gerald Corrigan, former president of the New York Federal Reserve Bank, said, the role of prudential policy is to help "establish an overall framework within which individual institutions can compete and flourish, but do so in a context that protects the safety and stability of the system as a whole."[1]

Prudential policy is generally defined as a collection of policies, including both regulation and supervision, designed to maintain the safety and soundness of the financial system. These policies fall into various classifications. For example, a distinction can be made between micro prudential policy, which attempts to motivate the prudential management of individual financial institutions and macro prudential policy, which intends to improve the stability and efficiency of the financial system as a whole. Micro prudential policy includes supervision of individual institutions and the lender-of-last-resort function of a central bank vis-à-vis a troubled institution. Macro prudential policy relates to such measures as the safe and efficient functioning of a payment and settlement system for minimizing systemic risks and a deposit insurance system to protect small depositors.

There is another type of classification, namely, ex-ante or ex-post prudential policy. Ex-ante prudential policy includes portfolio regulations such as capital standards and supervision. It aims at laying the foundation for prudent management of financial institutions and preventing the emergence of systemic risks. Ex-post prudential policy, such as the deposit insurance system and the lender-of-last-resort function of a central bank, primarily attempts to deal with systemic problems once they occur.

Of course, such a classification cannot be as clear-cut as is described in the effect of ex-post prudential policy. For example, the lender-of-last-resort function of a central bank categorized as ex-post prudential policy is said to have an ex-ante effect on the behavior of large banks in their funding and risk management mainly because it tends to create a perception that large banks are protected by the central bank in times of difficulties—the so-called "too big to fail" problem. The deposit insurance system, by guaranteeing deposits up

1. Corrigan (1990, p. 42).

to a certain limit, also has an ex-ante effect of preventing depositors from becoming panicky.

However, I think this distinction between ex-ante and ex-post prudential policy often becomes useful and relevant in examination of the regulatory agenda in both domestic and international contexts. For example, Herring and Litan argue that "if central banks prudently exercise their responsibilities as lenders of last resort, they can significantly reduce or even eliminate the threat of a systemic crisis." In order to reduce the threat of a systemic crisis, I think it is more appropriate to implement ex-ante prudential policy, not ex-post policy such as the lender-of-last-resort function.

Within ex-post policy, different measures have different intermediate objectives. The authors argue, "In principle, deposit insurance is not necessary to protect against contagion as long as the monetary authorities faithfully carry out their lender-of-last-resort responsibilities." Deposit insurance is a policy to protect small depositors in the event of a bank failure, while the lender-of-last resort function aims at maintaining the safety and soundness of the financial system as a whole. They are different in their intermediate policy objectives; they are not either-or policy measures. Since both create moral hazard, it is important for the authorities to achieve an appropriate combination of these two policies in a given situation to cope with the emergent contagion risk while minimizing moral hazard.

The effect of international harmonization on corporate structure may be different when we distinguish between ex-ante and ex-post prudential policy. The ex-ante prudential policy such as internationally agreed capital standards exemplified in the Basel Accord tends to have a large effect on corporate structure for financial institutions, which in turn affects their competitiveness in the respective countries. Though different countries might have different corporate structures, it would be desirable to level the playing field among financial institutions of various countries in a globally integrated market to avoid the endless competition between creating loopholes and making additional regulations. Therefore, "a minimum standards/greater autonomy option," which the authors consider preferable with regard to the activities of the Basel Committee, should be used in harmonization of the regulatory aspect of ex-ante prudential policy. Implementation of ex-post prudential policy is very much linked to historical, institutional, and social preferences, which differ widely among countries.

Furthermore, it tends to entail moral hazard, and the efforts toward wrong harmonization may exacerbate moral hazard. Though differences in the ex-post policy may lead to an "unlevel playing field," as Herring and Litan argue in the case of deposit insurance, any attempt to harmonize the ex-post prudential policy should be treated with utmost caution.

It is true that regulators and central banks tend to lag behind market developments. The authors assert, "Regulators are always trying to catch up with rapidly changing market practices." Regulators and central banks could not fully perceive the risks involved in the loans to less-developed countries and commercial real estate lending in the 1970s and 1980s. Neither could many banks at that time, I suspect. Furthermore, the authors correctly note, "Supervisors inevitably have much poorer information than the managers of the institutions they supervise. Moreover, they get that information with a time lag that is compounded by processing delays inherent in any bureaucratic structure." By compiling and analyzing the data of banks under their jurisdiction, however, regulators and central banks have an advantage over the private sector in obtaining a comprehensive picture of the development on an industry base in a relatively timely manner—more timely than generally expected—and in making an analysis from the viewpoint of prudential policy. This informational advantage, I think, is an important basis for implementing prudential policy effectively.

Herring and Litan took up five of the items on the unfinished international regulatory agenda: emergency liquidity assistance; the Basel Committee initiatives; harmonized standards for securities firms; the treatment of international financial conglomerates; and the role of market discipline.

Regarding the emergency liquidity assistance for internationally active banks, the authors advocate the following proposals: The lender-of-last-resort functions should explicitly acknowledge all the specific banks for which they recognize responsibility, without committing themselves to any course of emergency action; and central banks should announce publicly how responsibilities for dealing with liquidity problems of internationally active banks are apportioned. In relation to the second proposal, the revised Concordat of 1983 describes the apportionment of supervisory responsibility of liquidity, not the lender-of-last resort aspects of the role of central banks. For branches and subsidiaries, primary responsibility should rest with the host authority. The Concordat further stipulates that "within the framework of consolidated supervision, parent authorities have a general responsibility for overseeing the liquidity control systems employed by the banking groups they supervise and for ensuring that these systems and the overall liquidity control systems employed by the banking groups they supervise and for ensuring that these systems and the overall liquidity position of such groups are adequate."[2] I think this is the most that can be achieved from a practical viewpoint considering the "differences in local regulations and market situations as well as the complications of banks operating in different time zones and different currencies"[3] and the requirement that liquidity assistance must be provided in a prompt and timely manner.

I have rather strong reservations about the first proposal of explicit commitment policy. First of all, how can central banks reasonably determine a priori which bank should be covered by the lender-of-last-resort function and which bank should not? Herring and Litan seem to suggest that the size of a bank can be used as a yardstick for this classification. Size may be one criterion, but it certainly is not the only one. The lender-of-last-resort function should cover those banks that are "important" in various aspects including not only size but also character and the extent of their involvement in payments and settlement systems and international operations.[4] The importance of a certain bank would certainly change from time to time in a rapidly changing and globally integrated market. Therefore, the explicit commitment policy seems too mechanical in the rapidly changing financial environment.

In the description of the October 1987 stock market crash, the authors stated that "the Fed pressured major banks to continue their lending to securities firms, providing assurances that it would make liquidity available if necessary. More generally, the Fed immediately injected reserves into the banking system, bringing down interest

2. Committee on Banking Regulations and Supervisory Practices (1983, p. 8).
3. Committee on Banking Regulations and Supervisory Practices (1983, p. 8).
4. Corrigan stated, "Indeed, the experience with Herstatt and its long and painful aftermath seems to have provided the authorities in all countries with a lasting impression of the grave dangers associated with the sudden and uncontrolled collapse of an important financial institution, especially one with significant although again, not large by today's standards international operations." Corrigan (1990, p. 13).

rates." I think this injection of reserves into the banking system as a whole contributed greatly to restoring confidence in the financial system. Such an experience suggests that the explicit commitment policy targeting only a fixed segment of the financial system may not be an effective way to mitigate systemic risks.

If the explicit commitment policy is neither appropriate nor practical, what should be a policy for emergency liquidity assistance? I do not think there is a best policy. A policy of "constructive ambiguity" creates moral hazard. The explicit commitment policy would also create moral hazard even if publicly traded subordinated debt were introduced.[5] As long as a central bank makes a commitment, whether it is explicit or implicit, for liquidity assistance, moral hazard is bound to be created. As the experience of the 1987 stock market crash showed, the effectiveness of a policy for emergency liquidity assistance seems to rest on market confidence in the overall ability of a central bank, rather than on the explicit commitment by a central bank. Therefore, provided a central bank can maintain market confidence, which can be enhanced by effective supervision, I tend to support a policy of constructive ambiguity as the second-best policy mainly from the operational point of view.

I share the authors' view that there are limits to the Basel Committee initiatives in internationally agreeable rule making. This has been recognized by the Basel Committee itself. The Basel Committee has been and is a forum where central bankers and other supervisory authorities meet to discuss the issues of common concern, and its spirit lies in a pragmatic approach of recommending guidelines of "best practices which all members have undertaken toward implementing, according to the means available to them."[6] In this sense, the Basel Committee has been since its inception an information clearinghouse and "a forum in which supervisory authorities can exchange views about how best to measure and to control various sorts of risks," as the authors maintain. In this light, I agree with the authors' suggestion that the Basel Committee should work toward the

5. The authors contend that "depositors exercise only limited discipline against large banks in practice." This may be true for individual depositors, but experience indicates that large depositors, particularly interbank depositors, seem able to exert a strong influence over the management of a bank accepting these deposits. Furthermore, I suspect that holders of subordinated debt face a kind of asymmetry in downside risks and upside gains similar to that experienced by shareholders.

6. For example, Basel Committee on Banking Supervision (1990, p. 1).

harmonization of information requirements and the coordination of supervisory procedures, particularly to strengthen consolidated supervision. The harmonization of bankruptcy laws among countries should perhaps proceed more cautiously because it is deeply embedded in the historical and social setting of the respective countries.

It is important that the Basel Committee continues its efforts to refine the initial capital standards to make them take account of various risks that were not originally incorporated. Market risks exist, and they should not be left alone simply because supervisors do not know enough about them. Supervisors are now making tremendous efforts to understand the nature of these risks and to find a better way to measure them through close communications with banks. In the globally integrated market, multidimensional minimum standards incorporating various risks are necessary and useful for both supervisors and internationally active banks.

The most important area that needs international cooperation is the clearing and settlement system. The authors correctly point out, "The integrity of clearing and settlement arrangements may well be the most significant potential source of negative externalities." Both the public and the private sector have made a lot of progress in this area, and we should encourage further efforts toward a safer and more efficient clearing and settlement system. Securities firms are inextricably more involved in the clearing and settlement system than any other financial and nonfinancial institutions. As intermediaries in securities markets, they tend to hold a large quantity of securities portfolios at a given time, and they are more vulnerable than large banks to large and sudden fluctuations of prices, which may sometimes wipe out their net worth. In a tightly integrated global capital market, contagion risks are real rather than mere perception. The authors are skeptical about the merits of harmonized capital standards, but I think it is desirable to establish some kind of harmonized capital standards for securities firms. As the authors argue, these standards do not have to be the same as those for banks. However, given that securitization is progressing on a global basis and that both banks and securities firms are important intermediaries in the globally integrated financial market, capital standards should be based on common principles aimed at strengthening prudent management of individual institutions and promoting stability in the financial system. As the authors assert, confidence in the efficient functioning of markets should not be undermined by doubts about the solvency of important market intermediaries.

Another important area the authors point out is the harmonization of accounting standards and disclosure. I agree that market forces such as the demand by institutional investors for greater uniformity would put strong pressure toward greater harmonization on national systems. Nevertheless, coordination and cooperation as well as encouragement by the authorities across countries would contribute to promoting greater harmonization of accounting standards and disclosure initiated by the private sector.

The key question from the viewpoint of prudential policy is whether the failure of part of a financial conglomerate poses a risk of contagion to the rest of the conglomerate, thereby undermining confidence in the financial system as the authors suggest. I think this question of separateness is not only legal but also a matter of perception. If a subsidiary of a financial conglomerate fails, and if the market views the financial firm as indissoluble, large systemic risk will likely emerge. There is no guarantee that the strong fire wall between subsidiaries of the financial conglomerate will provide enough insulation for the market perception of separateness in times of severe financial distress. The fire wall may provide enough insulation, but we cannot take the risk of letting the whole process get out of hand since the social and economic cost of financial disruption is too high for this kind of indulgence. I take the view that prudential supervision must take place on a consolidated basis. Even though regulatory authorities may face limits in providing effective supervision, and they should not be optimistic about their capacity, it is their responsibility to do their best in not allowing such systemic risks to emerge in relation to financial conglomerates.

In the context of functional regulation, Herring and Litan propose a "narrow bank" option to minimize the threat of a disruption of the payments system. This option assumes that separateness of the financial conglomerate is possible. Even though I do not agree with the view that such separateness is possible, a narrow bank is an important concept, which raises one of the fundamental questions about what banking function is and what banks are, and should be examined in a broader context.

Banks have been regarded as special in the sense that they offer transactions accounts as a means of payment. However, as deregulation, computer technology, and communications progress, the competitive position of banks in providing payment services has been gradually eroded by the development of such alternative instruments as money market mutual funds. There still appear to remain psychological differences between payment services offered by banks and those offered by nonbanks. Yet there is a growing recognition that "banks are now far less 'special' than they once were."[7] There seems less and less reason why financial intermediaries other than banks cannot provide payment services, and the trend for nonbank financial intermediaries to offer payment services is accelerating. It seems important that the authorities strengthen their consolidated supervision to minimize the risk of a disruption of the payments system.

Finally, as I stated at the outset, I fully agree with the authors' premise that the better way to efficiently monitor the financial condition of banks and discipline the management of banks is to "place greater emphasis on discipline by the market rather than by regulators." Ultimately, the responsibility for minimizing systemic risks without dampening useful innovation rests with the self-discipline of financial institutions in their risk management imposed by the market mechanism. There are various ways to strengthen such self-discipline. It is a problem of corporate governance for financial institutions. Furthermore, as the authors suggest, "more timely disclosure of meaningful financial information" and "harmonization of financial reporting systems" are an important ex-ante ingredient in improving market discipline. Lowering the barriers to entry into financial services across countries should also be promoted to enhance competition and strengthen market discipline. In this regard, formal agreement of the GATT Uruguay Round on Financial Services is very much called for.

Financial institutions provide society with public goods such as the payments and settlement system. To the extent that they provide the public goods, there is a role for the authorities to play to protect against systemic risks. Toward this end, the authorities conduct prudential policy. Ex-ante prudential policy includes portfolio regulations and consolidated supervision. I think the regulatory aspects of such a policy should be harmonized across countries according to the principle of "minimum standards/greater autonomy." Ex-post pruden-

7. Greenspan (1993, p. 2).

tial policy such as the deposit insurance system and the lender-of-last-resort function of a central bank requires more communication, more cooperation, and more coordination among the authorities of various countries. The authorities should always be mindful that their ability is limited and that the aim of prudential policy is to maximize market discipline while minimizing systemic risks inherent in a globally integrated financial system.

Richard Webb

As a sailor examines the color of the sky to tell the weather, so the economist studies the balance of payments, chanting, "Foreign trade up—let's raise the cup. International finance is expanding—watch out for the landing."

Foreign trade and payments are both rising, but international financial transactions grew much faster than world trade over the past two decades. This is the starting point for Richard Herring and Robert Litan, and it helps to explain the focus of their paper. Usually economists favor even more rapid liberalization and cross-border integration. Herring and Litan, however, concentrate in their paper on the regulatory issues posed by the growth that is already occurring. That growth, they argue, has been driven by technological change and market forces. Deregulation has aided and abetted the expansion, but the driving forces, they say, have been technology and the market. Indeed, policymakers have been motivated to urge liberalizing and harmonizing steps by the realization that accommodation and partial surrender were necessary to salvage some regulatory control more than by a desire to further unleash the market.

The concern expressed by Herring and Litan may be paradoxical, but it is highly appropriate. Financial activity produces services that are consumed by households and that are also critical inputs to current production and to investment. As in any other productive sector, the output of financial services is cheapened, improved, and increased by specialization and by trade across borders. The peculiarly vital role of finance as an input, however, has made it prone to intervention; authorities everywhere have seen in finance a lever to improve one or another aspect of economic or social life, and the resulting regulatory zeal has been a barrier to specialization and to trade in the sector.

But the principal historical reason for the high level of regulation of financial activity and for the nervous reactions to rapid change in the sector is that finance is more than a producer of building blocks for economic activity; it is also the floor of the edifice. Herring and Litan have that collective good role in mind in their repeated references to

Richard Webb is a nonresident senior fellow in foreign policy studies at the Brookings Institution. He is working on a *History of the World Bank as a Development-Promoting Institution.*

systemic risk as a motive for regulation, and, even more clearly, when they define their terms of reference: "This book focuses on . . . measures designed to protect the safety and soundness of the financial system."

Since a discussion of financial stability raises both micro and macro questions, and because it is central to the entire theme of the larger study, Integrating the World Economy, the issue naturally crops up in other topics covered by the project. More especially, it is the subject of a full monograph by Ralph Bryant on macroeconomic policy coordination. Within that context Herring and Litan set the boundaries for their own book, taking the problem of exchange rate uncertainty, along with its underlying fiscal, monetary, terms of trade, and other roots, as exogenous facts of life and turning instead to an examination of more micro aspects of financial policy and regulation. Thus, when Herring and Litan measure the degree of integration already achieved by financial markets, using a helpful scale that is both conceptually clear and, in part, observable in market interest rates and premiums, they find that markets have gone a long way in surmounting the reduced, post-deregulation barriers, achieving a substantial degree of integration—up to the very edges of the mountain of exchange rate uncertainty. "Uncertainty over changes in the nominal exchange rate thus prevents the major industrial countries from reaching [a higher] level of integration," they conclude, passing the baton, as it were, to Ralph Bryant and the Bretton Woods Commission.

Yet the Herring and Litan study bears on the stabilization issue in a major way: financial instability is produced by an interaction between turns on the macroeconomic road and the internal, often volatile, dynamics of the financial sector vehicle. Two decades of financial integration have contributed to an even further weakening in the already imperfect capacity of authorities to dampen the financial sector's volatile responses to macroeconomic changes. The financial expansion produced by deregulation, market innovation, and cross-border financial transactions did not, of course, take the form of central bank liabilities. The growth occurred instead in money substitutes or noncentral bank liabilities, thus reducing the share of the financial market under direct control by the monetary authorities and increasing the need for indirect ways to exercise control over the nonmonetary components of M2 or M3.

The authors take up that challenge and pose one of the principal policy questions for the Integrating National Economies project: what can authorities do, at both the national and the international levels, to recover, to maintain, or to increase control over financial sector behavior to minimize instability? They review the record on regulatory modes and experience with regard, for instance, to capital requirements to strengthen institutions, to international cooperation to close gaps in the regulatory net, and to central bank commitments—or lack thereof—to bank depositors. In these and other pieces of the financial sector and of its regulatory machinery, they provide a guide for the policy efforts that must be directed at reducing the internal instability of the financial vehicle in a more fully integrated world. And the need for that guide is greater to the extent that advance toward international macroeconomic coordination continues to appear remote.

Though much of the book focuses on system stability, the authors discuss other aspects of financial integration and regulatory objectives. With instability on the cost side of an integration cost-benefit calculus, the principal expected benefits are allocative efficiency and aggregate savings and investment. These two potential and widely expected outcomes of economic integration, however, get little attention from the authors. The question of allocative efficiency is largely put aside with an early and explicit assumption that "restrictions against cross-border financial transactions are almost always unwise . . . impeding the transfer of resources to their best uses," and by references to other literature on the topic. The authors do note, however, cases where the level playing field norm may conflict with other regulatory objectives. The effect of integration on national savings and investment rates similarly receives only brief mention, in a reference to the strong correlation between national savings and investment rates. That observation suggests that the large and growing volume of international financial transactions has, for the most part, served a monetary and savings function, rather than a real investment purpose.

Perhaps it is as a former central banker that I find myself in considerable agreement with the authors' priorities, as expressed in their emphasis on stability, on the need for regulatory advances to keep up with the growing risks produced by financial growth and integration, and in their constructive discussion of the possibilities for improved regulation. I would, in fact, argue the need for an even greater concern. The authors' starting point—two decades of much faster growth in international transactions than in trade—brings to mind the recent debate regarding the sequencing of the financial and trade liberalization that took place in Chile, Argentina, and Uruguay during the 1970s. Over that period financial flows grew far more rapidly than trade, which in turn far outpaced the adjustment of regulation. During the succeeding decade, each of those countries suffered severe financial instability and collapse in production and incomes. Economists have concluded that a wiser course would have been for liberalization in trade to precede liberalization of financial flows. This piece of new conventional wisdom has no application to the broader situation addressed by Herring and Litan, in which financial integration has been driven principally by markets rather than by policymakers. But if financial integration cannot now be rolled back, nor, probably, slowed down, the Southern Cone experience can at least serve as a reminder that, in the financial sector, growth and allocative improvements are sometimes bought at a high price in instability.

Appendix

Permissible Activities for Banking Organizations in Various Financial Centers

See table on following pages.

Country	Securities	Insurance
Belgium	Unlimited; some activities through subsidiaries	Unlimited through subsidiaries
Canada	Unlimited through subsidiaries	Unlimited through subsidiaries
France	Unlimited	Unlimited, usually through subsidiaries
Germany	Unlimited	Unlimited, but only through insurance subsidiaries
Italy	Unlimited, but not permitted to operate directly on the stock exchange	Limited to 10% of own funds for each insurance company and 20% aggregate investment in insurance companies
Japan	Permitted through subsidiaries except for equity brokerage for the time being; banks allowed to own more than 50% of a securities subsidiary	Not permitted
Netherlands	Unlimited	Unlimited through subsidiaries
Sweden	Unlimited	Unlimited
Switzerland	Unlimited	Unlimited through subsidiaries
United Kingdom	Unlimited, usually through subsidiaries	Unlimited through subsidiaries
United States	Limited, through affiliates	Generally not permitted

Source: *Thompson's International Banking Register*, October 25, 1993, pp. 6–9.

Real estate	Bank investments in industrial firms	Industrial firm investments in banks
Generally limited to holding bank premises	Single shareholding may not exceed 10% of bank's own funds, and such shareholdings on basis may not exceed 35% of own funds	Unlimited, but subject to previous approval of authorities
Unlimited through subsidiaries	Permitted to hold up to 10% interests, with aggregate share-holdings not to exceed 70% of bank's capital	Permitted to hold up to 10% interests
Unlimited	Permitted with regulatory approval of interests in excess of 10%	Not prohibited, but such investments are generally not made
Permitted, subject to limits based on bank's capital; unlimited through subsidiaries	Limited to 15% of bank's capital; in aggregate limited to 60% of bank's capital	Permitted (subject to regulatory consent based on suitability of the shareholder)
Generally limited to holding bank premises	Not permitted	Permitted up to 15% of shares of the bank, subject to approval of the Bank of Italy
Generally limited to holding bank premises	Limited to holding 5% interests	Permitted, provided total investment does not exceed investing firm's capital or net assets
Unlimited	Subject to regulatory approval for voting shares in excess of 10%	Subject to regulatory approval for voting shares in excess of 5%
Generally limited to holding bank premises	Limited	Not prohibited, but such investments are generally not made
Unlimited	Unlimited	Not prohibited, but such investments are generally not made
Unlimited	Permitted subject to consultations with the Bank of England	No prohibitions contained in the Banking Act of 1987
Generally limited to holding bank premises	Permitted to hold up to 5% of voting shares through a holding company	Permitted to make noncontrolling investments up to 25% of voting shares

References

Acworth, William. 1994. "Derivatives Battle Renewed as U.S. Officials Push Bills." *International Banking Regulator* 6 (July 18).

Adler, Michael, and Bruce Lehmann. 1973. "Deviations from Purchasing Power Parity in the Long Run." *Journal of Finance* 38 (December): 1471–87.

Alesina, Alberto, Vittorio Grilli, and Gian Maria Milesi-Ferretti. 1993. "The Political Economy of Capital Controls." NBER Working Paper No. 4353 (May).

Aliber, Robert Z. 1973. "The Interest Rate Parity Theorem: A Reinterpretation." *Journal of Political Economy* 81 (November/December): 1451–59.

Bank for International Settlements. 1982. "Report on International Developments in Banking Supervision, 1981." Basel.

———. 1986. *Recent Innovations in International Banking.* Basel.

———. 1989. *59th Annual Report.* Basel.

———. 1990. *60th Annual Report.* Basel.

———. 1992. *Recent Developments In International Interbank Relations.* Basel.

———. 1993. *Central Bank Survey of Foreign Exchange Market Activity in April 1992.* Monetary and Economic Department. Basel.

Barth, Jarvis R., R. Dan Brumbaugh, and Robert E. Litan. 1992. *The Future of American Banking.* New York: M. E. Sharpe.

Basel Committee on Banking Regulations and Supervisory Practices. 1983. "Principles for the Supervision of Banks' Foreign Establishments." May.

———. 1985. "Report on International Developments in Banking Supervision, 1984." Basel.

Basel Committee on Banking Supervision. 1990. "Supplement to the Concordat: The Ensuring of Adequate Information Flows between Banking Supervisory Authorities." April.

———. 1992. "Report on International Developments in Banking Supervision." Report No. 8. September.

Benston, George J. 1993. "International Harmonization of Banking Regulations and Cooperation Among National Regulators: An Assessment." Emory University (June 27).

171

Benston, George J., and George L. Kaufman. 1988. "Regulating Bank Safety and Performance." In *Restructuring Banking and Financial Services in America*, edited by William S. Haraf and Rose Marie Kushmeider, 63-99. Washington: American Enterprise Institute.

Benston, George J., and others. 1989. *Restructuring America's Financial Institutions*. Brookings.

Bernanke, Ben S. 1983. "Nonmonetary Effects of the Financial Crisis in the Propagation of the Great Depression." *American Economic Review* 73 (June): 257–76.

———. 1990. "Clearing and Settlement during the Crash." *The Review of Financial Studies* 3 (1): 133–51.

Blustein, Paul. 1993. "'Real-Name' Policy Carries Real Costs." *Washington Post* October 21, p. D9.

Board of Governors, Federal Reserve System. *Flow of Funds Accounts*. Various issues.

Borio, C. E. V., and O. Van den Bergh. 1993. "The Nature and Management of Payment System Risks: An International Perspective." Bank for International Settlements Economic Papers, no. 36 (February).

Brittan, Sir Leon. 1990. "Opening World Banking Markets." Speech at the American Enterprise Institute. Washington. March 23.

Bröker, G. 1989. *Competition in Banking: Trends in Banking Structure and Regulation in OECD Countries*. Paris: Organization for Economic Cooperation and Development.

Bryant, Ralph C. 1987. *International Financial Intermediation*. Brookings.

Campbell-Smith, Duncan. 1982. "Clues Top a Banking Scandal." *Financial Times*, August 5, p. 16.

Catinant, M., E. Eonnai, and A. Italianer. 1988. "The Competition of the International Market: Results of Macroeconomic Model Simulations." In *The Cost of Non-Europe*, vol. 2, chap. 10. Luxembourg: Office of Official Publications of the European Community.

Cooke, W. Peter. 1981. "Developments in Co-operation among Banking Supervisory Authorities." *Bank of England Quarterly* 21 (June): 238–44.

———. 1990. "International Convergence of Capital Adequacy Measurement and Standards." In *The Future of Financial Systems and Services*, edited by Edward P. M. Gardner, 310–35. London: Macmillan.

Cooper, Richard N. 1986. *Economic Policy in an Interdependent World: Essays in World Economics*. MIT Press.

———. 1989. "International Cooperation in Public Health as a Prologue to Macroeconomic Cooperation." In *Can Nations Agree: Issues In International Cooperation*, edited by Richard N. Cooper and others, 178–254. Brookings.

Corrigan, E. Gerald. 1990. "Statement (with Appendices) before the United States Senate Committee on Banking, Housing and Urban Affairs," May 3.

Cumby, Robert, and Maurice Obstfeld. 1984. "International Interest Rate and Price Level Linkages under Flexible Exchange Rates: A Review of Recent Evidence." In *Exchange Rate Theory and Practice*, edited by John F. O. Bilson and Richard C. Marston, 121–51. University of Chicago Press.

Dale, Richard. 1984. *The Regulation of International Banking.* Prentice-Hall.

———. 1992. *International Banking Deregulation: The Great Banking Experiment.* Oxford: Blackwell Finance.

Doty, James R. 1992. "The Role of the Securities and Exchange Commission in an Internationalized Market Place." *Fordham Law Review* 60 (May): 80.

"EC Single Market in Financial Services." 1993. *Bank of New England Quarterly Bulletin* 33 (February): 92–97.

Feldstein, Martin, and Charles Horioka. 1980. "Domestic Saving and International Capital Flows." *Economic Journal* 90 (June): 314–29.

Frankel, Jeffrey. 1991. "Quantifying International Capital Mobility in the 1980s." In *National Saving and Economic Performance,* edited by Douglas Bernheim and John B. Shoven. University of Chicago Press.

———. 1992. "Measuring International Capital Mobility: A Review." *American Economic Review* 82 (May): 197–202.

Frankel, Jeffrey, and Alan MacArthur. 1988. "Political vs. Currency Premia in International Real Interest Rate Differentials: A Study of Forward Rates for 24 Countries." *European Economic Review* 32 (June): 1083–114.

Franks, Julian R., and Walter N. Torous. 1993. "A Comparison of the U.K. and the U.S. Bankruptcy Codes." *Journal of Applied Corporate Finance* 6 (Spring): 95–103.

Freund, William C. 1993. "That Trade Obstacle, the SEC." *Wall Street Journal* August 27, p. A6.

Friedland, John H. 1994. *The Law and Structure of the International Financial System: Regulation in the United States, EEC, and Japan.* Westport, Conn.: Quorum Books.

Fukao, Mitsuhiro. 1993. "International Integration of Financial Markets and the Cost of Capital." Economics Department Working Paper No. 128. Paris: Organization for Economic Cooperation and Development.

———. Forthcoming. *Financial Integration, Corporate Governance, and the Performance of Multinational Companies.* Brookings.

Giavazzi, Francesco, and Alberto Giovannini. 1989. *Limiting Exchange Rate Flexibility: The European Monetary System.* MIT Press.

Gilbert, Alton R. 1989. "Payments System Risk: What Is It and What Will Happen If We Try to Reduce It?" *Federal Reserve Bank of St. Louis Review* 71 (January/February): 3–17.

Goldstein, Morris, Donald J. Mathieson, and Timothy Lane. 1991. *Determinants and Systemic Consequences of International Capital Flows: A Study by the Research Department of the International Monetary Fund.* International Monetary Fund Occasional Paper 77 (March).

Goldstein, Morris, and others. 1993. *International Capital Markets: Part 1, Exchange Rate Management and International Capital Flows.* April. International Monetary Fund.

Greenspan, Alan. 1994. "Opening Remarks." Symposium sponsored by the Federal Reserve Bank of Kansas City, Jackson Hole, Wyoming, August 19–21, 1993, cited in "Changing Capital Markets: Implications for Monetary Policy" (Federal Reserve Bank of Kansas City).

Group of Thirty. 1982. *How Bankers See the World Financial Market.* New York.

————. 1993. Global Derivatives Study Group. *Derivatives: Practices and Principles.* Washington. July.

Guttentag, Jack M., and Richard J. Herring. 1987. "Emergency Liquidity Assistance for International Banks." In *Threats to International Financial Stability,* edited by Richard Portes and Alexander K. Swoboda, 150–86. Cambridge University Press.

Haas, Peter. 1990. *Saving the Mediterranean: The Politics of International Environmental Cooperation.* Columbia University Press.

Haggard, Stephan, and Beth Simmons. 1987. "Theories of International Regimes." *International Organization* 41 (Summer): 491–517.

Haubrich, Joseph, and Paul Wachtel. 1993. "Capital Requirements and Shifts in Commercial Bank Portfolios." New York University Salomon Center Working Paper S-93-47.

Hayward, Peter C. 1990. "Prospects for International Cooperation by Bank Supervisors." *International Lawyer* 24(3): 787–801.

Herring, Richard J. 1991. "Who Bears the Risk of Controls on Eurodeposits? Some Recent Developments." In *Protectionism and International Banking,* edited by Gerhard Fels and George Sutija. New York: St. Martin's.

————. 1993a. "BCCI: Lessons for International Bank Supervision." *Contemporary Policy Issues* 11 (April): 76–86.

————. 1993b. "'92 and After: The International Supervisory Challenge." In *World Financial Markets after 1992,* edited by Hans Genberg and Alexander K. Swoboda, 177–93. Kegan Paul International.

Herring, Richard J., and Richard C. Marston. 1977. "The Eurocurrency Markets and Their Interaction with the Forward Exchange and National Money Markets." *National Monetary Policies and International Financial Markets,* 79–105. New York: North-Holland Publishing Company.

Herring, Richard J., and Anthony M. Santomero. 1990. "The Corporate Structure of Financial Conglomerates." *Journal of Financial Services Research* 4 (December): 471–98.

Hewitt, Michael E. 1992. "Systemic Risk in International Securities Markets." In *Regulating International Financial Markets: Issues and Policies,* edited by Franklin R. Edwards and Hugh T. Patrick, 243–55. Boston: Kluwer Academic Publishers.

Horvitz, Paul. 1983. "Deposit Insurance after Deregulation." *Proceedings of the Ninth Annual Conference,* Federal Home Loan Bank of San Francisco. December.

Howell, Michael, and Angela Cozzini. 1990. *International Equity Flows, 1990 Edition: New Risks and New Products* (August). London: Salomon Brothers.

Hufbauer, Gary Clyde, and Jeffrey J. Schott. 1993. *NAFTA: An Assessment.* Washington: Institute for International Economics.

Institute of International Finance, Inc. 1993. "Report of the Working Group on Capital Adequacy: A Response to the Basel Committee on Banking Supervision 1993 Consultative Papers" (October). Washington.

International Monetary Fund. 1992. *International Financial Statistics* (July).

International Monetary Fund, Staff Team, Exchange and Trade Relations and Research Departments. 1990. *International Capital Markets: Developments and Prospects.* (April). Washington.

J. P. Morgan & Co. Incorporated. 1986. *Annual Report, 1986.*

Jack, Andrew, and Andrew Hill. 1993. "Liquidators try to put a brave face on BCCI ruling." *Financial Times,* October 28, p. 14.

Johnson, G. G., and Richard K. Abrams. 1983. *Aspects of the International Banking Safety Net.* Washington: International Monetary Fund. March.

Kane, Edward J. 1989. "How Market Forces Influence the Structure of Financial Regulation." In *Restructuring Banking and Financial Services in America,* edited by William S. Haraf and Rose Marie Kushmeider, 343-82. Washington: American Enterprise Institute.

———. 1992. "Government Officials as a Source of Systemic Risk in International Financial Markets." In *Regulating International Financial Markets: Issues and Policies,* edited by Franklin R. Edwards and Hugh T. Patrick, 257–65. Boston: Kluwer Academic Publishers.

Keohane, Robert. 1984. *After Hegemony: Cooperation and Discord in the World Political Economy.* Princeton University Press.

Key, Sydney J. 1989. "Mutual Recognition: Integration of the Financial Sector in the European Community." *Federal Reserve Bulletin* 75 (September): 591–609.

Litan, Robert E. 1987. *What Should Banks Do?* Brookings.

———. 1991. *The Revolution in U.S. Finance.* Brookings.

Loehnis, Anthony D. 1990. "Volatility in Global Securities Markets." *International Economic Insights* 1 (November/December): 16–19.

Maguire, Miles. 1994. "AIG Breaks Down Derivatives Exposure." *International Banking Regulator* 6 (June 13) p. 8.

Marston, Richard C. 1976. "Interest Arbitrage in the Euro-Currency Markets." *European Economic Review* 7 (January): 1–13.

———. Forthcoming. *Real Interest Rates in the Group of Five Industrial Countries: A Study of International Financial Integration.* Cambridge University Press.

Mashaw, Jerry L., and Susan Rose-Ackerman. 1984. "Federalism and Regulation." In *The Reagan Regulatory Strategy,* edited by George C. Eads and Michael Fix, 111–45. Washington: Urban Institute Press.

McCauley, Robert N., and Rama Seth. 1992. "Foreign Bank Credit to U.S. Corporations: The Implications of Offshore Loans." *Federal Reserve Bank of New York Quarterly Review* 17 (Spring): 52–65.

Merton, Robert C. 1989. "On the Application of the Continuous-Time Theory of Finance to Financial Intermediation and Insurance." *Geneva Papers on Risk and Insurance* 14 (July): 225–61.

Milner, Helen. 1992. "Review Article, International Theories of Cooperation among Nations: Strengths and Weaknesses." *World Politics* 44 (April): 466–96.

Mullins, David W. 1993. "Capital Standards and the Performance of the U.S. Banking System." In *Assessing Bank Reform: FDICIA One Year Later,* edited by George G. Kaufman and Robert E. Litan, 90–103. Brookings.

National Commission of Financial Institution Reform, Recovery and Enforcement. 1993. *Origins and Causes of the S&L Debacle: A Blueprint for Reform*, July 27. Washington.

New York Clearing House Association. 1986. "Clearing House Interbank Payments System."

New York Stock Exchange. 1993. "The Policy Implications of Stockownership Patterns: A Conference Summary and Research Agenda." Philadelphia: The Wharton School of the University of Pennsylvania.

O'Brien, Richard. 1992. *Global Financial Integration: The End of Geography.* Royal Institute of International Affairs.

Obstfeld, Maurice. 1986. "Capital Mobility in the World Economy: Theory and Measurement." Carnegie-Rochester Conference Series on Public Policy (Spring).

Olson, Mancur. 1982. *The Rise and Decline of Nations.* Yale University Press.

Organization for Economic Cooperation and Development. 1991. *Systemic Risks in Securities Markets.* Paris.

———. 1992. *Banks Under Stress.* Paris.

Pierce, James L. 1991. *The Future of Banking.* Yale University Press.

Quinn, Brian. 1993. "The Bank of England's Role in Prudential Supervision." *Bank of England Quarterly Bulletin* 33 (May): 260–61.

Rehm, Barbara A. 1993a. "FDIC Fund Expected to Hit Target by 2002." *American Banker* (March 24): 1.

———. 1993b. "FDIC Staff Sees Cut In Premiums by 1998." *American Banker* (July 9): 1.

Rekenthaler, John. 1993. "Adding to the Tool Kit." *Morningstar Mutual Funds.* (July 9): 1.

Restructuring America's Financial Institutions: Report of a Task Force. 1989. Brookings.

Roll, Richard. 1979. "Violations of Purchasing Power Parity and Their Implications for Efficient International Commodity Markets." In *International Finance and Trade*, edited by Marshall Sarnat and Giorgio P. Szego. Cambridge: Ballinger Publishing Co.

Santomero, Anthony M. 1989. "The Changing Structure of Financial Institutions: A Review Essay." *Journal of Monetary Economics* 24 (September): 321–28.

Santomero, Anthony M., Richard J. Herring, and Staffan Viotti. 1991. *Finanssektorn och Valfarden.* SNS Forlag.

Schaefer, Stephen M. 1992. "Financial Regulation: The Contribution of the Theory of Finance." In *The Internationalisation of Capital Markets and the Regulatory Response*, 149–216. London: Graham and Trotman.

Scott, Hal S., and Shinsaku Iwahara. 1994. *In Search of a Level Playing Field: The Implementation of the Basel Capital Accord in Japan and the United States.* Occasional paper no. 46. Washington: Group of Thirty.

Scott, Kenneth E. 1988. "Commentary." In *Restructuring Banking and Financial Services in America*, edited by William S. Haraf and Rose Marie Kushmeider, 386–91. Washington: American Enterprise Institute.

Semkow, Brian Wallace. 1992. "Foreign Financial Institutions in Japan." *Law and Policy in International Business* 23 (Spring): 331–414.

"The Skippers." 1984. *Economist.* September 22, p. Survey 49.

Spencer, David E. 1990. "Bank Liability under the UN Drug Trafficking Convention." *International Financial Law Review* 9 (March): 16–19.

Sproule, D. W., and Paul St-Denis. 1989. "The UN Drug Trafficking Convention: An Ambitious Step." *Canadian Yearbook of International Law, 1989,* 263–93. University of British Columbia Press.

Steil, Benn. 1992. "Regulatory Foundations for Global Capital Markets." In *Finance and the International Economy 6: The AMEX Bank Review Prize Essays,* edited by Richard O'Brien, 62–76. Oxford University Press.

Syron, Richard F. 1993. Testimony on June 22, 1993 before the U.S. House of Representatives, Committee on Banking, Finance and Urban Affairs, Subcommittee on Financial Institutions Supervision, Regulation and Deposit Insurance. Reprinted in *Federal Reserve Bulletin,* (August): 777–87.

Turner, Philip. 1991. *Capital Flows in the 1980s: A Survey of Major Trends.* BIS Economic Papers, no. 30 (April). Basel: Bank for International Settlements, Monetary and Economic Department.

Von Furstenberg, George M., and Bang Nam Jeon. 1989. "International Stock Price Movements: Links and Messages." *Brookings Papers on Economic Activity* 1989 (1): 125–67.

World Bank. 1989. *World Development Report, 1989.* New York: Oxford University Press.

Index

Abu Dhabi, 104
Accounting standards, harmonization of, 114–15, 160
Adjustable rate mortgages, 56
Adverse selection, 140
Allfinanz, 11
Allocation of credit. *See* Credit allocation
Antitrust legislation, 61, 74
Apartheid, xxvi
Arbitrage, xxiv, xxv, xxvi, 29, 44; interest, 32; regulatory, 7, 8, 66, 81, 88
Argentina, 166
Asset price integration, 29
Asset risk, 60
Asymmetric information, 84, 141

Bagehot, Walter, 97
Bahamas, 103
Bancassurance, 11
Banco Ambrosiano Holdings (BAH), 101–03, 129
Banco Ambrosiano SpA, 101–03
Bank capital, 8, 124–25
Bank failures, 1–2, 51, 75, 125, 126

Bank for International Settlements, xxviii, 25–26
Bankhaus Herstatt, 1, 95, 96–97, 98, 124
Bank holding companies: branching restrictions on, 60, 63–64; coordination of supervision and, 103; derivative instruments and, 68; rights of access and, 91
Banking crisis of *1974,* 95–96
Bank of America, 104
Bank of Commerce and Credit International (BCCI), 2, 67, 120; conflicts revealed by collapse of, 132–33; coordination of supervision and, 103–07; emergency liquidity assistance and, 129
Bank of England, 50, 97, 104, 106
Bank of Italy, 101, 103
Bank powers, 121
Bank regulators, 146–47
Bank runs, 51, 53, 67, 126, 127, 128
Bankruptcy laws, 101–01, 132, 133, 159
Banks, 9–11, 133; Basel Accord and, *see* Basel Accord; branching restric-

tions on, 60, 63–64; capital standards for, 159; central, *see* Central banks; commercial, 15, 63; consumer protection in, 75–76; coordination of supervision and, *see* Coordination of supervision; credit allocation and, 76–78; disclosure requirements of, *see* Disclosure requirements; distinction between securities firms and, 72–73; European Union and, 92–93; foreign, 18–19, 90, 106–07, 133; harmonization of regulations for, 8, 21; in-house, 16; investment, 15; loss of special position, 160–61; market discipline and, 147–50; mergers of, 59; money laundering and, 64, 118–19, 120; mutual recognition and, 90; narrow, 11, 146, 160; nonbanking activities of, 10–11, 63–64, 116–18, 121; North American Free Trade Agreement and, 91–92; prudential policy and, 154–56; reciprocity and, 94–95; rights of access and, 89; securities subsidiaries owned by, 117; systemic risk and, 51–52, 57–58, 59, 70, 95–96, 124–25, 153–54; technology and, 18–19; universal, *see* Universal banking

Bank secrecy laws, 64, 99–100, 101, 103, 104

Basel Accord, 4, 7, 8–9, 11, 107–13; credit allocation and, 77; disclosure and, 110, 133–34, 149; limitations of, 110–11; prudential policy and, 155; refinements and extensions of, 132–37; securities firms and, 9, 112–13, 136; subordinated debt and, 150

Basel Committee, 8–9, 10, 82, 86, 98–100, 120, 124, 156, 158–59; bank secrecy laws and, 99–100; on consolidation principle, 100–01; cooperation with, 125; credit allocation and, 77; financial conglomerates

and, 146–47; functions of, 132; limits on initiatives of, 158; money laundering and, 118; problems with coordination of supervision, 101–06; problems with information sharing, 136–37; prudential policy and, 155; retreat from position on market risk, 135

Basel Concordat, 99; on emergency liquidity assistance, 130, 156–57; refinements and extensions of, 132–37; revisions of, 101–05, 106

Basel Group of Experts on Payments Systems, 139

Bilateral netting, 111

Book valuations, 57, 59

Brazil, xx, xxvi

Bretton Woods conference, xx, 164

British-Israel Bank, 95

Brittan, Sir Leon, 22

Bryant, Ralph, 3, 164

Bush administration, 94

Canada, 21; capital controls in, 35; nonbanking activities of banks and, 116; North American Free Trade Agreement and, 4, 91–92; rights of access in, 90

Capital Adequacy Directive (CAD) of *1993*, 109, 111

Capital controls: Eurocurrency market and, 32; offshore markets and, 33–35; relaxation of, 35–36

Capital flows, 45–46; expanding, 23–29; real interest rate parity and, 40

Capital gains taxes, 20

Capital inflow controls, 34

Capital outflow controls, 34–35

Capital ratios, 109, 110, 133, 148, 149

Capital standards, 11, 77, 120, 125; Basel Accord and, 107–13, 133, 134, 136, 159; clearinghouses and, 55; harmonization of, 133, 136, 159; insurance companies and, 62; for securities firms, 112–113; systemic risk and, 71–72

Carter administration, 21
Cayman Islands, 5, 81, 104
Central banks, 9–10, 11, 125, 164, 165; clearinghouses and, 55; emergency liquidity assistance and, *see* Emergency liquidity assistance; as lender-of-last-resort, *see* Lender-of-last-resort; poor loan risks and, 156; settlement systems of, 70–71; stock market crash of *1987* and, 68; systemic risk and, 52, 53, 66–67, 68, 70–71, 72
Certificates of deposit, 20
Chile, 166
China, xx
Chlorofluorocarbons, xxviii
Clearing House Interbank Payment System (CHIPS), 23–24, 52, 55, 70–71, 72
Clearinghouses, 138–39, 159; Basel Accord and, 111–12; private sector, 53–55; systemic risk and, 51–52, 53–55, 70–71
Clinton administration, 94
Collateral, 69, 145–46
Collective action, 82, 85
Commercial banks, 15, 63
Commingling of funds, 72
Commissions, 6, 83
Committee on Banking Regulations and Supervisory Practices, xxviii, 98
Commodities Futures Trading Commission (CFTC), 114
Communication technology, xviii
Community Reinvestment Act (CRA), 63, 76–77, 78
Comparative advantage, theory of, xxiii
Competitive equity, 151–52
Concentration, 63–64, 116–18
Concordat. *See* Basel Concordat
Consolidation principle, 100–01
Constructive ambiguity, 10, 97–98, 126–27, 131, 158
Consumers/customers, 81, 113–15; domestic financial regulation and, 61–62; international financial regulation and, 74–76; of securities firms, 139–40; technology and, 14–18
Consumer sovereignty, xxiii
Continental Illinois Bank, 1, 127
Cooke, W. Peter, 100
Cooper, Richard, 3, 6, 66, 122–23, 124
Coordination, xxviii, 6
Coordination of supervision, 98–101, 132–33; consolidation principle and, 100–01; limitations of, 101–07
Corrigan, E. Gerald, 127, 145, 154
Counterparty risk, 110
Country premiums, 36, 45
Covered interest parity, 29–44
Credit allocation, 6, 62–63, 76–78, 81, 115–16
Credit risk, 68–69, 108, 113
Credit shock, 50–51
Criminal activities, 64, 76, 78–79
Cross-border spillovers, xxii, xxiv, xxvii, 65, 71, 120–21; from Banco Ambrosiano collapse, 102; credit allocation and, 76; criminal activities and, 78–79; direct, 6; emergency liquidity assistance and, 126; indirect, 6–7; public interest view on, 80
Currency swap contracts, 28
Customers. *See* Consumers/customers

Debt contracts, 72
Deep integration, xxi–xxiii, xxiv, xxv
Defined-benefit pension plans, 62
De jure seniority system, 149–50
Denmark, 113
Deposit insurance, 75–76, 81, 121, 154–55, 156, 162; systemic risk and, 53, 55–56, 59
Depository Institutions Deregulation and Monetary Control Act of *1980*, 21
Derivative instruments, 19, 20, 28, 108, 111; Basel Accord and, 134,

136; options-based, 69–70; systemic risk and, 68–70, 134
Diminished autonomy, xxii, xxiv–xxv, xxvii
Direct spillovers, 6
Disclosure requirements: Basel Accord and, 110, 133–34, 149; consumer protection and, 62; harmonization of, 114, 148–49; of insurers, 62; systemic risk and, 57–58
Discrimination, in rights of access, 90
Disintegration risk, 122
Diversity of regulations, 82, 85
Dollar, 23–24, 29, 32
Domestic financial regulation, 49–64; consumer protection and, 61–62; systemic risk and, 50–61
Dow Jones average, 73
Drexel Burnham Lambert Group, Inc., 9, 73, 138
Drug trade, 64, 76, 78, 118

Earthquakes, 74
Economic and monetary union, 36
Emergency liquidity assistance, 9–10, 66–67, 96–98, 120, 121, 126–31, 156–58; constructive ambiguity in, 10, 97–98, 126–27, 129, 131, 158; explicit commitment in, 10, 127–31, 157–58
Environmental issues, xxi, xxii, xxvi, 65
Equity prices, 63
Eurobonds, 20
Eurocurrency market, 45; covered interest parity in, 29–44
Eurodollar market, 74
Eurofranc rate, 34–35
Euromark rate, 34
European Community (EC), xxii, xxvii, 22, 35, 36
European Parliament, 21
European single-market initiative, 22
European Union (EU), xxix, 4, 6, 47, 86, 106, 109, 114; antitrust legislation and, 61; bank branching restrictions and, 60; Basel Accord and, 113; harmonization and, 8, 21; mutual recognition and, xxiv, 88, 90; nonbanking activities of banks and, 116, 117; reciprocity and, 93–94; rights of access and, 3, 92–93
Ex-ante prudential policy, 154–56, 161
Exchange rate uncertainty, 47
Explicit commitment, 10, 127–31, 157–58
Explicit harmonization, xxviii
Export subsidies, 63
Ex-post prudential policy, 154–56, 161–62
Externalities, xxv, 71, 80, 85; negative, 139, 159; political, xxvii; psychological, xxvi, xxvii

Fair Trade in Financial Services Act, 94
Federal Deposit Insurance Corporation, 53
Federal Deposit Insurance Corporation Improvement Act of 1991, 106, 133
Federalist mutual governance, xxviii–xxix
Federal Reserve System, 70; capital standards and, 107–08; coordination of supervision and, 106–07; stock market crash of 1987 and, 55; systemic risk and, 52, 53, 55, 59
Fedwire system, 52, 53
Feldstein, Martin, 44
FEYSS, 71, 72
Financial Accounting Standards Board (FASB), 58
Financial Assets Task Force, 119
Financial conglomerates, 121, 142–47, 156
Financial innovations, 84–85
Financial Service Act, 144

Financial service institutions, 18–19
Finland, 90
First American Bankshares, 107
Fiscal federalism, xxiv
Fixed exchange rates, 35
Fixed interest rates, 16, 28, 112
Floating interest rates, 16, 28, 112
Foreign banks, 18–19, 90, 106–07, 133
Foreign Bank Supervision Enhancement Act of *1991*, 106–07
Foreign exchange risk, 48
Forward exchange rates, 32
Forward premiums, 29, 37
Franc, 34–35
France, 21, 46; bankruptcy laws in, 132; capital controls in, 34–35; mutual recognition and, 8
Frankel, Jeffrey, 36
Franklin National Bank, 95
Free Trade Agreement (FTA), 91–92
Functional regulation, 142–46, 147, 160
Futures markets, 55

Gambling laws, 20
Garn, Jake, 94
General Agreement on Tariffs and Trade (GATT), xix, xxii, 78, 86, 120, 161; rights of access and, 3–4, 93; tuna fishing controversy and, xxvi
German Interbank rate, 34
Germany: capital controls in, 35; cross-border spillovers and, 65; derivative instruments in, 20; foreign banks in, 18; insurance funds in, 53; mutual recognition and, 8; nonbanking activities of banks and, 10–11, 116; systemic risk and, 53
Glass-Steagall Act, 116, 117
Global commons, xxv
Government bonds, 110–11
Great Britain. *See* United Kingdom
Great Depression, xix, 51

Greenspan, Alan, 70
Group of Seven, xxviii, 119
Group of Ten, 80, 124, 125; capital standards and, 108; coordination of supervision and, 98; emergency liquidity assistance and, 97, 129; money laundering and, 118; systemic risk and, 95
Group of Thirty, 139

Harmonization, 6, 7–9, 11, 85, 88, 125; of accounting standards, 114–15, 160; of bank capital, 124–25; of banking regulations, 8, 21; of bankruptcy laws, 133, 159; Basel Accord and, 109; of capital standards, 133, 136, 159; dangers of, 134–35; of disclosure requirements, 114, 148–49; explicit, xxviii; of financial conglomerate regulations, 143, 144, 147; market discipline as alternative to, 147–50; of prudential policy, 155–56; public interest view on, 81; of securities firm regulations, 121, 137–38, 140, 141–42, 156
Herstatt. *See* Bankhaus Herstatt
Hewitt, Michael, 50
Horioka, Charles, 44
Housing sector, 62–63, 77
Hurricane Andrew, 74
Hydrocarbons, xxii

Iceland, 90
Income taxes, 20
Indexed bonds, 84
India, 19
Indirect spillovers, 6–7
Indonesia, xx, xxvi
Industrial organization theory, 83–84
Inflation, 84
In-house banks, 16
Insider trading, 61, 114
Institutional investors, 16–18
Institutional regulation, 142–46

Insurance companies, 16, 64, 125, 141; consumer protection and, 61–62; European Union and, 92–93; rights of access and, 89, 91; systemic risk and, 53, 73–74
Insurance regulators, 146–47
Interest arbitrage, 32
Interest capitalization tax, 20
Interest-rate ceilings, 20, 60–61, 63, 83, 114
Interest-rate risk, 110
Interest rates, 6, 63; fixed, 16, 28, 112; floating, 16, 28, 112; nominal, 40
Interest rate swap contracts, 28
International Auditing Practices Committee (IAPC), 114–15
International bonds, 26
International Federation of Accountants, 114–15
International Lending Act of 1983, 107–08
International Monetary Fund (IMF), xx, xxviii
International Organization of Securities Commissions (IOSCO), 86, 112–13, 114, 115, 125, 136, 137
Investment banks, 15
Investors: institutional, 16–18; in securities firms, 140–41
Ireland, 19
Italy, 35, 101–03

Japan, xx, xxii, xxvi, 1, 5, 6, 15; antitrust legislation and, 61; Basel Accord and, 109–10; capital controls in, 35; cross-border spillovers and, 65; earthquakes and, 74; foreign banks in, 18; institutional regulation in, 143; interest-rate ceilings in, 60, 61; international bonds and, 26; keiretsu system in, 94–95, 116; nonbanking activities of banks and, 116–17; real interest rate parity in, 40; reciprocity and, 94–95; settlement systems in, 71; stock market crash of 1987 and, 67–68; tax structure in, 20; United States bank loss of market share to, 2

Kane, Edward, 83–84, 122
Keiretsu system, 94–95, 116
Kennedy Round, xix
Keohane, Robert, 123
Korea, xx

Lead regulator approach, 144–45
Lender-of-last-resort (LLR), 75, 97, 148, 150, 154–55, 156–57, 162; constructive ambiguity and, 126–27; explicit commitment and, 128–31, 157
Leverage ratio, 109
Liquidity shock, 127
London Interbank Offer Rate, 96
Loss-sharing, 70–71, 72
Luxembourg, 20, 101–03, 104, 106, 124; bank secrecy laws in, 101, 103; coordination of supervision in, 98

Macro prudential policy, 154
Market discipline, 9–10, 11, 121, 156, 161; constructive ambiguity and, 97, 98, 126, 129; explicit commitment and, 128, 129–30, 131; as harmonization alternative, 147–50; prudential policy and, 162
Market risk, 110, 111–12, 113, 134, 135, 159
Market shock, 135
Market valuation, 57, 58, 111
Marston, Richard C., 37
Mashaw, Jerry L., 80
Memoranda of Understanding (MOU), 114
Merton, Robert C., 84
Mexico, xx; North American Free Trade Agreement and, 4, 91–92; tuna fishing controversy and, xxvi
Micro prudential policy, 154

Milner, Helen, 124
Minimum standards, 8, 88, 90
Minimum standards/greater autonomy option, 155, 161
Money laundering, 64, 118–19, 120
Monitored decentralization, xxviii
Montreal Protocol, xxviii
Moral hazard, 140, 155, 156, 158
Mortgages, 56, 63, 77, 84, 109
Multilateral netting, 111
Mutual funds, 16, 64, 117, 141
Mutual recognition, xxvii–xxviii, 8, 88, 90, 91, 115

Narrow banks, 11, 146, 160
National autonomy, xxii, xxiv–xxv, xxvii, 88
National rates, 35–36
Negative externalities, 139, 159
Netherlands, 35
Netting of obligations, 69, 111
New York Federal Reserve Bank, 145, 154
New Zealand, 21, 149
Nominal interest rates, 40
Nondiscrimination, in rights of access, 89–90
North American Free Trade Agreement (NAFTA), xxii, 4, 86, 91–92
Norway, 90, 114

O'Brien, Richard, 3
Offshore markets, 29, 33–35, 45
Onshore markets, 33–35, 45
Operational risk, 110
Opportunistic behavior, 61
Options-based derivative instruments, 69–70
Organization for Economic Cooperation and Development (OECD), 61, 80, 110
Ozone layer, xxviii

Pakistan, 104
Partial mark-to-market accounting, 58

Payments system, 139; systemic risk and, 66–72
Pension plans, 16, 62, 141
Peru, 103
Political externalities, xxv
Political sovereignty, xxi, xxii, xxiii, xxv–xxvi, xxvii
Porpoise killing, xxvi
Portfolio risk, 110
Position risk, 55
Price shocks, 70
Prisoner's dilemma, 80–81, 85
Prudential policy, 17–18, 154–56, 160; ex-ante, 154–56, 161; ex-post, 154–56, 161–62; for financial conglomerates, 143–45; macro, 154; micro, 154
Psychological externalities, xxvi, xxvii
Public choice theory, 82–83
Public interest view, 79–82

Reagan, Ronald, 21
Real interest rate parity, 37–42, 43
Reciprocity, 90, 91, 93–95
Regulation Q interest rate ceilings, 61
Regulatory arbitrage, 7, 8, 66, 81, 88
Ricardo, David, xxiii
Riegle, Donald W., Jr., 94
Rights of access, 3–4, 88–95; discrimination in, 90; European Union and, 92–93; General Agreement on Tariffs and Trade and, 93; mutual recognition in, see Mutual recognition; nondiscrimination in, 89–90; North American Free Trade Agreement and, 4, 91–92; reciprocity in, 90, 91, 93–95
"Risk Management Guidelines for Derivatives," 136
Risk weights, 108–09, 110–11, 135–36
Roosevelt, Franklin, 53
Rose-Ackerman, Susan, 80

Safety nets, 75, 148, 149
Saudi Arabia, 104

Savings and loan (thrift) institutions, 11, 81; credit allocation in, 63; scandal in, 1, 56; systemic risk and, 53
Scandinavian countries, 1
Scott, Kenneth, 79
Second Banking Directive, 21, 92, 106
Securities: bank underwriting of, 64, 94, 116; consumer protection and, 61
Securities and Exchange Commission (SEC), 58, 114, 115
Securities firms, 125, 137–42; banks owned by, 117; Basel Accord and, 9, 112–113, 136; clearing and settlement systems in, 70–71, 138–39, 159; customer protection from, 139–40; European Union and, 92–93; harmonization of regulations for, 121, 137–38, 140, 141–42, 156; inefficient regulation of, 141–42; investor protection from, 140–41; rights of access and, 89, 91; systemic risk and, 51–52, 72–73, 112
Securities regulators, 8, 136, 146–47
Senior debt, 149–50
Separation fences, xix, xxi
Settlement systems, 70–71, 138–39, 159
Shareholders, bank, 128, 148
Sherman Act of 1890, 61
Socialist governments, 21
South Africa, xxvi
Spillovers. See Cross-border spillovers
Steil, Benn, 3
Sterling, 29, 32
Stock market crash of 1929, 51
Stock market crash of 1987, 51, 52–53, 55, 59, 157–58; international consequences of, 67–68; securities firms and, 73, 138
Subordinated debt, 111, 133, 149–50
Subsystem failure risk, 122
Swap contracts, 28, 111
Sweden, 20, 144

Switzerland, 124; bank secrecy laws in, 64; capital controls in, 35; coordination of supervision in, 98; financial conglomerates and, 147
Systemic crisis, 50–51
Systemic risk, 11, 50–52, 95–107, 109, 153–54; bank capital and, 124–25; banking crisis of 1974 and, 95–96; coordination of supervision and, see Coordination of supervision; derivatives and, 68–70, 134; domestic financial regulation and, 50–61; emergency liquidity assistance and, see Emergency liquidity assistance; financial conglomerates and, 160; insurance companies and, 53, 73–74; market discipline and, 131; minimizing, 52–61; payments system and, 66–72; prudential policy and, 162; securities firms and, 51–52, 72–73, 112; two related meanings of, 122

Taxes, xxiv, 20
Technology: consumers and, 14–18; financial service institutions and, 18–19; regulators affected by, 19–23
Thatcher, Margaret, 21
Thrift institutions. See Savings and loan (thrift) institutions
Tier II standard, 150
Timber cutting, xxvi
Tokyo Round, xix
Trade restrictions, 78
Trading risk, 110
Tropical rain forests, xxvi
Tuna fishing controversy, xxvi

Uncovered interest rate parity, 36–37
Uniformity of regulations, 82, 85
United Kingdom, 21; Bank of Commerce and Credit International in, 104; bankruptcy laws in, 132; bilateral accord with United States and, 108; capital controls in, 35;

capital standards in, 108; coordination of supervision and, 106; functional regulation in, 142; indexed bonds and, 84; lead regulator approach in, 144–45; mutual recognition and, 8

United Nations Convention, 118, 119

United States, xxii, 5, 6, 7, 15, 115; antitrust legislation in, 61, 74; bank branching restrictions in, 63–64; bank failures in, 1–2; bank mergers and, 59; bank regulation failure in, 11; bank runs in, 51, 53; bankruptcy laws in, 132; Basel Accord and, 109, 110, 111, 113; bilateral accord with United Kingdom and, 108; capital controls in, 35; capital standards in, 107–08; clearinghouses in, 52, 55, 138; coordination of supervision and, 106–07; credit allocation in, 76–77, 78; cross-border spillovers and, 65; defined-benefit pension plans in, 62; disclosure requirements in, 57–58; fiscal federalism in, xxiv; foreign banks in, 18–19, 90, 106–07, 133; institutional investors in, 16–17; institutional regulation in, 143; insurance market in, 74; interest capitalization tax in, 20; interest-rate ceilings in, 60–61; Memoranda of Understanding signed by, 114; mortgages in, 63, 84; narrow banks and, 146; nonbanking activities of banks and, 10, 63–64, 116–17, 121; North American Free Trade Agreement and, 4, 91–92; real interest rate parity in, 40, 43; reciprocity and, 94; rights of access in, 90; savings and loan regulation in, 11, 81; savings and loan scandal in, 1, 56; securities firms role in, 72; settlement systems in, 138; systemic risk and, 53, 57–58, 60–61; tuna fishing controversy and, xxvi

Universal banking, 11, 15, 92–93, 116, 117, 121, 143

Uruguay, 166

Uruguay Round, xix, xxii, 3–4, 78, 86, 93, 120, 161

Venezuela, xxvi

World Bank, 77

World Health Organization, xxviii

Zaibatsu, 116

Zengin, 71, 72